SOAR, ADAM, SOAR

SOAR, ADAM, SOAR

DISCARD

RICK PRASHAW

Cover image: Rick Prashaw; edited by Jennifer Scrivens
Printer: Webcom

"Be Not Afraid" Text and Music ©1975, 1978, Robert J. Dufford, SJ and OCP Publications. All rights reserved. Used with permission.
"You Alive," ©2014, Malik Ferraud, 2014. Used with permission.

Library and Archives Canada Cataloguing in Publication

Prashaw, Rick, 1951-, author
        Soar, Adam, soar / Rick Prashaw.

Issued in print and electronic formats.
ISBN 978-1-4597-4276-5 (softcover).--ISBN 978-1-4597-4277-2
(PDF).--ISBN 978-1-4597-4278-9 (EPUB)

        1. Prashaw, Adam. 2. Transgender people--Ontario--
Ottawa--Biography. 3. Epileptics--Ontario--Ottawa--Biography.
4. Ottawa (Ont.)--Biography. I. Title.

HQ77.8.P73P73 2019   306.76'8   C2018-902668-5
                                              C2018-902669-3

1   2   3   4   5   23   22   21   20   19

We acknowledge the support of the **Canada Council for the Arts**, which last year invested $153 million to bring the arts to Canadians throughout the country, and the **Ontario Arts Council** for our publishing program. We also acknowledge the financial support of the **Government of Ontario**, through the **Ontario Book Publishing Tax Credit** and the **Ontario Media Development Corporation**, and the **Government of Canada.**

Nous remercions le **Conseil des arts du Canada** de son soutien. L'an dernier, le Conseil a investi 153 millions de dollars pour mettre de l'art dans la vie des Canadiennes et des Canadiens de tout le pays.

Care has been taken to trace the ownership of copyright material used in this book. The author and the publisher welcome any information enabling them to rectify any references or credits in subsequent editions.
        — *J. Kirk Howard, President*

The publisher is not responsible for websites or their content unless they are owned by the publisher.

Printed and bound in Canada.

VISIT US AT

 dundurn.com | @dundurnpress | dundurnpress | dundurnpress

Dundurn
3 Church Street, Suite 500
Toronto, Ontario, Canada
M5E 1M2

To Adam's family and friends, for loving him home

CONTENTS

	Author's Note	9
1	Can't Wait!	11
2	"A No-Brainer" #seizurefree	17
3	A Beautiful Baby Girl	38
4	"MY Home!" and Facebook Dad	43
5	In Good Spirits!	63
6	The T Train #transman	68
7	The Boy in the Mirror	78
8	Hope Rising Up — Happy New Year!	86
9	The Cardinal, January 22–24, 2016	97
10	Dead Enough #beadonor	125
11	Tania	130

12   Soar, Adam, Soar   133

13   Heart, Kidneys, Liver, and   136
      Saint Jesus School

14   Celebration of Life   146

15   Angels in the Snow   163

16   Give Sorrow Words   166

17   The Brave Heart   187

18   Keep Us All Safe in the Storm   202

19   Fragments   219

      Postlude   245

      Acknowledgements   247

      Image Credits   249

AUTHOR'S NOTE

ADAM'S STORY IS both inspiring and complicated.

How else do you describe my kid — a kid whose mother intuitively recognized as a boy in the womb, who was then identified as a girl at birth by the doctor, was named Rebecca Adam by their parents, and spent about eighteen years going by she/her and, finally, about four years as he/him?

The kid who told us that he was always Adam.

It is not just writers who know that words matter. Names, pronouns, and language matter to every single human being. They tell us who we are and who we want to be. Words definitely matter to members of the transgender community who, as diverse as any group of people are, still find their fierce inner warrior when they meet people who want to erase them. I will let Adam name himself, explain and explore his own gender identity. In time, he came to accept his Rebecca years, sharing with the world his Rebecca pictures and stories.

The early chapters of *Soar, Adam, Soar* jump back and forth between the Adam and Rebecca years. Each trans person is unique in how they think about themselves pre-, mid-, and post-transition. I strive — out of respect for Adam and for all — for a consistency in names and pronouns as much as possible. I refer to Rebecca and use she/her for those early, Rebecca years, and Adam, using he/him, for the Adam years. There was no fixed date that this transition happened. Really, it happened over a lifetime. Adam is his name, as he will tell you, F-bombs and all.

Listening, learning, and loving worked well for Adam's family and friends. I highly recommend it.

CHAPTER 1

Can't Wait!

I KNEW I WOULD write a book about my kid. Just not this book.

Rebecca Danielle Adam Prashaw was born April 22, 1993, in Sudbury, Ontario. Suzanne, her mom, spent only seventeen minutes in labour, and then, *swoosh*, Rebecca slid into life's fast lane, never to put her foot on the brake.

As a record of her life and our relationship, I wrote my child a letter each year around her birthday. It took time to realize the letters might someday inspire a book. There was a story I wanted her to appreciate someday — hers, mine, ours.

I was a Catholic priest: a Roman Catholic priest who married when he was forty, becoming an instant stepdad to his wife's three children, and a year later, a first-time dad to one child, that kid with the interesting name.

I worked as a journalist, too. I like to tell and write stories, and I recognized a story here. The letters, I thought, would bind my story to Rebecca's story, so when the time was right, she would better understand the first chapters of her own journey. Or so I thought. That there was a book, too, was, well … more a dad's hunch, a crazy intuition.

The working title for this book idea was *Dear Rebecca: Love Letters from a Married Priest to His Daughter.* I knew that it wouldn't be on the Vatican's blessed books list. *That might work in my favour,* I thought!

Those annual birthday letters chronicled the year's events: celebrations, family trips to California and North Bay, camping, cottage visits, outdoor adventures, the pet dogs and rabbit, and a few mundane moments, too, that still somehow captured life's wisdom. They also recount some madcap misadventures — I confess to a few missteps as a later-in-life dad on training wheels. Memo to Dad: venturing out in winter with your five-year-old onto the Castor River in Russell, Ontario, without first checking the ice is not a good idea; the unexpected polar bear dip to my waist qualifies as "top shelf" in the family legends.

The fifth-year birthday letter reports the epileptic seizures that first appeared out of nowhere at the breakfast table — dark, ominous clouds on an otherwise sunny horizon.

The eighth-year birthday letter tells of my own heartbreak over my separation from Suzanne, the breakup of a marriage that I did not want to end. *Damn.* Now there would be stories I'd prefer to omit from my book.

More dad letters follow in the next few years, charting Rebecca's significant challenges in learning and at school, some clearly the consequences of the epilepsy. This would be the place where I would revisit a wickedly fun period of seven years when Rebecca played goalie for various girls' hockey teams in Kanata, in the west end of Ottawa. Unknown to anyone at the time, what she learned in the goalie crease would tutor my kid for life's adversities. Tales are emerging, too, of first jobs, hints of first loves, and more.

All in all, I recognized a story worth telling, a tale of a mischievous kid who was impossible to subdue or defeat, a kid wrapped in her parents' and her family's love; in hope, worry, and wonder.

But life, and my child, had other plans. Sickness, heartache, and unimaginable, enduring courage elbowed their way into the story. The book that I imagined writing is not the book I *am* writing. Adam emerged as the co-author.

Adam?

Our Rebecca.

First Communion: a dress and fancy shoes!

Remember the girl born in 1993 with the boy's name, Rebecca Danielle ADAM Prashaw? From very early on, Rebecca delighted in her boy's name. She never tired of hearing the story her parents told of how Adam became part of her legal name. Adam, of course, wanted this story, this book, to be something that he would help to write.

Rebecca was the quintessential tomboy. There were early signs of Adam everywhere — the short hair, cut pageboy-style some years; the "dressed down" rough-and-tumble look. We saw it but didn't see it. Rebecca was often thought *to be* a boy, as early on as age two. Rebecca's mom recalls the tough negotiation she had with Rebecca to get her to wear a First Communion dress. She made a deal that Rebecca could take the dress off right after the pictures — like a flash, Rebecca was gone, and the dress disappeared for a day or two before her mother found it under her bed. Before she pulled the dress off, we snapped the First Communion photo, a nick on her face from the latest mishap and, of course, the short crop of hair.

As friends came into our lives and we were asked the inevitable "number of children" question, Suzanne would say, "I have two girls, a boy, and a wannabe." In response to their inquisitive looks, she would add, "A girl who wants to be a boy."

I recall an early, fun conversation with my daughter when I asked her if Dad could at least see his daughter in a dress three times in her life. Could we agree on that? That semi-serious negotiation resulted in Rebecca committing to wearing a dress on three occasions — her First Communion (which she did!), her wedding day, and, hell, I can't even remember the third day she promised. It doesn't matter. She reneged. And in the story this crazy kid would live, there actually was a wedding day. Well, sort of, but it was one minus the dress. That story will be told here, in this new book that Adam and I are writing.

Things are clearer in hindsight.

Unquestionably, from that day at Sudbury General Hospital in 1993, it was love at first sight. I was forty-one years old, a new dad, "over the moon" happy. I never saw or had a need to see "Daddy's little girl" in Rebecca. Well, maybe a little, a nod to that "wearing a dress" negotiation! Indeed, I was punch-drunk ecstatic about being a dad of any child at all.

I guess the gender thing was there from the start. But it would take a lot of years, well into adolescence, for Adam to show up.

* * *

Adam made his official appearance in 2014, at twenty. His "coming out" was sandwiched between two major epilepsy surgeries in 2011 and 2015. We had called our kid Rebecca, or Becca, for short (and Bekkaa on Facebook), for almost twenty years, from birth through to 2014. I've sorted out my Adam/Rebecca story this way: the first happy, healthy childhood years, from birth to five (1993–1998); then the years during which the first series of smaller seizures occurred, from five to ten (1998–2003); then the more-or-less typical preteen and teen years, from ten to seventeen (2003–2011). The final part of the story takes place after the second series of bigger, more threatening seizures start in 2011. It is in the second, scarier epilepsy phase that Adam shows up, writing his own impressive new birth announcement. My co-author can't wait to tell that story.

There are other stories to tell, too — visits to the Montreal Neurological Institute and Hospital (many call it the Neuro), getting her driver's licence at sixteen, and a remarkable, life-changing conversation with her mother. Adam wants that in HIS book, too. "Her, she" is history. Adam will become my teacher on pronouns.

Somehow, bound and determined as he was to live a full, normal life, epilepsy and all, Adam, I sense, wanted to stay in the driver's seat, even after he lost his licence because of his seizures. This is his life, his story. It was him behind the wheel, driving his parents crazy at times in a madcap, fast-lane race to adulthood and the independence he keenly craved. As he endured the epilepsy surgeries, as he chose to come out and come in to Adam, I marvelled at a new meaning of courage.

And through it all, in what was undoubtedly a hard life capped by one cruel catastrophe, he wove in a heap-load of fun. He did it with amazing friends, the steadfast support of family, and most of all abiding steadfastness, as Adam saw it all through to the end.

This is the story of Adam (Rebecca).

Dozens of Adam's Facebook posts will help tell the story. I have not dared to change a single word. If it seems like Adam appears out of nowhere sometimes to jump into the conversation or start another conversation, well, that's my son. If you wince at some of his posts, know that I winced first.

Soar, Adam, soar.

Adam

January 19, 2016

Can't wait till I don't have to hide anymore. Time will come.... But the wait is hard. Definitely need and want to slim down though, need to work out more and get more pumped to. I need my hope to rise up more.... #wisdom #strength #passion #stages #transgender #myjourney #ftm[1] #dontstopliveitup #whereiam sofar #keepmyheadup

---

1. Ftm is social media shorthand for female to male.

CHAPTER 2

"A No-Brainer"

#seizurefree

November 25, 2015
Montreal Neurological Institute and Hospital

ADAM IS IN excruciating pain.

His bottom lip is quivering. Tears are rolling down his cheeks. His lower jaw convulses, shaking uncontrollably. I can't recall ever seeing him cry like this. I have definitely seen him cry before, watching sad movies and at stuff from life, like saying goodbye to favourite family pets: Murphy, our eleven-year-old yellow Labrador retriever; Molly, an Aussie cattle dog; Josée, Aunt Sandy's husky-terrier cross; and Oreo, a rabbit who was his "best Christmas present ever!"

But these tears tonight are nasty — pure hell for a parent to see — hinting at the pain that Adam is suffering.

We are at the Montreal Neurological Institute and Hospital. I have lost track of the days, but the calendar says it's Wednesday, November 25, 2015. In the late afternoon, nurses give us the green light to see

Adam in the recovery room. He is coming back to consciousness after an eight-hour surgery to remove a tiny section from the deepest region of his brain. The doctors wanted to completely remove the piece, which appeared to be triggering increasingly frequent and serious epileptic seizures that undermined Adam's stellar attempts at a normal life.

Bekkaa
October 22, 2012
"The purpose of life is to live it, to taste experience to the utmost, to reach out eagerly and without fear for newer and richer experience."
— Eleanor Roosevelt

Brain surgery for our kid. I must have missed that page in the parenting manual.

This operation is his second brain surgery in four years; the first operation happened in September 2011, done by the same doctors at the same hospital. I guess we are back in the same ICU. The big difference is that my kid is now called Adam, not Rebecca. I'll get him to tell that story when he's fully conscious.

Holding Adam's hand, stroking his hair, I'm a bit brain dead myself, numb, trying to recall the series of events that got us here. I look at my Adam on the hospital bed and see from long ago our tomboy, Rebecca. Rebecca Adam — both names are part of his legal name. It's complicated. He needs to wake up and tell the name story. He tells it so much better than I do.

Where have the years gone? He's twenty-two now.

Becca looking up to big sister Lindsay.

Lauren, Rebecca, and David on the first day of school.

As a young child, starting around five, our Rebecca Adam began a five-year period of smaller absence seizures, the kind the older generation called "petit mal" seizures. They started one morning at the breakfast table at our family home in the village of Russell, east of Ottawa. Rebecca was amusing her brother, David, and sisters, Lindsay and Lauren — a common spectacle. She was often the entertainer in the family, seizing centre stage as the youngest. She loved an audience. That morning, over and over again, she whipped her arm in a Ferris-wheel motion, holding a spoon of cereal. We laughed. It seemed part of her attempt to entertain, but in fact, a seizure was happening. Suzanne, Rebecca's mom, recalls the details better than I do: "Rebecca seemed frozen in time, just stopped, and was eerily still, barely breathing for what felt like an eternity — but, in reality, about five minutes. Then, with a very deep sigh, Rebecca slipped into sleep for hours from the strain on her brain and body."

That episode hurtled us through a frightening door: accompanying our child to specialists and hospitals and learning the names of a variety of epilepsy medications — Depakene, Dilantin, Keppra, Lamotrigine, Clonazepam, and others. Suzanne is far better than I am at remembering their names and dosage. Most of the absence seizures were brief, between five and fifteen seconds. We might have noticed a blank stare or vacant look. When those seizures were over, Rebecca often resumed what she was doing. But there were other, partial complex seizures in specific parts of the brain that left her confused when they ended.[1]

My letter to Rebecca written for her sixth birthday captured new worries.

June 9, 1999

I looked at you last night, your frustration and tears, your not being in good space, which is unusual for you, and I was worried, quite aware of my fears for you about the epilepsy, how much it will dominate your life, how long it will be with us. We have been told that the odds are good that you will grow out of it. Your first seizure occurred last September and scared us when you went rigid and fell into your trance. One day I hope you will know what that worrying and wondering is all about that we as parents store up in our hearts. We literally carry you in our hearts ... I thought ahead to the questions of driving a car and being pregnant and would any of this be affected.

The epilepsy meds would control the seizures, more or less. We would learn later that other seizures were happening in the brain that we did not observe. Together, all those seizures affected Rebecca — her memory, learning ability, and personality. There were mood

1. Now known as a "focal impaired awareness seizures," these start in one area of the brain and negatively affect sensory perception. Other symptoms may include automatic behaviour. Such seizures generally last between one and two minutes.

swings, too, some triggered by the meds. There were new frustra-
tions and tears. Yet she soldiered on. "Normal" — as in not sick and
like friends — was where she always headed.

Was it around age five that our kid started to fall behind? All
those seizures began to take their toll. The report cards coming home
in those early years had a common theme. Grade one: "Not taking
the time to complete her tasks," and "Sometimes accomplishes her
work with haste rather than care." Grade two: "Likes to hurry writing
without understanding assignment."

I typically rushed through those teacher comments to find the
other, inevitable note on my child being a pleasure to teach. Rebecca
attended French language school. The grade
two teacher commented: "Rebecca est gen-
tille avec les amis en classe." (Rebecca is kind
with her friends in school.)

A few years later, a school-referred
psychologist identified mild ADHD. His
report spoke of Rebecca's lack of concen-
tration and of her being overwhelmed by
homework, easily frustrated, wanting to

> Bekkaa
> July 19, 2011
> has had enough of the
> needles, machines and
> doctors and wants to go
> home!! <3

rush through work, and not easily retaining what had been learned or
read. The psychologist reassured us that it was mild ADHD, unlike,
for example, that of another of his patients, whose severe ADHD, he
said, was like "having five televisions on simultaneously in the head."

The mix of Rebecca's ADHD and the cognitive damage from the
seizures was a dangerous cocktail. School and life challenges were
emerging. At times, I suspected Rebecca misunderstood the purpose of school. *Don't I get bonus marks for being the first one done the
assignment, first one out the door after a test? What, you expect correct
answers, too?*

My Rebecca was in the fast lane, speeding. It started early. She was
in a shoulder harness at two years old for ten days after breaking her
collarbone, a harbinger of future misadventures.

My parental homework bribes worked short term for this kid who
lived always in the "now" and never the "later." I noticed Rebecca's
multiplication tables vastly improved whenever I dangled the promise

Bekkaa

December 16, 2011

it's fri-DAY, fri-DAY!! Going to get down on fri-DAY!!! oops omfggg whyyyyyyyyyyyyyy'd i put this for status... D= lmaooo oh well its true!! its friday!! and woot off all weekend <3 (: yay!

of Tim Hortons chocolate milk with whipped cream and chocolate sprinkles. The whipped cream on the nose and chocolate moustache made 9 x 8 bearable. Unfortunately, by the next day, she had forgotten 72. Well, no problem. More whipped cream and chocolate sprinkles.

* * *

Tonight, here in the recovery room after the brain surgery, we look around for nurses to relieve Adam's intense pain. I spy the cast on Adam's wrist and shake my head: this is minor, a sideshow fracture. A flashback to the collarbone shoulder harness Rebecca wore at two! Just five days before the scheduled brain surgery, Adam had informed me that he went to Emergency with a girlfriend late one night to have a wrist fracture confirmed.

Adam

November 23, 2015

Sucks that this happened Saturday night, broken/ fractured my wrist same week as my surgery, my fault though... Going to have two cast on as of Wednesday. Lol surely will be interesting... 😅 😵

Those first seizures, the ones that began at five, were called "atypical absences."[2] They produce a full stop in activity, last about a minute, and often end in a large sigh. Some go longer than others; some affect more areas of the brain.

Once, on the school bus home from École Russell, Rebecca exited the bus in a trance, going around the front and heading across the street

---

2. Such seizures result in a loss of awareness: the sufferer will seem to enter a dreamlike state. Unlike typical absence seizures, atypical seizures begin and end slowly, last longer — up to several minutes — and are accompanied by a loss of muscle tone, which can result in slumping or even falling.

before her brother grabbed her. Other seizures stiffened her muscles, bringing on episodes of jerking and relaxing, rapid blinking, or staring.

The doctors continually worked to identify the best medication to help Rebecca deal with the seizures. I think she was ten when the doctors deliberately reduced Rebecca's meds, hopeful that she might grow out of the seizures. Despite minor seizure activity on the EEG, the doctors noted that she could live a normal life without taking any more medications. That was terrific news. The doctors told us the seizures might return with puberty, but with life being much more normal now, we put that possibility out of our minds. Indeed, the visible seizures disappeared and life returned to an ordinary childhood schedule of school, sports, hobbies, and friends. We were ecstatic, believing that the worst was behind us. This was the beginning of the second healthy phase, much like her first years, from birth to five.

Bekkaa
November 18, 2009
boreeedd!! thinking about doing the vow of silence but it would be extremely hard for me

Those birthday letters I wrote from ten on are devoid of seizure stories, so different from the previous five years. They include trips with her mom and other family members to the Dominican Republic and Cuba. Swimming and martial arts classes, singing, arts and crafts, braces, the Russell Fair, a switch to Harry Potter glasses. Me surviving an Avril Lavigne concert with Rebecca on the edges of the mosh pit on the arena floor. Summer drama and horse riding camps. Accounts of rocketing down Vermont hills on sleds. A trip to the East Coast with my sister Jude, as Rebecca and her cousin Alec sang a bilingual "O Canada" a few hundred times in the back seat. Rebecca collecting forty pins at her sister Lauren's Canada Winter Games national curling championship in Bathurst, New Brunswick, in 2003. Rebecca, Suzanne, and I cheering for Lauren's silver medal.

Those were good years. Life was a highway whether she was with her mom or her dad. Rebecca never seemed part of the "in crowd" in school, but she typically found good friends. It was an early hint of her total acceptance of people. She genuinely liked a wide range of different types of kids. Rebecca had an Individual Education Plan at Holy

Trinity Catholic High School in Kanata to help her — this gave her more time for an exam or fewer questions, and help with homework.

One day, Rebecca announced that she wanted to play hockey. Up to ten, her favourite sport had been soccer. She loved being the goalie or keeper for the Nepean Hotspurs Soccer Club. Why was I surprised, then, when after the first hockey practice, she walked out of the dressing room hauling the heavy goalie pads? She clued in to the fact that the goalie crease is where the action is. It may have been a friendly house league level of play, but our Becca was fiercely competitive. She wanted to stop every shot for her teammates. She was not happy when she allowed a goal.

By the time she was a teen and a good height for her age, she filled up most of the net when she wore all the goalie equipment. Despite her size, she was agile, shooting a leg out or doing the splits for a spectacular save. Sitting in the stands, we could hear her shouting encouragement at her teammates. She was flat on the ice as much as on her skates, scrambling from post to post or on her back, lifting a goalie pad in the air to block a sure goal. I played sports and coached baseball, but I was instantly smitten by girls' hockey, certainly this house league version in Ottawa in which we immersed ourselves.

Once, Rebecca stopped forty shots in a heartbreaking 2–1 loss. I headed to the dressing room, wondering how the girls were handling the defeat. I heard hooting and hollering, laughing, comments about the ref, about a boy, about the parents in the stands. The girls were oblivious to the loss. Did they know that they had lost? I wasn't sure. Some didn't seem to know the final score. Regardless, they were over it. And Rebecca was in the middle of the dressing room taking off the goalie pads, regaling everyone with a funny story from the game.

She did play a higher-skill level of competitive hockey one year for her high school team but gravitated back to the recreational league. From the opening whistle to the final horn, my kid wanted to win, but

> Bekkaa
> April 26, 2009
> On the count of three let's all burst out laughing and make people think there's something really funny. 1..2..3 AHAHAHAHAHA-HAAHAHAHAHAAHAHAHA * everyone turning out to be really laughing* AAHA-HAHAHA ....2 mins later what were we laughing at again?? LOL best

Our Carey Price. Life's lessons in the goalie crease.

Bekkaa
December 12, 2009
first of many
hockey games this
weekend+monday
tonight! lol : this
should be fun!

once the game was over, it didn't matter anymore. It was all fun. Life was pitch-perfect between the goalie pipes. On the drive home, Rebecca tolerated me when I reported exactly how many shots she had stopped and what her GAA (goals against average) was. I failed miserably in trying to turn her fun into a math lesson, suggesting she figure out her GAA — dividing the goals allowed by the games played. At home, she threw the latest First Star or Tournament All Star medal on the growing pile in her bedroom.

*   *   *

Time flies by so fast. At sixteen, soon after her birthday, Rebecca got her driver's licence, another rung in her climb to independence. She liked having part-time jobs, and getting behind the wheel birthed a new teenager, one who accelerated her fast drive to adulthood. When she noticed her older teammates driving to the hockey arena alone, she proposed that I find another ride to the game so she could take my car by herself! These suggestions came with a "love you, Dad" look.

Hockey and driving and part-time work were all big deals for Rebecca, and she wrote about them and much else on Facebook and other social media sites. I suspect many parents can identify with Rebecca's Facebook posts for these years — teenage angst of boredom, broken phones, a Farm Boy job;

Bekkaa
May 26, 2009
Got My G1!!! =D woooo lol && braces are coming off next tuesday!!

updates like "text me," "who wants to chill," "fml"(fuck my life), "braces off," and "too much homework": and, for my kid, hockey, hockey, hockey.

Bekkaa
July 31, 2009
camping was awesome :) saw a porcupine<3<3 he was sooo cute :3 work tomorrow 9-5.//.text mee

Bekkaa
December 3, 2009
school hockey game tomorrow, then driving lesson at 6:00pm, after that tanya sleeping over and we're making the most amazing video of all time!!<3 lol all weekend long! no joke : P

Bekkaa

December 22, 2009

try not to text me too much guys!! or my mom will spazz @ me for a extremely high phone bill!! which i don't wanna see the consequence for :P lol {3moredaystillchristmas} :) <3

Bekkaa

February 24, 2010

soooo effing bored -_'

Fast forward to three weeks before her eighteenth birthday. March 2011. Rebecca was working the cash at Farm Boy grocery store in Kanata when she felt nauseous and asked her supervisor if she could go home. She was halfway up the employee stairs at the back of the store when a seizure struck.

It was one of what used to be called the "grand mal" type — major, dangerous. The worst ones are life threatening. The arms go rigid. The eyes roll back. Such seizures can last a few minutes. We learned a new language for these seizures: "generalized tonic-clonic" is the term for what Rebecca suffered at Farm Boy. There are also other, more common "partial complex seizures," as they were called at the time. These do not involve convulsions, but they impair awareness or consciousness. During the seizure, the person may be unable to respond to questions. A doctor will tell us later that the bigger seizures, which last a few minutes and include loss of consciousness, leave the patient as exhausted as if they had run a marathon.

After seven apparently seizure-free years, we were now back in the world of epilepsy. I say "apparently" because the doctors reminded us again that not all of Rebecca's seizures were visible. During those years when Rebecca seemed seizure-free, she may, in fact, have been suffering small, but unnoticeable, seizures.

I am learning to distinguish the seizures. There are two main categories: *generalized* and *focal*. The terms are used to distinguish between a seizure that is diffuse and one that is restricted to networks in one brain hemisphere at the onset. The sufferer usually loses consciousness during a generalized seizure. There is a period of confusion when the seizure ends, often leaving the individual very tired and in need of rest. The term *tonic-clonic* describes the effect on the muscles: *tonic* refers to increased muscle tone or stiffening, and *clonic* refers to a series of alternating contractions and relaxations.

The fine technical distinctions were not much help for us, though. Our fears returned. How much would epilepsy dominate our kid's life? How long would this phase last? This was devastating: the independence that Rebecca craved was gone in a flash. Gone, too, were jobs for a while, the wages she liked and needed, hockey, the driver's licence — perhaps, too, the ability to work with children, something she keenly wanted to do. She loved kids. Kids loved her. She was terrific with them.

Bekkaa

October 26, 2011

ever since my epilepsy left when i was 9 my life became great, i always happy, going out to places, seeing my friends, traveling, seeing family lots, having fun everyday … now just because it had to come back in March'11 … and ever since be in hospitals lots, can't drive, not being able to go to college so losing friends, contact with people, always alone … things have just been miserable and i wish i could just have what i use to have back.

The seizure recurrence obviously affected Rebecca's quality of life. It robbed her of a good deal of her independence, but it also affected her memory. In this second epilepsy phase, and likely throughout Rebecca's teen years, she suffered scores of small seizures that had an impact on her social, work, and academic life.

Within weeks of the new seizures, an Ottawa neurologist referred us to Montreal and to an extraordinary medical team under the supervision of Dr. André Olivier. We had a consultation on possible surgery. The doctors felt that Rebecca would be a good candidate. They determined that there were abnormal cells in our child's hippocampus that, if removed, might cure the seizures or, at minimum, allow her a normal life with medication.

We were learning fast as parents. Surgery is out of the question for some epilepsy patients. A colleague on Parliament Hill, where I worked for a New Democratic Party member of Parliament, was happy for Rebecca but jealous of my news. My colleague had been denied surgery.

Dr. Olivier wrote to our Ottawa neurologist, saying that "the current evidence strongly suggests hyper-intense T2 and Flair signal in the left mesial temporal structures associated with a hippocampal and amygdala asymmetry, the left being larger than the right." I sometimes deliberately lost myself in the medical jargon; it seemed to anesthetize me from all my fears. I'd memorize every medical term if it meant beating epilepsy. All I knew was that these new seizures were much bigger and more dangerous than those we had dealt with when Rebecca was a child. Dr. Olivier recommended a repeat MRI, some neuropsychological testing, and that she be admitted to the telemetry service for long-term tracking and measuring of her brain activity. Rebecca was keen to co-operate, motivated to reclaim her independence.

During the investigation, it was confirmed that those seizure-free years from the time she was ten were a bit of an illusion; her seizures had never fully stopped. Even though she might have felt sick to her stomach at times during those years, it was unclear whether the nausea was related to epilepsy. She did have occasional dreams and visual hallucinations where she appeared to be in a *Scooby-Doo* cartoon — yes, *Scooby-Doo*. In fact, this "dream" seemed to be her aura before having a seizure, which then caused the nausea. We did not spot those seizures, which were hidden compared to the trancelike "petit mal" or epic "grand mal" seizures that visibly surfaced. And Rebecca was not always very good at recognizing them when they occurred.

The doctors made no promises but were hopeful.

The first surgery, in November 2011, appeared to make a difference. It was amazing to watch her fast recovery. Her youth and fitness helped. Things were looking up. I was optimistic, gauging the strong recovery, new meds, and some stability on the health care front. She was seizure free for ten months. Rebecca was wrapping up high school and starting studies in Early Childhood Education (ECE) at Algonquin

College. She chose ECE because of her love for kids. I suspected that someday she would land a job working with kids or animals.

Only two months after her first surgery, Rebecca was delighted to get the green light to fly to the Dominican Republic for the destination wedding of her cousin Natalie Prashaw to Stephen Ramon. Rebecca inhaled the fun week in the sun, playing pool volleyball every day and tagging along with older cousins for nighttime clubbing and dancing.

Then, on a June afternoon, *bam!* The seizures started again. Dr. Olivier was upset when we notified him. *Failure* is probably too strong a word to describe the first surgery; the operation likely cut the number and the severity of the big seizures. Still, we were disappointed. The miracle never happened. Rebecca was the one most upset, though. Citing her tears and pain, she tells her Facebook universe on April 29, 2012, that life is mostly downhill. She is convinced that ending the seizures is her ticket to happiness.

The seizures after the first surgery were rare at first, then occurred more and more frequently. The trips to Emergency became more frequent; the medication changed and increased. Farm Boy had initially placed Rebecca as the express counter cashier. She had been good there with customers, friendly and fast. She knew all the produce codes to punch into the cash register. Now she struggled a bit to remember those codes, or how to do inventory, a chore she had handled routinely before.

There were other serious consequences of this new bout of epilepsy. Rebecca had to interrupt her ECE studies. She would return to Algonquin a year later and would choose a lighter workload to complete a one-year certificate program in Community Studies.

Losing her driver's licence to the seizures was nothing short of catastrophic in her teen universe. She had gotten her G1 weeks after her sixteenth birthday. She loved to drive and was a good driver. She especially enjoyed the "adult" part of being a driver: her independence and ability to pick up friends. One Saturday night, though, we learned the hard way that, on occasion, even without the licence, Rebecca was still driving.

My kid had a new girlfriend, Ciarra, in 2014. Still identifying as Rebecca at the time, she had responded to another friend's request to help Ciarra move. Well, Rebecca moved Ciarra in and, *carpe diem*, she decided to move in, too! It was time to leave Mom's place.

Rebecca had borrowed Ciarra's car to get some laundry done at her mom's. She slyly parked a block away from the house to hide the fact that she had driven there. However, in the walk from the car to the house, she had a seizure, fell backward, and hit her head, cracking her skull. A neighbour called an ambulance.

When we got to the hospital to comfort Rebecca, we learned what had actually happened. *Okay, Rebecca, please recover from this seizure so I can kill you for driving!* We were furious. Rebecca's relationship with Ciarra was still new and Ciarra did not yet totally appreciate the seriousness and unpredictability of the seizures. As a typical teenager, there were days when Rebecca didn't understand, either; in her desire for "normal" in her life — no more seizures, meds, hospitals — she took a few foolish risks. We made it clear how dangerous it was to drive, how it jeopardized her life and the lives of others if a seizure happened while she was driving. Ciarra quickly became an ally in helping Rebecca live with epilepsy.

The new seizures and visits to Emergency created a vicious circle — the more often she forgot her medication, the more seizures occurred. Those seizures increased her memory loss, causing her to be more likely to forget her meds. Over time, though, with a new neurologist and by learning to manage the memory issues, her health stabilized.

*   *   *

Tonight, in the recovery room after the brain surgery, I look at my kid and recall the turmoil of those teenage years, Rebecca becoming less expressive and more withdrawn after that first surgery in 2011. Those were hard years, from seventeen to twenty. Had it been typical teen angst? The meds? The surgery? It appeared to be more than that. Her mom sensed that something in Rebecca's life was not quite right. It took time and lots of patience and love, but eventually Rebecca told her mom that she liked girls, not boys. She said she was a lesbian. Later, Jessie Lloyd, a girl

> Bekkaa
> September 9, 2013
> Fml :(why does this keep happening to me ...

my kid went out with for several months, told me the story of that morning when Rebecca found the courage to come out:

> To most it appeared we were the best of friends. That's the way it stayed until one Sunday morning late winter, we woke up in her purple basement room as we usually did on weekends. The difference was Rebecca woke in an odd mood. She said she was tired of hiding. That she was tired of not being honest with family, herself, and me. She told me she had had a dream of coming out to her family and telling them that not only was she a lesbian but that she and I had been a couple for several months. She told me she could remember the fear and the anxiety as if it were real life and not a dream. She told me that upon telling her mother, she felt like a weight had been lifted and she felt free. She decided today would be the day she announced who she is.
>
> The day that she came out, Rebecca, along with Suzanne, her partner, Mike, and I, went to the Meadowlands Pub and Eatery for breakfast as we did most every Sunday. We all laughed and ordered our food as any other day. When our food arrived, Rebecca grabbed my hand under the table and let out a big breath. I still remember the way she looked down at her food as she said, "Guys, there is something I need to tell you."
>
> Suzanne and Mike listened intently as Rebecca continued and finally told them she was a lesbian. At first, they didn't say anything, taking in what she said, I remember her holding my hand harder through the silence. Suzanne looked Rebecca right in her eyes and said, "That's okay, but we need to discuss sleeping arrangements when Jessie sleeps over from now on."
>
> Her hold on my hand lightened and she laughed. We continued to eat as if nothing had happened. Rebecca cried when we got back to her house. She was so relieved that she was accepted, no questions

asked. She cried because she felt free, because she was happy, because she, at this time anyway, was who she felt like she was. She was finally in the open, no more secrets.

It would be another few years of teen turmoil before my kid declared publicly that he was a boy and wanted to be called Adam. It came in stages. Suzanne recalls a conversation on her deck when she asked seventeen-year-old Rebecca if she felt gender confusion: "She told me then that she was happy to be a girl but she would never be a 'girly' girl." But that self-understanding was also changing. Gradually, my boy realized he did like girls, but as a boy likes girls, not as a girl might. He told his mom and took his grandfather aside to tell him personally.

I got the right body parts as a boy. Adam didn't. My boy was changing. And my boy would change his parents. We fastened our seatbelts for the ride of our lives.

Wake up, son, before I tell your whole story.

> Bekkaa
> March 7, 2011
> Gaga concert was sooo fucking amazing!! I love you so much Mother Monster you made me proud to be born this way! <3 keep kicking ass!! Xoxo

* * *

Locally, we were happy to be dealing with a new neurologist in Ottawa, Dr. Rajendra Kale, an epilepsy specialist at the Ottawa Civic Hospital. It had not ended well with our previous neurologist in Ottawa, whom we had seen during the beginning of the second phase of our kid's epilepsy. At one of our first meetings back in 2012, he had told us that the three biggest triggers for seizures are alcohol, tiredness, and stress. He declared that Rebecca should avoid those.

Good luck with that, I thought to myself then. *He is an older teenager.*

We were, however, grateful that this doctor had introduced us to Dr. Olivier and the Neuro. But, during appointment after appointment with this first neurologist back in Ottawa, there were lectures on Rebecca's failure to take the meds sometimes, or to take the right dosage. These were difficult appointments, made more so by the fact that

Rebecca came to them not always aware of what meds she was taking. The doctor requested that we bring in all Rebecca's medications and prescriptions each time.

I appreciated his frustration. These were our messages, too. If the doctor's admonishments were difficult to accept at times, what was much more difficult was his response to the changes in Rebecca's condition. With each new meeting and report of further seizures, this doctor had one, and only one, response. Up the meds. He reasoned that no matter what the context or situation, if the meds failed to stop the seizures, then they needed to be stronger.

One seizure episode proved to be the breaking point. Rebecca was working at Subway, where one of her bosses would make her close one night and then come back several hours later to open the next morning. Rebecca's stress, tiredness, and panic triggered a seizure. We felt that the meds were working fine. It was the back-to-back closing and early shifts that were the culprits. When that doctor prescribed stronger meds, we looked for a new doctor.

Bekkaa
February 13, 2013
Hmmm so Lent begins, what to give up ... junkfood? overthinking? worrying? 😕 homework hmmm sounds nice lol but I won't ... UHMMM what what what..

Dr. Kale was different. At a lengthy intake appointment, after Adam had announced his true name and identity, Dr. Kale let Adam talk at length. Dr. Kale took notes on Adam's gender identity, name, his epilepsy, and soon-to-start transgender medication. Kale did not anticipate any pharmaceutical or medical problems in the interaction between the different medications for epilepsy and the testosterone for transitioning to a boy. He told us that he would check with a doctor who had more experience with epilepsy for transgender patients. He also surprised us with his recommendation that we go back to Dr. Olivier for an assessment for further surgery.

I almost broke my neck, though, during the initial appointment with Dr. Kale! The consulting room was crowded, and I was perched on a bed. At one point, he asked my son if he drank much alcohol. Adam shrugged. "No," he said. My head snapped in a low twist as I looked over to him.

For most of his teens, Adam had not shown much interest in alcohol, but I knew that he had started to like beer in the last few years and was enjoying drinking with his friends at the clubs. Two nights earlier, we had been at Jack Astor's at TD Place on a Wednesday night to celebrate his twenty-second birthday. The playoff game between the Ottawa Senators and Montreal Canadiens at the Canadian Tire Centre was on all the television screens at the restaurant. He had his Carey Price sweater on; I, my Sens jersey.

> Adam
> April 22, 2015
> Partying for my birthday and sens and habs game at my favorite place with my dad! 🍺 🎉 🎂
> GO HABS GOOO !!

That birthday night, he drank a couple of thirty-two-ounce half growlers — "howlers," they call them. I went to the bathroom thinking that we were done, but much to my surprise, I spotted a third howler in front of him when I returned. As anxious as I was on the epilepsy front — "alcohol, tiredness, and stress" — I shut up, not wanting to rain on his birthday celebration. He may have needed the third beer, too — my Ottawa Senators beat his Habs and Carey Price 1–0.

As we left Dr. Kale's office after the appointment, I told Adam what I had been thinking when he told Dr. Kale he didn't drink much alcohol:

Adam's twenty-second birthday. Wearing our team colours.

Adam
October 10, 2015
Being an adult is the dumbest
thing I've ever done.

it might be good for his health that he was too poor to celebrate too often.

* * *

The doctors back in Montreal were in favour of a second operation, more certain this time about what still needed to be removed. All of the scans captured a flare of brainwave activity in the seizures that is typical of those originating in a single place deep in the brain. This report made Adam a good candidate for surgery to remove the seizure trigger. I rooted for a cure.

I remember the family conference with Dr. Olivier. Adam was twenty-two. He was given a choice — surgery with a 50/50 chance of being seizure-free, and much better odds, perhaps higher than 70/30, at controlling the seizures. But with surgery came the risk of additional memory loss. The doctors also stated that skipping surgery meant deterioration of other cognitive faculties was likely. Adam made the decision himself. It was a "no-brainer." I smiled at those words.

Adam craved normal: who knows, he thought, he might be able to drive, star as a hockey goalie again, get a full-time job, even resume school studies, work with kids. He took a chance on a normal life rather than continuing with seizures, trips to Emergency. He wanted an end to all these interruptions. He wanted to make more important decisions on the questions emerging in his life.

Adam
November 19, 2015
HATE needles!!! So
many in one day!!

We supported the decision for further surgery. We had been noticing his gradual deterioration. In my visits to the Neuro, I watched the other outpatients on the unit: a few young adults like Adam, but also others who worried me more, these much older: middle-aged and a few seniors. I noticed their failing health, their physical and seeming mental health challenges. Was this our son's future?

* * *

We are through the second surgery now. Tonight, standing beside the bed, I do wonder and worry about what shape his brain will be in now.

Adam will focus on other things, like becoming Adam.

On Facebook, the day before this 2015 surgery, Adam shared his nervousness, his so wanting the surgery over. He wrote that he was taking a "deep breath ... I've done this before. I can do it again."

Right now, Adam desperately needs relief from this pain. His head aches from the incision and surgery. His back is screaming from being on a surgery bed all day. The nurses start the morphine drip. It works its magic, taking him to a better place to numb the pain for the night.

Adam
September 25, 2014
I have such amazing people in my life, and you all know who you are! :) So happy you guys are here with me through it all and no matter what there's always smiles and laughs

We bask a little in Adam's confidence in this surgery. We give him the water he is allowed to drink. Lindsay and Lauren come in for a quick visit, to say goodnight, to add their love. They have shared the long day of waiting and worrying. As Adam lets the morphine take him to a better place, I, too, drift away, to a Sudbury hospital bed a long time ago. That is where Adam will pick up his story.

Adam
February 17, 2015
Anyone wanna hang with this guy tonight?

CHAPTER 3

A Beautiful Baby Girl

April 22, 1993
Sudbury General Hospital, Sudbury, Ontario

IT IS LOVE at first sight.

We are at the Sudbury General Hospital late in the afternoon. Suzanne has had a ringside seat for those nine months leading up to today. This is her account:

> Rebecca was born on a cool April day after staying in the womb a little longer than I expected. She was my fourth child; she was ten days overdue. The night before she was born, I took a long walk, frustrated with the false labour leading nowhere and eager to hold her in my arms.
>
> Of course, at the time, I thought she was a he. Many of you have heard the story of me being so convinced I was carrying a boy I called my growing belly

Adam for nine months. I was shocked when the doctor said, "Congratulations, you have a beautiful baby girl." I was truly stunned; I had had no doubt that baby was a boy.

When she decided it was time, she entered the world so fast it was over before I understood the labour. That Thursday afternoon, I was walking the halls of the hospital before 4:00 p.m., worried it was more false labour, and then seventeen minutes later, Rebecca entered the world. In many ways, this was the story of her life. She was slow to jump into anything, but once she decided to do something, she jumped into it with gusto.

Typical of stories, I have my own version of the pregnancy and birth.

This kid, Rebecca Adam, is indeed my first child. I had married Suzanne the year before, choosing to leave active ministry as a Roman Catholic priest. It was a willing, magical jump into the deep end of family life; I was an instant stepdad of three children — Lindsay, Lauren, and David. In truth, as "with it" as I liked to think that I was as a priest, I knew next to nothing about birth and babies, even though I had baptized hundreds of them. Suzanne was the expert, with three kids already. She said we were having a boy, and that was good enough for me. We put a name on that "growing bump in the belly." For close to nine months, I enjoyed talking directly to Adam and with Suzanne about our Adam.

The labour is short. I hold Suzanne's hand too hard. She tells me to look south or I will miss the quick birth. An intern catches the baby. No doctor could be found fast enough. The intern breaks the news of the gender of our child. Mom is gobsmacked. A third girl? Where did our Adam go? Suzanne sits halfway up on the delivery table, looking for a second opinion. The intern, the calmest in the room, announces that although it is the first baby he has ever delivered, he is confident that we are parents of a "beautiful baby girl!"

But moms know best, right?

* * *

When Adam came out as a boy years later, he told his own amazing, heartfelt version of how he came to have the name he loves. And he fashioned the news into his own birth announcement on Facebook:

Adam
September 13, 2014

... this is something that has been bugging me for a while.... and I do mean awhile... since I was a baby even in my mom's womb, I always considered myself a boy. I got used to Rebecca or Becca only because that's what I was born with and called all around. But my real full name is "Rebecca Danielle Adam Prashaw." Danielle was for my pepère [grand-father] whose name is Daniel but my parents added "le" to it to make it feminine but gave me Adam because they didn't want to have a ultrasound to see what I was because my mom had already had two girls and they were at the bottom of her belly and then had my bro and he was at top of her belly ... so when she was having me she felt me up in her stomach for a while, not below like my sisters. So she and my dad expected a boy and came up with Adam for me. But when it was time I came out, it was total opposite, I was a girl ... and they were shocked but still happy and of course with my dad's past life he came up with Rebecca and they gave that to me.

As I grew up I felt like it just sounded odd, and inside I always loved boy things: playing with boys, playing video games, being Prince rather than princess, hated Barbie, built forts and played lego with my bro, power rangers etc! It has been very difficult for me to speak my mind and what my heart and mind wants. And been afraid of losing people or

making people laugh at me... but thanks to a lot of
newer friends and close friends I've had for a while
some I call "bro" lol love them all ... but now I want
to start being who I really am... I've had to hide it
well all my life... and felt uncomfortable till now and
I just want now my family and friends to still be
there and love and accept me for who I am..

So everyone, as of today as you saw already
on my FB name I am a transgender named Adam.
I was born with that name for a reason and so it is
kept in as my name now.. this is Adam Prashaw
Thanks :P means a lot.

Quite the birth announcement from our Adam! Better than the
one we wrote for the *Sudbury Star* in 1993. Get my kid wound up
and there is no end to what you will hear. And never doubt a mother's intuition. Adam delighted in telling people that his mom knew
before he did that he was a boy. Years later, on his Facebook page,
I joke that he must have smart parents to have known who he was
from day one.

So, in one way, I guess our Adam "came out" and "came into"
himself when he was in his late teens and early twenties, but he
says it best: Adam was there all along. We somehow knew that, too.
However, accepting the doctor's declaration and what our eyes saw,
we did name our "girl" Rebecca. It evolved into Becca. She spelled it
"Bekkaa" on her first Facebook page. We included Adam in the legal
name. Call us crazy. I have often wondered if Adam was up to some
early mischief influencing this unusual choice, or was it that we parents were smarter than *we* thought?

Growing up, our Rebecca was into Legos and building things,
action figures — never dolls. She liked boy shirts. Forget makeup. If
we were ever separated in a department store, I never bothered checking the girls' clothing section. I smiled when I saw my Rebecca next
to a "girly girl" classmate or neighbour. That was like gender shock
therapy for this dad.

In his "I am Adam" 2014 Facebook post, he referred to his dad's past church ministry to explain the choice of the name Rebecca. He was right about that. I admired Rebekah in the Old Testament of the Bible. Rebekah figures prominently in Israel's story (Genesis 24–27). Mate of Isaac, mother of Jacob, she was destined to become ancestor of Israel. In a patriarchal world, she seized power, taking an active role in the many negotiations surrounding her family. This was certainly a foreshadowing of my child's character! My kid became proficient at seizing power in family negotiations.

This biblical Rebekah was strong, courageous, an independent thinker, and knew how to exercise power. I wanted my kid to have a strong name, be confident as a child, and grow into a strong woman. We would not be disappointed, although we were not necessarily thrilled every time this strong-willed kid came knocking. A girlfriend called him "hard-headed." That is Adam.

I went back to the early pages of the Old Testament to find that name. Who could imagine that, one day, our kid would trump that and turn back to the first page of that sacred book, to the story of creation, for his name.

And none of us could ever imagine how strong our kid would be.

Bekkaa

April 4, 2013

forget the risk and take the fall, if it's what you want, then it's worth it all ♥
[Malik Ferraud, "You Alive"]

CHAPTER 4

"MY Home!" and Facebook Dad

November 26 to December 31, 2015
Ottawa, Ontario

AS WITH THE FIRST surgery four years earlier, Adam's recovery is remarkably quick — the plus side of being young. Right after the surgery, the nurses tell us that he will be out of the Intensive Care Unit and back on a regular ward the next morning, and likely be discharged the following day, less than forty-eight hours after the all-day brain surgery.

Back in the hospital early the next morning, I see a very different Adam. No tears. He is awake, sitting up, eating applesauce, his pain better controlled but his head still hurting. Both the tube in his arm and the catheter are out. I plan to have a short visit and then say goodbye, making sure to text his mother the morning-after update that he's doing better. My stay is brief because I have to head home to Ottawa to retrieve Adam's dog, Dallas, who is staying with family friends. Dallas is a three-year-old puppy and can be a handful!

Amazingly, the next day after surgery, Adam is indeed in a regular ward room at the hospital. And, of course, he is on Facebook.

Adam
November 26, 2015
Just wanna say operation went fine yesterday, was sleeping all day yesterday and today and could still go back for more. Head hurts, of course and feel sick but I hope begins to feel better soon. Thank you all for the love and support. Means a lot and can't wait to feel better and be home.

Adam goes home to Ottawa on Friday, to his mom's place first. He plans to be back to his Elgin Street apartment by November 29, less than a week after the surgery. That sets my anxiety soaring — despite his perpetual quest for normal, Adam is still recovering, and even in good times, he is not always the best at caring for himself. There are epilepsy meds to take, although this is made easier with a new automatic, blister-pack epilepsy-pill dispenser that pops out the right pill and dosage each morning and night. Some epilepsy patients can get confused about meds. Adam certainly did. At different stages in his epilep-

Adam
November 27, 2015
So much pain 🙁 ugh....

sy, he wore MedicAlert bracelets and set alarms on his mobile phone to remind him when to take medications. The seizures can mess up thinking, too — what to take, when, how much — as doctors adjust the meds after new seizures.

Adam needs a lot of rest. That will be a challenge to my kid, a young man in perpetual motion, someone who has struggled with maintaining good sleep habits most of his life. Plus, being Adam, he needs to see everyone!

Texting will be our lifeline, as it is with his mom. There are multiple daily messages — news, questions, favours, and more. I hear more from Adam via texts than through emails or phone calls.

It is one of life's many ironies. When he comes over for supper or to see visiting relatives, I am constantly reminding him to put away that distracting phone. But that same phone proves to be the most precious lifeline to my son during his recovery. That "infuriating" phone allows me to communicate with him more than I ever remember communicating with my dad, as good as that relationship was. In those days, being "out of sight" usually meant no communication, except for the infrequent, long-distance phone calls during my university studies. Now, for this dad in search of his son, Facebook and texting serve as welcome umbilical cords.

"Dad" Adam with Chelsey's Landon.

Adam is heading back to be with a girlfriend, Chelsey. They started going out eight months earlier. She lives in another apartment in town with her two-year-old son, Landon, but she is at Adam's place a lot. Is it in most (or all?) parental DNA to judge our kids' romantic partners? They never seem to quite measure up in the first, rash judgments. I certainly have misgivings. Adam seems drawn to those who are vulnerable. Perhaps he sees a bit of himself in them. Perhaps it is his amazing, total acceptance of people that we have seen since he was a child. He has tended to accept people, period, rather than be bothered much by their faults. This is another of life's ironies, though; as Adam returns to Chelsey, this comforts me. He will not be alone. What the hell? Worried about the girlfriends and yet happy he will be with one. Theory and practice are not always in sync for parents! Adam is fond of Chelsey. He is crazy about Landon.

Adam
December 4, 2015

Really gotta say I'm the luckiest guy ever! Gosh do I love these two! I got to spend part of my time healing with Chelsey and Landon for two days/one night feeling like a true family. I sure do love every moment with these two and can't wait for what the future will bring us three!

A few days later, Adam posts the first post-surgery selfie, proof of his "hell and back" physical appearance — his shaved, puffed-swollen head, black eye, stitches. He looks like a war casualty. Indeed, he has been in battle.

Adam
November 28, 2015

So for anyone that's curious this is what I look like after my surgery on Wednesday 24th. Back home finally, but still in extreme pain, been hard to sleep, appetite been up and down, non-stop headaches but it was definitely worth it. Just the wait of it to

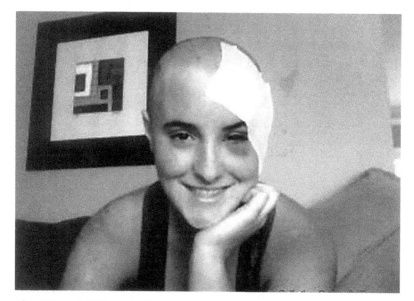

After Rebecca's 2011 surgery. Battered but never beaten.

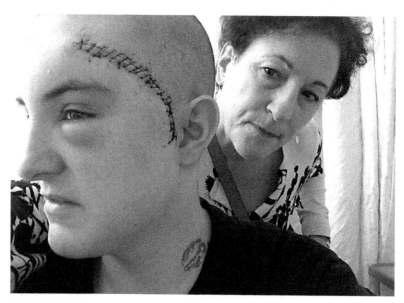

Mom checks Adam, post-surgery, 2015.

heal will be the hell of me, plus being stress for so much doesn't help out. Anyways just thought I'd share what I look like and keep posted since I'm not fully 100% and hard to msg [message] every-one. Let's just hope this goes by day and my stress leaves me. (and don't mind my silly sister she was truly trying to make me smile while in hospital.

The "silly sister" is Lindsay, mugging for the camera in the hospital room, loving her brother back to health.

Adam's post-surgery fighter picture reminds me of another photo Rebecca posted after the first surgery in 2011. It is one of my favourite pictures — Rebecca with this gorgeous smile, a bandaged head, a black eye, and a "not going to stay down long" look up against the epilepsy. Tired, battered, but never beaten. Even though it is a 2011 photo, I see both Rebecca and Adam in that face.

I get to see Adam's posts because I am Adam's friend on Facebook. I know other parents who are FB friends with their kids, and I know others who marvel at this feat, jealous of my connection, sad because they don't have that link. And then there are some who do not want that experience, who do not want to be part of that world. Parental ig-norance might be bliss! For the most part, visiting Adam's Facebook page demands that I keep my Facebook Dad in check for any incoming or outgoing adolescent missiles, learning that I do not have to call 911 after every post, knowing instead the value of offering a thumbs-up "like" or shutting up and surviving the roller-coaster ride. I am more spectator and cheerleader than spy, rarely opting for a timely intervention and doing so only when necessary. His Facebook posts often do confirm my suspicions. I play catch-up to my kid's news, the first to suspect things but the last to know. How ironic is it that Facebook helps me better un-derstand the kid who for so long lived in the very next room!

Adam's return to Facebook, his second home, was quick. The boy lives online. His good friend Kendra Borthwick once joked that she took a five-hour break from being online and returned to find fourteen new posts from Adam and Chelsey.

Adam and Kendra Borthwick. So many best buds.

If he wanted to, Adam might complain. He certainly has grounds. When he does complain, it is done quickly, and he is over it. I don't see him feeling sorry for himself or wanting anyone's pity.

He posts another post-surgery selfie. He's handsome, scars and all. The bandages are his badge of courage. It's been a bit amusing to his parents that, even when he was a little kid, Rebecca never tired of telling people about the latest hospital or medical adventure in the greatest detail. The stories are unreservedly epic. They are his bragging rights. My kid may not want pity, but he always courts an audience.

* * *

2015 is coming to a close.

Again, back in his Elgin Street apartment, Adam is keen to see his friends and get back to normal, at least his normal. Recovering from brain surgery and continuing his transition from a woman to a man may not be the norm out there. It is Adam's. And, given Adam's irrepressible personality and his sometimes impulsive choices, his norm appears at times more "SNAFU": situation normal, all fucked up.

Adam is also keen to return to work. Doctors tell him that he will need several weeks to recover before returning to work at the upscale boutique Nature Café at the Canadian Museum of Nature. He has worked there almost a year as a chef's assistant, telling his Facebook family after his very first shift that "I can tell already I'll love this job and good hours."

Bathed in natural light and surrounded by the imagery of natural elements, the café is refreshingly easygoing, spacious, and inviting. It's been a treat to see Adam in his chef's assistant outfit, flashing a grin my way from behind the counter. He's learning how to make the specialty coffees. This regular job is pivotal for Adam. I suppose that's true for any kid, but it's particularly true for transgender kids. Adam craves the stability that working offers; there's the money he needs but, equally, the self-worth and meaning it brings.

It is a far better place to work than the "sandwich artist" jobs he has had in the past few years at two sub shops. These jobs were okay for a while. There, he might be in early to put the coffee on, prepare the breakfast sandwiches, and clean up. He also often had a closing shift, cashing out and cleaning as I, at times, waited and watched from the parking lot. He would chat with the regulars, including a few seniors who nursed their coffees or read a newspaper.

I watched him through the windows thinking of a few summer jobs of mine — cleaning at the Voyageur Hotel in North Bay or dropping six bolts into each engine gasket in an assembly line at the Windsor Ford factory. If nothing else, I hoped the experience of those jobs in the sub shops might encourage my kid to stay in school. My summer jobs did!

Rebecca, too, grew to despise those sub-shop jobs. Employers demanded many opening and closing shifts, at dawn and past midnight, shifts that robbed her of much-needed sleep. The sleep deprivation then triggered more seizures.

The café where he works now is a block from his apartment. His epilepsy rules out full-time work, but the café offers him four or five shorter shifts each week. Better still, none of those start before 9:00 a.m. — something that suits Adam perfectly. Best of all, the café staff completely accept him as Adam. That is huge. For the first time, he has Adam on his ID tag. He's proud about that.

Adam recovers from the surgery fairly rapidly. Facebook tells the story of his first weeks back home. The posts cover his typical array of loves, friends, clubs, wicked humour, work, angst, never-ending stress, current events, and more. From reading his posts, I admit I've all but given up on my efforts to persuade him to keep his private, intimate moments to himself and not post them on Facebook; weird for the parent in his sixties to be passing on instructions to his kid in his young twenties on how to manage his Facebook account to limit who sees what he posts online of his latest pillow talk or fight with a girlfriend. Of course, I realize that he knows all about Facebook. In his impulsive spontaneity, he simply prefers to post everything to everyone. *I am who I am. Love me or unfriend me.*

Most important, though, I pay attention to the hashtags ending his posts.[1] My boy is like enough kids, sometimes tight-lipped with his parents on how he truly feels. He may be an open book or a closed book in the same hour! He may or may not even recognize how he feels. And if he does, it might be easier to tell the universe on Facebook than his parents. Those hashtags reveal his thinking and feelings. They are highways to his heart.

Adam
November 30, 2015
Brain Surgery & broken wrist within same week. Break wrist over November 21-22 weekend and then go to get brain surgery Nov 25 for my epilepsy I feel so drained and uncomfortable especially when I am around random people when I go check mail, or have to go up to see landlord or leaving for somewhere

1. For those not on social media, hashtags are the words or phrases strung together after the symbol # at the end of a post.

(which I can't do much, I need to rest!). Woman in elevator today said I looked like I was in accident and I said no surgery she said oh wow ok well you also look like a fighter. And made me smile a bit cause I rather show that I was or am tough than be a wimp or weak. I hope the healing processes fast and I can just feel better. Stitches removed Wednesday 4th and then wrist checked the 7th. Help me pray for quick recovery! #brainsurgery #mysecondone #epilepsy #painandstruggles #fight #staystrong #friendsandfamilysupport #careandlove #bestgirlfriendever #surgery2015 #maythisbethelasttime #seizurefree #timewillcome #mcgillneurology #montreal

Fight.
Stay strong.
Friends and family support.
May this be the last time.
Seizure free.

He's back in his own apartment, posting on Facebook that he is happy to be in his own bed and reunited with his girlfriend and his dog, Dallas. He is eager to have his stitches removed on December 4. Indeed, Adam looks like a prizefighter. He has this inner steel. Epilepsy smacks him down and then he gets up off the canvas to smack it right back. Whether from seizures or mistakes, he gets up, smiles, and carries on. He vows to stay strong. Family and friends surround him in support. He wants nothing more than to be seizure free.

Adam shared a photo
December 1, 2015
If robbers ever broke into my house and wanted money I would just laugh and search with them

I laugh at many of Adam's posts. In the midst of incredible pain, he inevitably cracks a joke, looking for a ray of sunshine.

Adam

December 2, 2015

Just want this pain to stop!! It's not even my head anymore, my head feels fine and stitches off Friday unless needs little more time. But no, it's my F***ING ass and I legit mean ass!! I walk like an idiot and can barely sleep or sit and get up and can't always stand. I just want this pain to stop so I can finally just say I'm fine!!

He elaborates on this pain in a text. His lower back is like "throbbing electrical warm feelings … makes me feel weak and I can't walk, legs shake so I gotta stop and hold something for a bit. Hurts to get up too. Anything hurts."

Adam

December 5, 2015

Stitches finally off! There's still some swelling going on, but I can't complain too much, just happy my bandages and stitches are finally removed. Now it's just the time it'll take for the swelling, and stitches residue to clear off. And soon back to looking normal and not have people staring at me so awkwardly.

Adam

December 12, 2015

Update on my process of recovering. Things looking good, little swelling still but scarring healing, and wrist cast off the 30th! Happy hair's growing back quickly too! Lol never liked it this sort miss my spikes. But back soon #brainsurgery #epilepsy #curingepilepsy #surgery2015 #healing #happy #loveandsupport #trans #ftm #strength #takestime #alliswell #support #grateful

His posts mirror his life, pain, and love, with a shake of humour.

"Love and support," "takes time," and "healing, happy" leap from my computer screen. Good words for a parent to read. These are words that Adam does not often use in speech. He is back mixing his two epic journeys — conquering epilepsy and transitioning from a woman to a man. The two seem joined at the hip. The seizures and surgeries frustrate Adam's primary agenda to be, in his words, "all boy."

*   *   *

Adam announces a new Snapchat name: DarkKnight.[1] He adores Batman, and his crazy love for the winged crusader is made plain with images everywhere in his apartment — on cups, hats, T-shirts, underwear, posters, pillows, and more. It's like the Batcave. Now every friend knows that he IS Batman. My letter for Rebecca's second birthday told of the time when, after I told her Polkaroo or Bear and Marigold were not on TV, she "matter-of-factly asked for Batman."

He has a tattoo of Batman, too, one of a dozen or so adorning his body. I wince at each new picture posted of another personal tattoo; the tattoos mostly drive me crazy. I think first of the money, blown so soon after the last discussion on how to save money and get out of debt. I worry that his tats will cover him head to toe. Will he regret having them someday?

Now, those tattoos also make me grin, rubbing my own first tattoo on my right shoulder, the paw mark and name of our Labrador retriever, Murphy. On the sad day that Murphy was put down, Adam first took an ink print of his paw. We later visited Adam's tattoo artist, Dolly, for an unforgettable "Dad and Adam" moment. Of course, Adam told those stories about Murphy's death and our memorial tattoos on Facebook.

Bekkaa

May 5, 2014

So surprised it's been 11 years. you've helped

---

1. Snapchat is a popular mobile app that allows you to send videos and pictures, both of which will self-destruct after a few seconds of a person viewing them. It's also a fun messaging app.

me through a lot of times, good and bad, kept me happy and comfortable. We traveled together, spent a lot of time together, but now is the time for me to say goodbye... even though you'll always be in my heart and memories forever and always ♥ ♥ R.I.P Murphy ♥ you were such an amazing dog, son, and best friend!! I love you so much and say hey to your family up there with you now to keep you happy and joyful :) <3 but please be my angel ♥ ♥

Bekkaa
May 15, 2014
Me and my dad got our amazing best friend and dog for 11 years paw and name tattooed today! Was my dad's first tattoo aha! Gotta say pretty impressed how easy he took it! And well my 9th lol.. more to come :P but was truly amazing experience and great memory to have and share with my dad :) thanks to Dolly for doing them & Ciarra for being there ♥

Nine tattoos and "more to come." Cue another Dad head shake.

* * *

As the new year approaches, Adam is preoccupied with his usual priorities — friends, a relationship, transitioning to being a boy, job, money, and family — all with the inevitable heaping side-helping of stress. So many things bug him. He worries about everything.

Like enough other young people, Adam doesn't think much of himself, at times, or believe he has many friends. He is sensitive to what others think about him, how others might react if he told them who he truly is. He gets down on himself.

Through conversations and reading, I am learning how self-esteem and maturing are huge issues for trans kids as they struggle to figure out their identities. Until Adam showed up, I hadn't given it much thought. I supported trans rights politically in my work for the New Democratic Party on Parliament Hill, but there were so many other issues competing in a busy life. Now, it's personal.

Adam responds with a thumbs-up sign to a meme about someone who does not have a lot of friends but who knows a lot of people.

Bekkaa
April 26, 2012
Stress stress
go away please
come back
when... Well wait
no, never...

He posts a Tumblr quote on being sad and stressed "since 2012. 2016 better be it."[1] He wishes his stress would disappear, forever.

From 2012 to 2016 — five years bookended by the two surgeries and their recoveries. This second round of epilepsy has loitered a long time.

On Facebook, Adam is like many of his generation: transparent about his struggles. Annoyed. Frustrated. Bored. I read those words a lot. When he shares his latest stress or that he is down or depressed, his good friends immediately shower him with love. He always seems to reply with a thank-you and a "love" sticker back. He struggles on.

On December 15, he posts a picture of himself in an elf hat with his beloved pépère and mémère, Suzanne's parents, Dan and Jeannine Corbeil, who are visiting from North Bay for an early Christmas. There's no such thing as a countdown to Christmas for my kid. He starts celebrating early and often, opening presents well before December 25. He

Bekkaa
October 9, 2010
Gotta love life....

posts pictures of Chelsey and himself exchanging gifts that they bought and opened after unsuccessfully trying to hide them from each other. Adam has told Chelsey that he also bought Justin Bieber concert tickets for a May 18, 2016, show at the Canadian Tire Centre in Ottawa. I make a mental note for another budget talk.

Adam is enjoying the relationship with Chelsey's son, Landon. On December 21, he shares on Facebook an image with the text, "The greatest feeling in the world, being called Dad." Adam has been going to parenting and support classes with Chelsey. They've become a little

1. Tumblr is a microblogging and social networking site. The service allows users to post multimedia and other content to a short-form blog.

family. On Christmas Day, enjoying Ottawa's warm weather and green Christmas, Adam snaps a picture of himself wearing shorts, Landon on his lap, Adam flashing a big grin. At a downtown diner during the holidays, I mention those Facebook posts and how he appears to be enjoying this "dad" experience. He glows, without saying a word.

Christmas Day, a favourite time of his, arrives. Having separated parents has an upside for him — at a minimum, two Christmas and birthday celebrations each year, scoring double the presents. For years, the kid has somehow magically grown his birthdays into week-long parties. Now, living on his own, it seems that these seasonal parties have morphed into three or more celebrations, partying with his downtown friends, whom he cherishes.

On December 27, he posts, "Psychology says the person who tries to keep everyone happiest often is the loneliest." He says this is true for him. On December 28 he writes, "Just ever feel like running away grabbing shit and going."

I didn't know then that his relationship with Chelsey was ending.

I am playing catch-up again with my son. With Adam enjoying his downtown, independent phase, I feel that I am the last person on Earth to learn his news. My empty nest in the Ottawa suburb of Kanata is my own struggle. Driving, you can be downtown in a half-hour; it can take up to fifty minutes if you go by bus. It seems a short distance to me, but in Adam's galaxy, Kanata might as well be next to Pluto. Kanata was the centre of his high school universe, but not now. Adam is thriving downtown. Most days, I remember why that is. Downtown, Adam is his own person. He is master of the ship, paying the bills, going to work, falling in love.

However, far worse for my parental ego is that it seems his friends, the Facebook universe, and Mom are often ahead in the line for actual contact with Adam. He can be short with me when I press for details of a story he has already told others, stories that I may have missed or forgot. They might only be a day or two old, but those events are ancient history to him. He doesn't want to tell me the "Chelsey breakup" story. "I told everyone!" he snaps.

Adam
December 25, 2015
Merry Christmas everyone!! 🎄🎁 😊

This makes me think of a visit the previous year from a nephew and his partner, who is a psychologist. In a brief meal at a restaurant, that psychologist easily picked up on the avalanche of stress falling from Adam. In an informal meeting afterward, he mentioned to me how he thought that biofeedback therapy would help Adam to relax, something that would have the side benefit of reducing the seizures. Adam told me that he was open to going, but this turned out to be a smokescreen to please Dad. I kept him informed as I checked out local biofeedback therapists and coordinated a few possible appointments that he asked me to arrange. But he never followed up. He wasn't really interested, and said no in his way, making sure it never happened.

In fairness to Adam, my son had had his fill of doctors and counsellors.

I joke with friends that Adam had enrolled me in a Ph.D. course on parenting at age forty-one. And those friends know that, for all my complaining, I would not have it any other way. Well, maybe, if anyone asked, I would change a few things. *Will you listen more, Adam? Will you agree with me now and then? Will you park that stubborn, hard-headed personality?*

For all I can see, the kid doesn't have a malicious bone in his body, but he can be stubborn, and yes, hard on me. On the one hand, I recognize the hard-headed thing is a survival skill. I want to cut him some slack, appreciating that I might be seeing him when the wind is out of his sails, tired from the latest seizure or from the meds that might dull his emotions. But on the other hand, frankly, there are times when he will not even try to meet me halfway, or any way. Call it adolescence, immaturity, rebellion, whatever. I feel that there are times when there should be no excuses.

Despite our ups and downs, I still want to see him. He may be twenty-two and on his own, but I find myself craving more contact. I so enjoyed those high school days in Kanata when, as Rebecca, my kid spent most of her time with me because her school, friends, hockey, and job were all there. Now, with Adam in his early twenties, and downtown, the half hour to my place is light years away. Complicating matters, I don't own a car at the moment; instead, I rely on booking a car for errands and downtown visits. As much as I try — through love, guilt, and yes, the odd parental bribe — most of the infrequent get-togethers happen downtown. When I occasionally dump my parental woes on his mother, she puts it all in her perspective, reminding me that I won the "separated parent" lottery in those high school days of ample access in Kanata. She adds that she doesn't see much of Adam, either. He is in the same town but busy with friends, doing his thing. It isn't malice; he doesn't think of us if we are not directly in front of him, and getting in front of him is a constant challenge. He might throw me a Facebook "Happy Birthday," but he may not come out for a celebration that day. Those messages are sincere. They are also so fleeting.

On the positive side, we text incessantly back and forth, as Adam does with several other family members and friends. I am "in his life," following him on Facebook. We speak on the phone frequently. For all my missing him, we are still intimately connected. Perhaps it is one of those parenting contradictions — so close and yet so far away, influenced by feelings and perceptions on both sides.

Thinking about all of this, I have a "Rick at twenty-two" flashback that puts things in perspective. I remember how seldom I beat a path to my parents' door.

So much has happened since then.

What a leap it was, in 1990–1991, to jump from a celibate life to fatherhood, Father Rick to Dad; to become a stepdad of three kids and then the father of Rebecca Adam. I recalled a priests' meeting in the diocese of Sault Ste. Marie in northern Ontario when the bishop, Marcel Gervais, became quite uncomfortable listening to a few priests raise their concerns (and struggles) about living compulsory celibacy.

At the front of the room, Gervais, a very smart man, a biblical scholar from London, Ontario, was getting a northern baptism. The North has its own unique attitude and spirit in many ways, including in our faith communities.

He shrugged off the priests' concerns, commenting that if we thought we had it bad as priests, we should talk to married couples and parents.

The comment, I guess a joke, gets a few laughs, but others shake their heads.

Thinking back to the bishop's comments, I now laugh, too, recalling I *did* take his advice. I talked to those parents. Sunday nights, after a full weekend schedule crammed with confessions, weddings, several masses, and baptisms, I typically re-energized myself by heading to one of those families' homes for dinner. The families to which I gravitated tended to have kids, many with normal, irreverent teens who delighted in trying to shock the young priest with their stories or bold questions. Those suppers were often a saving grace, sampling the normal mayhem of family life. The time spent with couples did not make me listen to the bishop's counsel, nor want to race back to the refuge of the rectory. They were "Harry meets Sally" moments; I wanted what they had: family life. A desire for my own family, apparently buried deep down decades ago, surfaced.

Of course, the dream life I've chosen has had its difficult times. And I sometimes appreciate the irony of having my own irreverent kid challenging me when it had been my decision to leave the priesthood and choose family life despite a bishop's warning that the grass might not be as green on the other side.

Now, I'm the parent of the irreverent kid, eager to talk about most of his shenanigans. This kid is my "show and tell" for life's sweet, simple delights. I fondly remember the early days of a child squealing at a full moon, finding the brightest star in the country sky, counting all the yellow school buses, devouring with Dad a pan of warm chocolate chip cookies just out of the oven.

*   *   *

The year 2015 is ending.

We are at another important juncture. Adam is twenty-two. As parents, we worry. We read his periodic Facebook comments on alcohol and sex, uncertain if they are reporting news or if they're just youthful bravado and humour. I message him with my worries that he is adopting unhealthy behaviours, seems to have little time for family, and appears to be unaware of the consequences of being irresponsible. I tell him that he has to think about more than only

> Adam shared
> June 29, 2015
> such a nice day i think
> i will skip my meds and
> stir things up a bit

himself and think through what the "normal" he craves actually means, assess whether he is heading to true adulthood or self-destruction. I know that I am not the only parent doing this. We are a little scared.

As I message him, a memory pops into my head. I am Adam's age. My buddies are literally carrying me up the stairs at the Carleton University residence after a night of drinking "across the river" in Hull, Quebec, where the legal drinking age is eighteen. Inebriated, I hear distant talk from my pallbearers of "alcohol poisoning," "last rites," and debates about what they will take from my room after my demise. They lay me in bed and light a few votive candles, as only "true friends" would do. This flashback from my college drinking days makes me pause. It doesn't make me think that I am a hypocrite, nor does it mute my parental objections now for Adam. It does give me perspective, though. I wouldn't be too worried about the drinking if it weren't for Adam's epilepsy, knowing that alcohol can trigger seizures. That is what I worry about. That is one of the things that Adam hates about his epilepsy.

I need to step back a bit and give Adam some space. Still, I cannot shake the feeling of dread, as though I am constantly standing under a high-wire act, watching my artist son teeter and totter high above his audience. He has a life-threatening illness and still an Everest to climb to become who he wants to be.

I watch, hope, pray, and frequently check in. I suspect his mom is doing likewise. Suzanne and I may be separated but we still collaborate as parents on several health care issues and school events. We do most of the parenting solo, directly with Adam, but occasionally we share urgent intel via email or in person, figuring out what our kid might actually be up to, finding ourselves united as we react to his latest escapades or the newest hole that he has fallen into or dug for himself. We are ready to intervene whenever a new crisis might come. And come they do. This job of parenting — part balancing, part crapshoot — consumes me. Years ago, in Russell, Suzanne typically argued that we should allow the kids wider latitude to learn from their experiences and mistakes. That seemed reasonable. I just didn't see it working for Rebecca all the time. I err more on the side of intervention and rescue, which has its own set of mistakes. Suzanne and I are different and see the world differently, though we both love our son deeply.

I act at times like Molly, my former Aussie cattle dog, herding my kid away from the various cliffs or predatory shadows nearby. Epilepsy is THE predator. Epilepsy feels like a home invasion, something that lurks in the shadows, a dangerous stranger who has burst into our lives, impossible to control and refusing to leave.

We are all relieved that this second surgery is over.

Adam shared
August 3, 2015
I wonder if clouds ever look down on us and say,
Hey look! That one is shaped like an idiot

CHAPTER 5

In Good Spirits!

AS 2016 APPROACHES, my eyes are wide open to the challenges ahead in the new year, but I like how things are coming together. Adam notices that change is coming.

The balmy Christmas weather also has Adam in good spirits.

The surgery is over. As much as the Neuro in Montreal felt like a second home to him when he walked through those doors on University Avenue off Sherbrooke, he is happy to think that he will never have to return. There will be a few follow-up appointments in Montreal, but Adam will mainly be dealing with Ottawa doctors.

Adam is optimistic about other developments, too. Apartment-wise, he expects to be out of his pricy Elgin Street apartment in a few months. He first moved into a bachelor apartment there with Ciarra. Now he is down the hall in a one-bedroom apartment and

> Adam
> June 29, 2015
> We don't do drugs. We are drugs. We'll make the most out of tonight and worry about it all tomorrow.
> 😉 👍 👊
> [— Salvador Dali]

is searching for another place. He is a few months from the end of the lease his mother co-signed.

Work-wise, he steps back from his usual panic and returns to the Nature Café at the museum. From time to time, he finds it awkward going back when a seizure has happened at work or when he's had surgery. Eventually, Adam wants to exit the fast food industry. Unsure of what to do, he goes in to talk with his boss, Joel Frappier. He meets his new supervisor that day. After their chat, not surprisingly, he reports that he is pumped, ready to return to work on Monday, January 25th.

His dog remains with me almost a month after Adam's surgery. Adam is too weak for the long walks and energetic play this three-year-old pup needs. We are also nervous about Dallas jumping on Adam's head stitches or surgery scar. In December, still not feeling 100 percent, Adam asks me to run his bi-monthly claim for the Ontario Disability Support Program (ODSP) over to the Ontario government office on Prescott Street.

Bekkaa
October 2, 2012
Human Sexuality teacher showing us powerpoint about penises and internal structure and all of a sudden "Looks like an Aero bar doesn't it?" Okay yeah no more Aero bars for me now thanks... lol

Adam is getting ODSP benefits. The support is essential for a kid who has decided to live on his own and has only part-time work. He never has enough money. Like many in his generation, he's living cheque to cheque, with minimum wage and precarious jobs. The rent, food, phone, internet, dog food, laundry card, and other bills have him on a steep learning curve for household budgets. But he is learning. I smile at one Facebook post where he comments on two consecutive 5:30 a.m. shifts working as a labourer with Mike, Suzanne's husband, telling friends he now understands why adults are tired after work. He says he feels like a zombie and is heading to bed early.

Doing a budget with his mother is new. It's a nice surprise to notice files in his apartment for pay stubs, ODSP, taxes, and more. Sticking with the budget is another matter. He is poor — Bieber-concert-tickets poor, now. His money woes usually mount in the second half of each month. I get heartfelt thank-you messages when I, occasionally, bail him out.

Adam is proud of his independence. He's trying to make it on his own, following his own counsel. The ODSP benefits started in 2014. How he qualified and what we learned has shone a light on Adam's current difficulties as he recovers from surgery and prepares to return to work.

The Ontario government rejected Adam's initial application. His disability was not visible or obvious. Even when a seizure occurred, it appeared to be only a temporary interruption in an otherwise healthy, normal life. He always seemed to find work. He did his jobs well. It took a while for an employer or friend to recognize the genuine disability, made harder, too, by Adam himself, as he is often the last person to want to talk about what he can't do.

When the Ontario government turned Adam down in 2014, a family friend put us in touch with Glenn Webster, a Toronto psychologist who we understood had helped some others to successfully appeal their ODSP decisions, framing clear evidence of disability into those rigid government definitions.

It was weird preparing Adam to meet Glenn. I wanted Adam to focus on his disability, which is the last thing in the world he wanted to do. Adam does not see himself as a person with a disability. He will wear a MedicAlert bracelet, take his meds, visit the doctors, and life goes on. His seizures, surgeries, and setbacks are stuff to soldier through, get over, and forget, so he can get back to his life. Much like other kids, he wants to fit in. And, many days, he does.

But the disability is obvious to his parents, as it was to a professional like Webster. Adam cannot work at any jobs that involve driving a vehicle. He cannot work anywhere where he needs a car to get to the job site, such as outside the city. He has learned that he cannot hold down two simultaneous jobs or work more than twenty-four to twenty-eight hours maximum a week, or do repeat or constant late-night or early morning shifts. All those work conditions typical for young people trigger tiredness and more seizures. Worse, when he has a seizure, sometimes he has to take the next day off to recover.

Bekkaa
March 20, 2013
These times are hard but they will pass, and soon become times of happiness <3

Preparing to meet Glenn, I petitioned two Ottawa hospitals for my kid's medical records. The sheer volume of Emergency Department Triage record sheets astonished us — a few hundred pages, a testament to the total number and frequency of hospital visits after seizures.

Glenn met Adam during a weekend, and saw him for a total of four and a half hours, testing him and talking to his parents, too. There was nothing in Glenn's report that surprised us, although the cold, clinical language was tough to read (this is just before the early stages of Adam recognizing he is a boy, so all references are to Rebecca): "The triggers for epileptic seizures, stress and tiredness, the effects of medication, condition limits employability ... limited to part-time, minimum-wage jobs, many whose conditions do not enhance her seizure prevention guidelines, i.e., rest, regular sleep, avoid stress and exhaustion ... [There are] cognitive memory issues that [signal] a clear disability." Glenn's report put the pieces together to frame the disability.

> Bekkaa shared
> September 25, 2012
> If you're just yourself,
> you'll never lose

Still, in an odd way, the report reinforced my pride in this unstoppable kid. He does cope in amazing ways. He shrewdly finesses a way through a maze of difficult workplace and school challenges. He keeps moving forward. He does so with a smile on his face.

Part of Glenn's report included a letter from an employer who let Adam go after a short probation. In 2014, before he found work at the museum café, the Mags & Fags (currently named the Gifted Type) on Elgin Street hired Adam. (Adam didn't know the British slang word for cigarettes. He found the name funny!) It was a busy store, where people dropped by for quick purchases. Employees had to be on top of their game and familiar with the merchandise. When the store let Adam go, his boss explained that he could not handle all the tasks required of him. However, like every teacher in school had, the employer liked Adam and asked if there was anything he could do to help him. He wrote a timely letter for the ODSP appeal to underscore how the disability messes up Adam's thinking and memory.

Memory is definitely becoming a concern. One time, working at the sub shop, Adam called his mother, crying. He had forgotten how to do an inventory, a chore he had performed dozens of times. Ciarra went in occasionally to help. Chelsey, his later girlfriend, also noticed the memory loss. Adam would ask her something and then come back into the room five minutes later to ask again.

The seizures take their toll. It feels like a vicious, cruel circle. Adam's epilepsy has likely ruled out the career he covets in Early Childhood Education. He needs more education in order to obtain the better paying jobs, but school studies are a problem.

Adam's thoughts are elsewhere. He is thinking about his epilepsy ending, getting back to work, and how to start the physical changes he craves for his body.

Adam shared 92 PRO FM's photo
October 8, 2015
Do you ever start telling your parents a funny story and then remember what happened was illegal?

CHAPTER 6

The T Train

#transman

INDEED, ADAM IS FEELING optimistic about his number-one priority, becoming "all boy."

We like his trans health team at the Centretown Community Health Centre. This clinic is a community-based, multi-service health centre. Centretown's LGBTQ+[1] and Trans Health programs are offered to help people stay well, get better, and meet others.

Adam has been on quite the gender journey, especially since the middle of 2014. He is discovering who he is and finding his voice to tell us about it. Naturally, it has been gradual. He is figuring things out for himself: where he has been and what he is becoming.

The journey began with Ciarra in 2014. Rebecca confided to her girlfriend that she felt more like a boy. Ciarra encouraged Rebecca Adam to wear the clothes he wanted to wear, to be who he wanted to be. It was with Ciarra that Adam found the strength to begin the journey home to himself. This special girl's love led the way.

---

1. Lesbian, Gay, Bisexual, Trans, Two-Spirit, Queer, and other sexual and gender identities.

Adam D. Prashaw

June 9, 2014

So …. I have made a long wanting decision that I hope everyone will accept and respect. As of now I ask if everyone can refer to me as Adam and use "him or his." I hope everyone can respect that while I start this interesting journey. Please and thank you.

Coming out.

Coming in.

Coming home.

All with a polite please and thank you. Adam wants to identify as a boy, have a boy's body. It's clear from his Facebook posts that he didn't wake up one day and decide that he was transgender. He has recognized the boy in him for a long time, even as a kid. He knew that there was something different about him. There's nothing wrong with him. He just has the wrong body. It took time, though, sorting out who he is. Like her girlfriends, Rebecca went through the phase of pinning the "cute boy" pics on the bedroom wall in Kanata. As Rebecca, she became interested in girls, which made her conclude that she was a lesbian. But still something was not right. High school is a confusing time for most kids — who to like, coming to like yourself. How much harder must it be when, at the same time, you are figuring out core gender identity issues, who you truly are? He knew that the "girl in the mirror" was not him.

Adam

September 27, 2015

"didn't chose to be transgender , but I did chose purposefully to be comfortable in my skin and be authentically happy" (Anonymous)

I suspect that you can know who you are for a long time but not know the terms of your identity. And not dare to be who you really are — understandable given the conflicting, overriding desire we have to fit in. Adolescence can be a tortured, twisted time — the shades of grey and angst playing themselves out sexually and other ways. Adam may have felt more like a boy but he still wanted to fit in. He had no models for becoming someone other, for identifying otherwise, for transitioning, for questioning gender assumptions. He was only ever surrounded by cisgender people.[1] How could Adam take the risk to imagine otherwise when he didn't see himself anywhere? He got the constant messages, too, about the two distinct worlds of boys and girls. The locker rooms, bathrooms, sports. "It's a boy!" or "It's a girl!" is the first declaration we hear when we are born. Boy or girl — this is society's great divide. "You have a beautiful baby girl," the intern declared that day in Sudbury. So many of us use gender as the basis for looking at others. So, I suspect Adam and others might hide their true selves, might even try to deny themselves, question and doubt their very selves, adapt, attempt to fit in, improvise, and follow society's script. Sadly, such coping strategies produce an identity that is often far away from their true one. Society's norms leave little room for play, discovery, trying things on, or being okay in the "in between" place of transition. Individuals can end up lost, torn apart.

But I see now that Adam is not going to deny himself any longer. This is Adam's big breakthrough. For years, Adam seemed to drop hints about his identity, through his choice of clothing, hairstyles, and interests — the kid's go-to language when family or community don't recognize what's going on below the surface. He begins the transition now more intentionally. He starts with the informal name change, with his announcement on Facebook. He will change his name on Facebook from Bekkaa to Adam D. Prashaw. The *D* is for Daniel, for his pépère. He changes his middle name from Danielle, knowing that this middle name was actually for his grandfather, anyway. He will inquire into legally changing his name but will not get around to doing anything for another year. From my theology and biblical studies, I appreciated the intrinsic value in a name and in naming someone. "I have called you by name. You are mine" (Isaiah 43:1). Adam's name and gender were assigned without consent at birth. He's fixing all this, and I am listening and learning.

---

1. A term for people who have a gender identity that matches the sex they were assigned at birth.

The long, agonizing wait is over. Centretown Community Health Centre calls in January 2015. He will begin health care and counselling appointments soon.

The T train leaves the station. *T* is for testosterone. Testosterone can be taken one of three ways: by injection, skin patch, or pill. The testosterone injections are intended to speed up the transition. In time, Adam will see the changes he craves to see — facial and body hair, a deeper voice, fat and muscle mass redistribution.

Adam chronicles online all that happens this year.

Adam is feeling amazing
January 15, 2015
Could this really be starting?! The journey will soon begin 8 weeks and I'll get call back for a transitioning counselling referral.

Adam
February 19, 2015
Transitioning song from a favourite glee show Unique performs from "Where I Have Been" beautiful! I hope someday I can be finally who I want to be and not have to disguise it @Rick Prashaw & @Suzanne Corbeil

Adam is feeling positive
February 23, 2015
oh do I hate being on waiting lists but hey Trans Health Center was very kind to have just called me apologizing for the wait explaining how there's been sudden increase on being busy they weren't expecting but they told me I'm like 11th on the list which isn't so bad than what it could be. But told me should get call within 4-6 weeks. It's slowly beginning :)

Adam

April 10, 2015

May be a bad start to the day at work and crappy weather but ain't stopping me from having a smile on and excited for 3pm!! My Trans Health Counselling Begins!! 💪👍😆😆

Adam

August 6, 2015

Just saw my Trans Health Doctor and I can say that I will finally be beginning T. I am so excited and happy, it's finally starting for me. can't explain how much this means to me!

That last post references his first testosterone treatment, an oral pill. Four months later, he's cheering his first testosterone needle.

Adam

December 16, 2015

Got my first T shot today!!! I was on the pills before because of my other medical stuff, I felt comfortable with it but wasn't too happy with how it was going. But now I'm so happy I changed over to shots, this will definitely be much quicker and happier for me.

Apparently, this kid likes some needles better than others!

Not surprisingly, Adam finds this T train excruciatingly slow. He wants everything at once. Now! He cannot see all of the physical change yet, even though he is excited to be moving forward. Adam wants to see the muscle and body changes, hear the voice drop, find the hair on his face. He wants changes yesterday. To me, as a parent, the T train is rocketing forward, much like the TGV across France. In eleven months, he has moved from the waiting line to counselling, to talking to a social worker and a doctor, to taking first oral testosterone pills, and then to injections. Pivotal this year are his first meetings with his counsellor, Nichelle Bradley, and his doctor, Jennifer Douek.

Nichelle Bradley is the social worker, a godsend who, while wrapping up a contract at the Centretown Community Health Centre, agrees to meet with us when we ask for information to better understand and support Adam's journey in the months and years ahead. It's a bit amazing, I feel, but Adam is cool about his parents coming to his meetings. He's learning a lot. I am learning, too, growing in my understanding of his issues as he grows to understand them himself. I know there are plenty of gaps and misunderstandings on my part. I suspect that there is some unlearning ahead.

We are seeking professional reassurances that Adam is making the right choice. We tell Nichelle about Adam's patterns of impulsive behaviour, related to maturity and perhaps personality. Is this adolescent rebellion, another "leap before thinking," or rather, is Adam genuinely pushing back against what he feels is being dictated to him as normative? At one point, Suzanne tells the counsellor that this is a "pretty drastic" change for Adam and we had better be certain that it be the right change. I add: "Drop the *pretty*. It IS drastic!" As a parent, I suspect that too often I may be thinking of this "girl to boy" transition as something that will take place within a set period of time. I am not sure whether Adam thinks that is how it will happen. It seems at times more like a lifelong process than one specific change. We support Adam, and yet we want professionals like Nichelle to spell out all the consequences and options.

> Bekkaa
> October 31, 2010
> i don't look like me
> at all lol

Nichelle indicates that this is exactly her role. She will conduct an assessment, following standard tests by WPATH, the World Professional Association for Transgender Health.[1]

She says that this assessment is necessary to assess and diagnose the presence of gender dysphoria: gender-identity distress over the sex one is assigned at birth. To determine this, a psychosocial history and a gender history are completed, usually over six sessions. There are no shortcuts.

---

1. WPATH describes itself as a professional organization devoted to the understanding and treatment of gender identity disorders. They work to promote evidence-based care and education.

Nichelle advises us that she is morally and ethically bound not to make the recommendation unless she is certain Adam is right about being a man. Adam insists he is a man and has a strong desire to be male. These are indicators for beginning a positive assessment. Adam is consistent also in his presentation as a man and in his distress about having female parts on his body. Nichelle explains that these tests and indicators will be used to determine if Adam has gender dysphoria, a diagnosis that is a prerequisite for any referral to a physician to begin hormone therapy.

During this appointment and the reading I do later, I find myself bouncing between healthy respect for the professionals and wondering about the very real danger of losing Adam to the science or to this medical diagnosis. Will the tests and international criteria miss or underappreciate what is happening in my son? Can a test capture this extraordinary life-affirming "becoming" that is happening? Although Nichelle observes that Adam is a trans man and has worked this through, she also says she will not recommend any trans health services, drugs, or surgery unless Adam "passes" the test's stringent criteria.

Geez, I never had to pass any tests to be me! I wonder later what this must be like for Adam and for others like Adam — needing professionals to "legitimize" you, having to fit a scientific consensus to qualify for the gender you claim.

Adam appears to benefit from the psychotherapy he is required to undergo to help him adjust to the numerous life changes that occur in the process of transition.

At this meeting, Suzanne becomes emotional, recounting a conversation she had with Adam. He did not see any change. He was upset that he was not seeing "a boy in the mirror." There were those breasts. Suzanne said, "I can't imagine anyone looking in the mirror and not seeing themselves." That gets me teary, too — then, and later, whenever I recall those words.

A boy in the mirror. How many times do we look at ourselves in the mirror? Most of us see ourselves. We may not always like what we see, but the reflection is us, good days and bad days. Trans kids don't get to see themselves for the longest time. That's all Adam wanted, to be himself, to see a boy in the mirror, to love who he loves. Who doesn't want that?

I wonder how much Adam looks in the mirror these days.

Nichelle gives us some reading material: *Families in TRANSition — A Resource Guide for Parents of Trans Youth*;[1] *Trans Care Gender Transition — Hormones: A Guide for FTMs*;[2] *Trans* Ally Workbook: Getting Pronouns Right and What It Teaches Us About Gender*;[3] *Transgender Visibility: A Guide to Being You*.[4]

Nichelle says that transgender people may "go the entire route" — hormone treatment, mastectomy, and one or more sexual organ transplants. There are those who go halfway; some will need less assistance and some more to link bodies to gender identity. There are those who act quickly and those who go slowly, putting off the hormone treatment or surgery for several years or even forever. She has known very few people who regret surgery.

Huge for the trans man is the mastectomy, to be rid of the breasts that are not him. The boy in the mirror. I sense that this is all Adam is focused on now, along with the hormone treatments. At least with me, he has not spoken of anything else yet.

Both at the beginning and end of our appointment, Nichelle affirms our support for Adam. She is adamant that we continue be there for him. We *do* support and love Adam through his journey without hesitation. Nichelle also comments that this kind of support is rare, unfortunately. She doesn't see many parents; some remain on the sidelines and a few are outright opposed. It is sad to hear this. Last year, I read of a couple who even took their opposition to their child's grave. They refused to put their seventeen-year-old's girl name on the tombstone after she committed suicide. God forbid. Suicide and self-harm are real threats. Support from parents, friends, and workplaces significantly reduces the risk of suicide. It is reassuring to see the immediate and extended family support for Adam. His special friends also have his back.

Unwittingly, Nichelle sends my fears through the roof, confirming the discrimination that exists against transgender people in terms of rights, laws, and services. Rights for the trans population trail behind the progress made for gays and lesbians. Transgender people routinely

---

1. Central Toronto Youth Services (Toronto: 2008).
2. Olivia Ashbee and Joshua Mira Goldberg (Vancouver: Vancouver Coastal Health, 2006).
3. Davey Shlasko, Think Again Training and Consultation, 2014, www.thinkagaintraining.com.
4. Human Rights Campaign Foundation, 2014, www.hrc.org/transgender.

Adam
August 12, 2015
[Accompanying photo of Robin Williams]
finally someone knows how i feel "i think the saddest people try to make people happy because they know what it is like to feel absolutely worthless and they don't want anyone else feeling like that"

experience discrimination, harassment, and violence, which significantly affects their health and well-being. I've informed myself by reading and talking to professionals, but this also takes me back to being a kid in my bedroom with the bogeyman I feared. Then, as a scared kid, I turned on the lights and the ghosts disappeared. But when I turned off the lights, I still heard new noises. I hear those noises now as a parent. Worries chasing worries.

I want my kid to be happy. That's every parent's wish, no? A tough road lies ahead.

Nichelle recommends to both Dr. Jennifer Douek and Dr. Wallace Archibald, the wonderful family doctor in Russell, that Adam begin hormone treatment. She also requests that they use male pronouns and use the name Adam from now on. Nichelle also puts Adam on the long waiting list at the gender reassignment clinic in Toronto. Adam's name is at some ridiculous number on the list, like six hundred plus. Gender reassignment surgery may be years away, given that there is, at the time, only one clinic in the country designated to approve and carry out the operation. OHIP covers its cost if you wait for that lengthy approval. Going ahead privately will mean a bill in the thousands and thousands of dollars.

Adam
December 12, 2015
I may seem "ok", but that's just how I go about every day and may seem. But really, I can't wait till I can truly feel happy and confident of myself. And I feel it'll be awhile.

One day at work, Adam is very upset when a woman at the café corrects her son when he calls Adam "sir."

Adam is 😠 feeling aggravated
October 29, 2015
When a little boy is smarter than their parent and correcting them when they say "she'll help you"

"give it to the girl/give it to lady at the cash" and say "that's a boy mom or that's a boy dad!" and yet the parents said "just because SHE had short hair doesn't mean she's not a girl! Girls have short hair too! Look your a boy but have long hair doesn't mean your not a boy!" Why are there such stereotypical, rude, people out there?! you don't judge a book by its cover! My name is ADAM! it says on my fucking name tag! I'm a guy, makes me feel so hurt seeing how others see me, and then I see all my trans friends getting surgery done, voice way deeper than me, and much quicker facial hair growth. And me NOTHING cause clearly if people still say I'm a girl nothing has changed... people have no idea how much this hurts. Why can't I be lucky as my other fellow trans friends and appear to have a much more obvious change in gender showing who I really am. Fml

It is hard to avoid misunderstandings, but it kills Adam to be mistaken for a girl. He's upset at the hostile, rigid expectations of what men and women should look like.

Days before Christmas 2015, he posts pictures from his favourite party place, the Lookout Club. He goes on stage for one song with the Capital Kings, a drag king troupe. He enjoys their entertainment — the lip-synch songs and dancing. As performers, they draw trademark beards and moustaches on their faces. I comment on his new "beard" on Facebook: "Is this your Movember hair? Nice. David, your bro has some real competition." Adam answers: "I wish it could be my real movember hair but sadly not yet. After my surgery changing to [testosterone] shots will make it faster."

Adam
February 25, 2015
I need to get this all fixed

CHAPTER 7

The Boy in the Mirror

AS ADAM'S GENDER transition and epilepsy collide full force toward the end of 2015, there is a remarkable change in him. An adult is emerging, a guy with a stronger voice.

Adam
February 2, 2015
Slowly starting to feel more comfortable and truly happy for who I really am.
#transgender #feelingcomfortable #strong

Adam strong!

Adam is getting his T meds supervised by his trans doctor, Jennifer Douek. We meet Dr. Douek in November 2015, again wanting to understand the health care side of his journey. We made sure this appointment was before the epilepsy surgery scheduled for later in the month. While the Montreal surgery took precedence, we didn't want Adam to lose hope or stop moving forward on his real goal.

Dr. Douek is young, perhaps in her early thirties. She is working a shift at Centretown Community Health Centre. She is in jeans. Adam has already told us that he likes her.

At one point in the interview, Adam stresses that he wants things to go faster, that he wants to switch to the injections for the testosterone. She agrees to this but wants to talk to him about the pace of the transition.

"Adam, I know you want all of this to happen now, like yesterday, physically. That's understandable. But you are not growing into Adam only physically. You are growing into Adam emotionally, psychologically, in so many other ways."

I resist the strong urge to get up and hug this doctor.

Slow down, Adam! Be sure, Adam!

I am relieved to hear Dr. Douek's pep talk on the necessity of a slow transition so that Adam will grow into all that he is.

Dr. Douek tells Adam that even she, a young woman, is "still growing into being Jennifer."

Bekkaa shared
May 6, 2012
About all you can do in life is be who you are. Some people will love you for you. Most will love you for what you can do for them, and some won't like you at all.
[— Rita Mae Brown]

"Hell, I'm sixty-four and still growing into being Rick," I added.

I wonder, though, if Adam actually heard his doctor, what with his mild ADHD, memory impairment, and all. A few days later, at his favourite diner, the Elgin Street Diner, the signature clubhouse sandwich in front of him, I brought up the conversation with the doctor.

I am my usual, subtle train wreck with him.

"I like your doctor," I say, between sips of coffee.

"Yeah, she's good."

"I like what she said about how important it is to go slow."

"Yeah."

"You know what she said?"

At which point, Adam, finding the right "I know, Dad" sarcasm, repeats Dr. Douek's message word for word. It was like I was listening to a tape recorder. My kid was listening. Adam is growing up.

It was in those doctor and counsellor meetings that I felt his remarkable willpower guiding us all forward. It was there, when I closed my eyes, when I listened to my son speaking, that I heard a young man speak, finding his voice, a maturity awakening.

Listening to Adam, I begin to appreciate where he is and how far he has come. I read someone else's trans blog one day, and it seems to catapult me inside Adam's world:

> Transgender people go through a long process....
>
> The years of agonizing about who you are. The nights lying awake, trying to understand how you could feel the way you do, think the way you do, be the way that you are. Knowing society will freak out. Fearing that, fearing for your safety. Fearing your own self. Then reaching that point. Some trigger within you. Knowing you can't do it anymore. Knowing that to keep trying, keep lying to yourself, is killing you slowly. That you would rather end your life than continue as you have.
>
> The self-doubts initially. The worries. The fear of losing everyone and everything you love. The determination that even if it does cost you everything, you have to do it, or you may as well just kill yourself. The first tentative steps. The growing determination to see it through. Fighting through a system designed to prevent you from succeeding. Succeeding anyway. The joy of seeing yourself in the mirror and no longer hating who you see. Being happy. Loving yourself for the first time in your life.
>
> We don't just wake up one day and decide we are transgender. We have known something was different about ourselves for a very long time, many of us our entire lives. We have agonized over what it means. Argued with ourselves. TRIED to fit within the gender norms of society... and yet... we never can. We never can because our minds, our thoughts, our way of thinking... is so alien to our physical bodies.

It's not a choice. We are not given any choice in the matter. WHO we are, is not what is between our legs. It is what is between our ears. We would prefer that they both matched. But they don't. We would prefer that we don't have to face the constant barrage of hate thrown at us. But we do. We would prefer that our bodies matched our minds. But they don't. And while medical science can't magically change us so everything matches the way it should … it can help us change enough so that we can manage to have a normal, happy life. It can change us enough so that rather than hating ourselves, we can love ourselves. It can change us enough to help us be happy…. And that IS all we want. To be happy. With ourselves. About ourselves. In our own skin.[1]

The joy of looking in the mirror and no longer hating who you see. Right, Adam! This makes sense to me and binds me to more of my son's actual experience: his feelings — agonizing, worrying, doubting — his lying in bed at nighttime and wondering.

Doctors like Dr. Douek and Dr. Wallace Archibald initiated us into this maze of health care and new worries. In a visit to Adam's hometown of Russell, Suzanne peppered Dr. Archibald with questions on trans health risks involving both the testosterone and the likely gender reassignment surgery down the road. I grimaced at references to the short-term and unknown long-term side effects, such as relatively minor cancer risks or possible bone deterioration in midlife. There are other references in my reading to mental health challenges for these transgender kids.

Geez! *Kapow*, Batman! My head is spinning.

When Rebecca told us that she thought she was lesbian, I had no judgment, but I did have Dad worries and fears for my child. The parental worries went nuclear with the transgender news; although, again, I accepted Adam's news without judgment. There was talk of breast amputation, penis construction, and lifelong testosterone shots.

---

1. Elain Corrine Mora, "The Living Hell of Being Transgender," 2015.

But Adam's thoughts were in another place on this visit back home. He wanted to stop by the Castor River where that picture of the tomboy Rebecca, in the leather jacket, was taken many years ago. Down at the river, he got back on this favourite rock for a picture of the new boy.

Bekkaa
March 31, 2013
keep looking back at this photo and laughing :) my fav baby photo of me! <3 lol if I go put my leather jacket on and sit on rock in river I'd look like my baby self just taller :P

(left) Adam's favourite Rebecca picture: on a rock by Castor River in Russell, Ontario. (right) Adam returns to the Castor River rock.

I looked at him on the rock. He's so much more now than a tomboy. Adam felt like an alien living in another body. That is changing.

Adam also scored lunch at his favourite place, Russell Restaurant, ordering, of course, a club sandwich and a chocolate milkshake with whipped cream. Leaving Russell, I sorted through the surgeries and medical events ahead for Adam. Testosterone treatment has begun. Epilepsy surgery in November. I calculated that most of 2016 would focus on his T injections and more counselling, but now, for the first time, I add to my list the likelihood of the first gender reassignment surgery: top surgery to remove all or part of the breast tissue, to reconstruct the chest. There's no definite timetable yet. Later, bottom surgery might follow for penile and other corrective surgery. There is no doubt about Adam's "yes" to the top surgery. Those breasts are the visible reminder, publicly and privately, that he does not look like a boy. He can't help but see how so many people in this world are fixated on breasts.

> Bekkaa shared
> February 3, 2012
> When life hands you lemons, bust out the tequila and salt!

Adam has started binding, wearing the undergarment that flattens the breast tissue to create a smaller and less noticeable chest. He binds his breasts to appear more as a man. But it's a temporary illusion, and he tells me that the cheaper binders are painful. They can cause rash and infection and can be hard to wear for a long time. I meet Adam at the Venus Envy store on Bank Street to buy better binders. Adam's binders are short-term, stopgap measures and he is growing tired of them.

He dreams of being shirtless.

From the neck up, he is boy. Some new friends tell him they are surprised when they learn that he is trans and not biologically a boy.

I do get a smile out of him before the second Neuro brain surgery, suggesting as the doctors prep him that they perform the trans surgery the same day! He is ALL for that!

We are learning to use the right pronouns for my kid. *He, him,* and *his*; not *she, her,* and *hers*.

This change is difficult for me. I have been referring to my kid as "she" or "her" for nineteen years. Now, it's "he" and "him." Suzanne once acknowledged that I was doing well on getting these pronouns right, but I make mistakes, noticeably more when I talk *about* Adam to others than when I speak with him. Perhaps his death stare keeps me on track! When I get a pronoun wrong with him, he makes quite the face. He looks like I have stabbed him in the heart. I guess I have. Pronouns matter. I start noticing my mistakes more and more. It feels like I'm undertaking a conscious reprogramming, hard but worthwhile work. I learn to appreciate what it means to Adam and to others in transition. We all like to be identified properly; above all else, by the right gender. Who doesn't want that? I'm "fuckin' Rick," eh, Adam?

The right pronouns come with practice. And I guess that Adam sees us trying. That matters to him.

Humour always helps, too, although my kid doesn't think I am funny. (I think I'm hilarious.) When I caught up with Adam at the Elgin Street Diner downtown after he came out on Facebook and announced that he is Adam and wishes to be called Adam, we have this exchange.

"So you are a guy, right?"

"Yeah."

"You like girls because you are a boy?"

"Right."

"So, you are not a lesbian, eh?"

"Yes, Dad."

"Whew, thank God, I am so relieved. So, you are not gay, just trans?"

He doesn't smile.

It was actually a serious joke, on a few levels. His family has never had an issue with having a lesbian in the family. We are all different! Now, as Adam did, I had to sort out the crucial distinction between his sexual orientation and his gender identity. Both as Adam and as a younger Rebecca, the real attraction is to girls. Initially, Rebecca concluded that this meant she must be a lesbian, that this was her sexual orientation. Now, as Adam recognized the boy he had always been, he was claiming his gender identity. All that teen confusion about his sexual orientation had to do with gender identity. The term *transgender* is an umbrella one, used when referring to a wide group of people. Adam wants to bring his body in alignment with who he is. I got a boy's body. Adam didn't.

I tried my comedian routine another time when he was declaring himself to be Adam and I was mixing up names and pronouns. I begged for his patience while I was getting his name and pronouns right, joking that this was like teaching an old dog new tricks.

"Adam, you know that when you were Rebecca, you had a nickname?"

"What?"

"I called you Becca for short."

"Yeah."

"Well, now that you are Adam, is it okay sometimes if I call you by a nickname?"

"What?"

"Becca?"

"That's not funny, Dad."

I thought it was.

Humour, Adam's humour, gets him through many days. He loves being silly. His friends tell me that he lights up the room when he walks in. There is no containing his excitement or enthusiasm.

Indeed, he is beginning to post pictures of himself shirtless, or with his top pulled down, his arms or a phone strategically placed to cover the breasts. He is done hiding. There is no doubt now who he is and what he wants. There is no stopping him.

On Christmas Day, this Facebook post:

> **Adam shared a link**
> December 25, 2015
> Scientists create a human penis in lab, could change trans men's lives forever https://www.gaystarnews.com/article/scientists-create-human-penis-lab-could-change-trans-mens-lives-forever071014

Merry Christmas, Adam! Another item for my revised parenting manual.

> **Adam**
> March 22, 2015
> People drive me nuts sometimes

CHAPTER 8

Hope Rising Up — Happy New Year!

I AM AGAIN FEELING conflicted as a parent after Adam's break-up with Chelsey in the last few days of 2015. If things were normal, my counsel to him would be to take time before jumping into another relationship, something he seldom does. In this new adult gig, I want him to learn from past relationships. But things aren't normal. I imme-diately worry about Adam being alone in the apartment.

His beloved dog, Dallas, is back with him — great company, getting him out walking, exercising. The kid I caught five years ago taking a bus one block to work at Farm Boy now walks miles with his dog along the canal; and in the coldest part of winter, he skates the entire 7.6-kilometre length of the Rideau Canal and back. As a young kid, Rebecca became a good skater, bribed to keep skating to the next BeaverTails pastry kiosk on the canal. BeaverTails taught my kid to skate!

Bekkaa
December 13, 2009
Life is complicated ....lol

However, Dallas is not a seizure dog. She may bark, but she is otherwise unlikely to rescue Adam or alert others when a seizure occurs. Because she is not a service dog, she is not permitted in his apartment building pool area. Several years earlier, I inquired with the Lions Club and service animal organizations about a seizure dog for Rebecca. At the time, our kid was starting to have the more serious, partial complex seizures. There were not many of them at first, though, and the service dogs appear to be for people with frequent attacks. We seemed to fall through the cracks.

It's New Year's! Adam parties 2016 in. He is revelling in the real change in his life. On New Year's Eve, he posts an impressive list of resolutions.

Adam is 🎉 celebrating New Year's Eve
December 31, 2015
My goals for 2016 are: to get in shape, have my T to start showing more changes, find new job I love, hope results stays the same and pray for no more seizures, don't rush things, find my true friends, and just to always have good times and a smile on my face!

I smile, reading a new, determined resolve in those resolutions. This is the same kid who only two years earlier posted when he announced he was Adam: "It has been very difficult for me to speak my mind and what my heart and mind wants. And [I have] been afraid of losing people or making people laugh at me."

As Rebecca, my child fretted about telling her parents that she was lesbian. Now he is "coming out" a second time, with more determination. He knows what his heart and mind want. He's happier. He has a few things he wants to change still, but there is a sense he is getting more and more comfortable in his own skin. We are even more optimistic after Adam has the first post-surgery checkup assessment in Montreal on January 4, 2016, with Suzanne.

Dr. Olivier is pleased with his progress. The news is all good. Adam's mother reports:

Adam seems to be progressing and is happy to hear [there is] no seizure activity. Dr. Olivier said the swelling and bump on the head will take time to go down; it is the muscle that has been stretched and cut during the surgery, but likely will always show to some extent. Dr. Olivier is still confident he got all of the abnormal cells and will continue to monitor him but is optimistic the seizures will be controlled or maybe even gone. No change to medication for a year.

Adam will go back in June for cognitive tests to see if there has been any impact on memory or other deterioration since the last test in 2012.

Suzanne tells me that Adam is happy. He is "on top of the world" hearing the medical news. He is excited to get back to work and get on with life. Adam and his mother discuss his return to school in September. He wants to speak to a counsellor about programs suitable for him. This, too, is good news. He is optimistic, perhaps for the first time in a long time.

His hope is rising. There is new energy. Nothing can hold him down for long.

On January 10, he posts:

Adam

January 10, 2015

My body does not define who I am. I am a boy, but my body may show different. I know who I am, and I don't need anyone to tell me and call me what I'm not. But whether a person is gay or Transgender or straight, it doesn't change the fact that they are trying to lead their own life. #ftm #trans gender #steppingup #livingtherightlife #myjourney #sacrifices #time

Those hashtags!
Stepping up.
Living the right life.
My journey.

Time.

He posts another picture of himself, shirtless, holding his phone in front of him, with the hashtag #cantwaitfortheday. He wants to act on his goals.

He is telling everyone that he is Adam. He is a boy. Soon enough, his body will show it. There is a new-found resolve, stronger, more vocal. All of this he shares with his friends downtown.

While waiting for further news on his epilepsy and for the next stage in his transition, Adam is determined to enjoy his life now. His new home is one of the things he relishes. He lives on the twelfth floor of his apartment building. He loves the downtown location and the pool, gym, and hot tub on the penthouse floor with its solarium windows.

But Adam is not a homebody. He lives for going out with friends. Fridays — Friday nights in particular — are something he treasures. It isn't the typical, "end of the work week" weekend excitement. Like many of his friends, Adam might have weekend shifts. No, the cheer for Friday night means meeting up with his best friends at the Lookout Club or Zaphod's in the Market area of Ottawa. The Lookout proclaims itself "Ottawa's favourite gay bar." Adam's late-week and Friday posts inevitably fire up his friends for the party.

At the Lookout or Zaphod's, Adam is Adam, spending a few hours to unwind and party with friends, many around his age, including those like him on their own journey home. Alex Tetreault, a friend, told me how they met there. Adam apparently stared at Alex a long time. Adam came over and asked if he could ask him a personal question. Was he trans? Was he, like Adam, a trans man? Alex confirmed he was. Adam was "over the moon" happy to meet someone else who understood. Always excited, enthused, Adam sat down for a long conversation, and in no time, he was showing him his Rebecca pictures.

Adam is home there. Adam likes watching the Capital Kings perform there. He goes on stage from time to time as a "baby King."

Adam

January 16, 2015

Finally back at the Lookout tonight for the Capital King's 3rd year anniversary!! Going to be a great

night with my gf and friends and King's and yes
even some of the yes-man in Ottawa tonight at
lookout! If you got nothing to do I'd say come to
lookout it's so worth it!! :)

It is a "sacred place" where, for a few hours, they can be them-selves, be accepted, and immunize themselves against the judgment, stares, hurt, and stupid hate they sometimes encounter in the city. My parent worry isn't for those clubs. I worry more about Adam's walk home afterward, through the Ottawa Market, through the pub scene, onto Elgin Street, and home on those late Friday and Saturday nights when the beer-fuelled guys come out of their pubs. The hate for trans people and the hurt they feel scares me. Adam doesn't stand out much, physically, from those lads. What frightens me is his strong-willed determination to be himself in public, anywhere. Unlike many trans kids, who may avoid using public washrooms, feeling obliged to reassure people that they are in the right place, Adam is determined to assert his right. Much more importantly, he is determined to show his love for those he loves. He is determined to hold hands or share a kiss with a girlfriend. In a way, I admire him for that. He should have that experience, but I know my town and some of the people living here. He is deaf to my pleas to exercise caution, to remember this is small-town Ottawa, not a cosmopolitan city like Vancouver, Toronto, or Montreal.

I recognize how stressed he is but do not always appreciate what his life is like now. He enters a Hot 89.9 radio contest that profiles trans kids living in Ottawa. Here is what he writes in his contest entry:

I feel right as a boy. The counselor did all the testing required to be sure of my identifying as a boy. The counselor so agreed with me on being Adam. I have started the hormone drugs but it will be a long jour-ney with lots of challenges. People confusing who I am, the washrooms, the legal names, it can be a real headache. The stress is always there.

He congratulated the winner of the contest — Serena, a man transitioning to a woman — noting "wish it was me, and would have been amazing and felt like a miracle, but doesn't mean I'll stop, it'll just be [a] journey that hopefully can end someday."

Although Adam is enjoying his return to his regular life in Ottawa, I think he might appreciate a short break. I am heading to California for a three-week holiday, to my sister Pati's place, and I ask Adam to consider coming along for a holiday. After all, he's had a rough six weeks since his surgery, recovering and enduring a breakup with his girlfriend. He has enjoyed a few vacations there, liking the sun, the beach, and his cousin Mack. But this time he says no. His friends are in Ottawa. He needs to get ready to return to work.

And, as usual, his stress is through the stratosphere. He has butted heads recently with his landlady over balcony and pool incidents when friends visited.

The new year's Facebook posts pick up on familiar themes, laced, of course, with humour.

Adam

January 9, 2016

Great night tonight! With bunch of friends, and some I got to bump into as well! always greats nights when it's times like these! Can't wait for much more!

Adam

January 10, 2016

What is Your Motto for 2016? You can only reach your goals when you act towards them.

Adam shared 101.3 The Brew's photo

January 11, 2016

I like you so much that if our boat was sinking and there was one only one life jacket, I would miss you a lot.

Adam shared Tygieria's photo

January 11th, 2016

Getting into a relationship may seem like a good idea but so was getting on the Titanic and look what happened there.

Days before I leave on holidays, Adam texts me that he is lost somewhere near the Ottawa International Airport looking for the FedEx parcel office. I am downtown on errands myself and offer to find him. On our way to a Harvey's lunch, I look at the FedEx envelope on his lap.

"Bieber tickets?"

He grins. Yes, the late-arriving Christmas present tickets for his now ex-girlfriend, about which he told her well before Christmas. Truth can be stranger than fiction for my son. Dropping him off at his apartment, I lean over for a fast hug as he leaves the car.

A few days later, and now in California, I continue our texting. I joke that his strange father is probably the only person in California watching the Scotties Quebec curling championships on the internet. Lauren's team is winning, tied for first place at 5–2 in the standings, and heading to play the other top team to determine weekend playoff positions. Lauren has Adam's competitive genes in spades. It's been a wonder to see a quiet, rather shy girl become a very good national women's skip, shouting at her teammates, on the ice and in the house with the likes of Canada's (and the world's) top curlers Jennifer Jones and Rachel Homan.

On January 12, Adam texts to suggest that I check out a website that has boxers and briefs he likes, plus the "thing to stand to pee and stuff is interesting and i would really appreciate and use. Especially for me using the men's washrooms and not always going to the stalls."

We text about Dallas, work, how he is feeling. One day, out of the blue, I ask Adam if he believes in God. I am sure that he does, but we haven't talked for a while about his beliefs. He replies that he understands God. It is me who he does not understand!

The boy can make me laugh.

I text him to be patient: "U have gone to hell and back. All the pain in body has to come out. Just think about driving again!"

I tell him that I like the picture he posted from the pre-Christmas celebration with his grandparents. Adam has his red plaid lumberjack shirt on. I tell him to wear that shirt to our Ottawa Redblacks CFL games next year.

"I love this pic. Your smile. Shirt. U look like Adam."

"Cause I am."

"Yep and it's showing."

I tell him that Aunt Pati and his California family so appreciate his courage and his goodness.

The next day, I text him that President Obama said he wants a country where everyone can marry the person they love.

I sense that he is texting madly with his mom and friends, too.

I keep him posted on the long recuperation of his idol, Montreal goalie Carey Price, from a knee injury.

> Adam
> January 18 , 2016
> Can't wait till I'm back to work Monday; in need of food most of all, but help for my bills, etc. I hate this sick leave and the pain of no job.

I share a funny birth notice correction sent out by a family when their trans son came out as a teenager. It reads:

> **Birth notice correction. Oops it is a boy. A Retraction — Bogert**
>
> In 1995 we announced the arrival of our sprogget, Elizabeth Anne, as a daughter. He informs us that [we] were mistaken. Oops! Our bad. We would now like to present our wonderful son — Kai Bogert. Loving you is the easiest thing in the world. Tidy your room.[1]

Right they are! Tidy your room, kids. The rest is negotiable.

We exchange emails on the new gender reassignment surgery rules recently announced for Ontario and the hope that the long waiting

---

1. "Parents Place Retraction to Birth Announcement to Show Support for Trans Son," *Brisbane Courier-Mail*, December 2, 2014, couriermail.com.au/news/queensland/mum-takes-out-classified-ad-to-show-support-for-son-kai-bogert-who-used-to-be-a-daughter/news-story/e123195ddaf755c58410855b956edda8.

lines might shrink, but there's still confusion about what it all means and which doctors are going to be certified, among other things.

I send him this tweet posted by @HilaryClinton: "We need to say with one voice that transgender people are valued, they are loved, they are us."

On January 19, he posts this exquisite personal anthem that seems to say everything about where he is at, who he is, and where he plans to go.

Adam D. Prashaw
January 19, 2016
Can't wait till I don't have to hide anymore. Time 🕐 will come… But the wait is hard.. 😑 Definitely need and want to slim down though, need to work out more and get more pumped to, I need my hope to rise up more. You only got one life, I'll be a fool to take a seat, I got one life and don't stop live it up! #wisdom #strength #passion #ftm #stages #transgender #myjourney #dontstopliveitup #whereiamsofar #keepmyheadup

Adam will not take a seat on his one life. But sometimes, that life does wear him down, and then, as frequently happens on Facebook, his friends jump in to cheer him.

Samantha Meier You're amazing inside and out, I know who you are. Because you've never gave me any other choice but to believe you're an amazing man!! Which so much to look forward too. Always shine

Jessie Lloyd Well said. It doesn't matter what you are outside… It's what you feel inside that counts and i am so proud of you for realizing and following your true self. You are a brave soul, Adam Prashaw. Never give up and never settle for less than what i know YOU KNOW you deserve. <3

These posts help, but they can't drive away all the hurt and sadness. He has plenty on his mind the next day, January 20. He shares a meme: "Sometimes you try so hard to take care of everyone else you forget to take care of yourself" and adds this comment: "yep, pretty well all the time."

He posts two pictures, a little girl who then transitions to a young guy with the comment: "I was a human then and i am human now. #transrights Adam TRUTH!"

Then this:

Adam shared
January 20, 2016
Death is not the greatest loss in life
The greatest loss is what dies in us while we live
[— Norman Cousins]

When he is not sharing life wisdom, his humour sees him through everything.

Adam shared Lezbehonest's post
January 21, 2016
I always carry a knife in my purse you never know, cheesecake or something

It is now a late January weekend. Friday. Will he be at a club with his friends this Friday night? He posts a beautiful selfie while posing in the hot tub, wearing no top, the sun shining down on his head from the window, slanting on the side and roof to the sky.

Adam D. Prashaw
January 22, 2016
Hot tub time 😎 😁 #hottubtime #confidence #goodtimes #ftm #presurgery #timewillcome #transgender

Adam's January 22, 2016 selfie, 3:52 p.m.

CHAPTER 9

The Cardinal, January 22–24, 2016

Friday, January 22, 2016
California

MORRO BAY, CALIFORNIA, is my go-to winter paradise. I may have had as many visits there as Adam has tattoos.

Plunked roughly halfway between Los Angeles and San Francisco, this seafront community of ten thousand permanent residents is snookered between the ocean and the volcanic range of the "Nine Sisters," or Morros Mountains, trailing over to the city of San Luis Obispo. Morro Rock climbs majestically out of the water in Morro Bay — an iconic figure rising to greet visitors. There's an idyllic twelve-month moderate climate, 15–29 degrees Celsius, but if you drive east over one mountain range inland, the temperature climbs to well beyond 38 degrees on the hot summer days. Tourists flock to this central coastal region for its spectacular beach and nearby wine country.

Every winter visit, I try to head north 50 kilometres to the Cambria seal rookery to marvel at the 900-kilogram female elephant seals and

2,200-kilogram male seals who crash on the beach each November, exhausted after their marathon swim from Alaska. I've already been to Cambria this trip. Those seals beach there for three months of sleep, sex, and the birth of their pups. On one visit, I learned the perils of venturing onto the beach during mating season. Those two-tonne passionate males move like Usain Bolt out of the starting blocks. I scampered back quickly to the viewing deck. A few miles north of Cambria is the opulent Hearst Castle, the late newspaper magnate William Randolph Hearst's estate, which served for many decades as a playground for the rich and for famous stars and starlets from Hollywood, whose private planes landed on the estate's airstrip in the mountains.

My real Morro Bay attraction, which is not in the tourist books, is my favourite sister Pati. I have three favourite sisters, but Pati and I share a special kindred spirit of adventure, playfulness, and humour. Even when life bites, as it often does, we have figured out ways to bite back. Pati is a nurse. During one of those exoduses of Ontario nursing students in the late seventies, she landed at a hospital in Houston, Texas. A few years later, she fled the Houston humidity to find work at a hospital on the central coast of California.

On this Friday, I am two weeks into a three-week vacation. I have just wrapped up work as a legislative assistant for Nickel Belt MP Claude Gravelle after his defeat in the October 2015 federal election. I do wish Adam had come for this holiday. He's visited California three times; his cousin Mack is my boy's own favourite attraction.

This trip is perfect — daily beach walks with anywhere from three to five of the dogs that Pati has in the house, and now a new addition to the itinerary, in fact, an addiction: the sport of pickleball. Shrink a tennis court, put a large-size paddle in your hand, add a perforated polymer ball like a Wiffle ball to hit, and welcome to North America's fastest-growing sport. The older crowd enjoys the doubles format, the strenuous workout, and the informality of the sport. Pati is a nice person until you put a pickleball racquet in her hand when, with the nickname of "The Wall," she defeats me regularly, along with many of her opponents.

This Friday, we squeeze in the pickleball and beach dog walk early and leave for Costco, as Pati has a cleaner coming to the house. Our nephew Kevin O'Connor and his partner, Asia, are driving over from

Santa Cruz. We have plans for a happy hour, supper, and then a book-store concert with an Aussie folk singer. Tomorrow morning, of course, more pickleball!

Back from Costco at Pati's, I take a quick dip in the hot tub to soothe the aching pickleball muscles. Midafternoon, my phone rings, a 613 Ottawa area-code call, although I don't recognize the number. On this U.S. vacation, I am unsure what add-ons are covered on the phone. I had added text roaming, wanting to keep in touch with Adam. I don't answer the call.

A few minutes later, Pati's phone rings and she answers. She keeps looking over at me. I don't like her look. My brother Jon, in North Bay, tells us that Suzanne has urgent news. I need to call her right away. There has been an accident.

I redial that Ottawa number. It's hard to listen, with Suzanne's emotions and my lousy hearing on phones. *Adam. Pool. Underwater. Emergency. Hospital.*

Nooooooooooooooooo!

Energy swooshes away. Suzanne promises to keep in touch, and as soon as I get off the phone, I text her to establish contact. Suzanne confirms that there has been an accident in the hot tub at Adam's building. Adam was underwater. Paramedics resuscitated him. An ambulance whisked Adam to the Ottawa General Hospital. Suzanne only learned the details herself when she arrived at the hospital. When she got the call, she had assumed that this was one more typical visit to Emergency for our son. A nurse tells her the far worse news.

I can't think straight. A fog rolls in. The words tumble around — *accident, drowning, resuscitation, hospital, seizure.* Damn, not a seizure. God, the surgery was only two months earlier, almost to the day. There have been no seizures since then.

Not again!

I am frantic after the call. I sink to the kitchen floor. Pati hugs me. Life is bleeding away. Is this shock, despair? I need to find a picture of Adam and any picture of my late parents. Dad and Mom must help to save my son.

I am 4,000 kilometres away, 2,800 miles. I desperately need to be with him, NOW.

I have to get a flight home, NOW. I bounce madly from collapsing in tears to stints of clarity and making plans.

My return flight is scheduled a week from today on a combined Air Canada–United Airlines ticket. Pati and I call United Airlines to see if I might be able to fly home tonight. It's already 3:00 p.m. here in California, on a Friday heading into the weekend. That means that it's 6:00 p.m. back in Ottawa. This will be difficult.

My heart is racing, my brain mush. The United Airlines telephone attendant cannot locate San Luis Obispo Airport, a small, commuter airport a half-hour south of Pati's home. He thinks San Luis Obispo is in Central America. Once he does find the airport, he cannot find any seats to get me home tonight. I can fly all day Saturday, arriving in Ottawa Saturday night. I want to scream at him but I need this man to help me. Late Saturday night seems too late. How bad is Adam? Pati says there is certain to be damage from his being underwater. We are unsure how long he was in the water. Did I hear it took three times to resuscitate our son? I dread not getting home in time. I want to be with Adam.

Kevin and Asia arrive. Pati has already given them the bad news in a phone call. They have this well-deserved family reputation for working miracles with airlines. They don't take no for an answer. After they walk through Pati's door and hug me, they hear my pessimistic update on the flight challenges. They grab my phone and head into separate rooms. In forty minutes, they have me booked on three separate flights — leaving in two hours for the short trip from San Luis Obispo to LAX Airport in Los Angeles, then a red-eye flight from LAX to Toronto, and then over to Ottawa first thing in the morning. This will put me at the hospital at 9:00 a.m., instead of twelve hours later. These "angels of the airlines" wisely booked three separate flights rather than ask for one trip with stops in Los Angeles and Toronto.

I feel like a zombie. Kevin and Asia put my airline tickets and boarding passes into my shirt pocket. They arrange to have a United Airlines attendant greet me at the arrival gate at the gargantuan LAX Airport to drive me across one terminal to a bus that will take me to the right terminal and right gate. It all happens exactly as Kevin and Asia plan, with time to spare despite the tight connections.

The gods are with me, I think. But are they? I sense a nastier conversation beginning. I want my God to get me home tonight. Pati, Kevin, and Asia seem to be an answer to those prayers, but this is the same God to whom I entrusted Adam, praying for this last surgery to end the epilepsy seizures once and for all. I've been asking this same God every night to keep Adam safe.

Enough. I need to get home fast. I plead for Adam to be all right, for him to make it through this accident.

As Pati, Kevin, and Asia drive me the half-hour to the airport, I drift in and out of their conversation. As Pati turns into the San Luis Obispo Airport parking lot, she grabs my arm. "Hon, we want the best for Adam, that he be well. But, if it is not to be, he is a young man with healthy organs. I am sure he wants others to have this gift from him."

She is right. I, too, believe that Adam would want that. But my Adam is not going to die. That is not on!

The flight home is uneventful. At each airport landing, I turn on my cellphone for any news. There is none. I decide that no news is good news.

I try to sleep despite the incessant "good Rick, bad Rick" chatter going on in my brain. Are there two angels on my shoulders competing for my attention and, worse, for my Adam? The "good Rick/good angel" reassures me that friends and paramedics found Adam in time, that any damage to his brain or other organs is minimal, that it might take time but he will recover. His brave, strong heart will see us through yet another herculean medical adventure. His parents, siblings, and friends will be there for him.

But "bad Rick/bad angel" creeps in, nipping at my positive prayers and thoughts.

Death, funeral, burial plans all jump into my head. I wince and expel those awful thoughts. But they keep returning. They circle me through the flight, wolves in the black, bleak night that I see out the plane window.

Damn, this kid has suffered enough! So many setbacks have dogged his recoveries. He has endured these major surgeries. He is well down the road to having a body that aligns with his gender. And now he is fighting for his life in an Ottawa hospital. Damn it, God. This is so wrong!

The family members in Ottawa brave out the long, hard Friday night at the Ottawa Hospital – General Campus, getting updates from the doctor and nurses, hearing a first, poor prognosis, comforting Adam, alerting family and friends, making their own plans. Lauren, competing at the Scotties Quebec curling championship, is now on her way home. Her rink will be short a player for their weekend playoffs. Lindsay, who lives in Ottawa, joins her mom at the hospital. David, who works for a helicopter company out of Edmonton, is arranging to fly home the next day.

On the flight home, I drift back to the November epilepsy surgery several times.

* * *

Saturday, January 23, 2016
ICU North — Room 28, Ottawa Hospital – General Campus

Sarah Martin, daughter of my good friend and former member of Parliament boss Tony Martin, meets me at the Ottawa airport. She brings me to the hospital.

Now there is no more denying. I have erased the 4,000-kilometre chasm between father and son, but now I begin to dread the final few steps to his side. I linger a moment. If I don't go into the hospital, and into the room, maybe all will be well. Crazy thinking. On the floor, I find the ICU and am buzzed in. I navigate the maze of corridors and see I-28, spotting Suzanne first, then Lindsay and Lauren, Suzanne's husband, Mike, and others all around the bed. I go in and lean over to kiss my boy.

Oh, Adam.

Noooooooooooooooooooooooo!

I have to touch him, hold him.

There are hugs and hellos all around. Everyone has endured a long, long night. The love for Adam fills the room. There is so much to process but, like that first call in California, little is making sense. Looking around the ICU room, I can see that Adam is clearly receiving excellent health care. Family members mention the good doctors and nurses. The machines, tubes, computers, and intravenous lines are pumping, beeping, and gurgling, an orchestra of sounds all working for him. I'd been in dozens of these rooms as a priest, witnessed emotional life-and-death moments, including some with a few parishioners who were close friends. It surprised me back then how professional and detached I could be, bringing calm, peace, and confidence to others who were distraught.

Not here, not with my son hooked up to all of these machines.

I catch bits and pieces about the accident from the day before. On Friday afternoon, Adam was with a friend on the penthouse floor where the pool is located. Another friend outside joined them. Those two went to get something in Adam's apartment. The seizure happened in the short period that Adam was alone.

Damn.

I did wonder on the flight home if he was in the pool and hot tub alone. We talked to Adam about this danger. He tried to have friends with him. We knew of no seizures since the Montreal surgery. He shared our confidence that this was all behind him.

Taking off a coat and throwing a suitcase in the corner, I notice a note on the whiteboard on the wall. Up in the corner, with an asterisk and a box, are the words, "Patient is known as Adam." In the midst of this awful tragedy, this note is strangely and deeply consoling. During the flight home, I worried about how Adam would be recognized and what he would be called in the hospital. His health card says Rebecca. That is still his legal name. He's been living as Adam for three years, but he is still in transition in many ways. An application to change his legal name is sitting on a table at his apartment.

"Adam is my fucking name," he screamed on Facebook in October 2014.

I didn't want to have to scream his declaration at any doctor or nurse. I am tired. I sense that the red-eye flight and my son's tragedy have me raw and in a mood. I was braced for a fight about his name, knowing that this was Ottawa, a government town where bureaucratic mentalities can kill common sense.

Thank God, Adam will be Adam to everyone at this hospital. We are spared further, unnecessary grief. It is an early blessing.

I am able to take in more of the medical news now. On Friday night, doctors ordered induced hypothermia, putting a cooling blanket on Adam. They want his body temperature to be between 34 and 36 degrees Celsius. The cooling can increase the chance of survival and a favourable neurological outcome in post–cardiac arrest patients.

Adam is fairly cool when I touch his skin. He has mechanical ventilation and pressure support. He is intubated with an endotracheal tube. His stomach is a bit distended from water in the body. There is an arterial line to his heart.

We are in for a long Saturday, waiting, worrying, and wondering, letting the health care — the meds, the fluids, and the chemicals — work. It is a day of waiting to see how Adam will respond. I hurried home to now slow down, stop, and join family and friends in this vigil of love, care, prayers, and those never-ending, meandering, messy thoughts.

No one says the words "life support" but life support is what my eyes see. No one will speak those words.

The nurses are often in, checking the feeds, tubes, and drips, fixing a monitor or a beeping signal. From time to time, we leave to give Adam and the nurses their privacy. There is a nursing station right outside our room with a window for the nurses and doctors to also observe.

We are often six to eight visitors around his bed, a few times even more.

Like others, I suspect, I treasure my alone time with Adam, a chance to be intimate and whisper what I need to say to him. I caress and hold him. The touches of his mother, sisters, their partners, and everyone else keep him company.

Given the size of Adam's extended family, the ICU staff are magnificent in waiving the usual rule of two people in the room at any one time. There will be a parade to and from his bed all day and night.

Dr. Pierre Cardinal will update us on Adam's condition. I meet Dr. Cardinal and I am immediately struck by his compassionate, professional demeanour. He appears to be in his late fifties or early sixties. There is a gentle calm. He gives me a warm handshake and touches my shoulder when we meet. I will experience this touch, this gentleness, over and over again in the next twenty-four hours. Adam is in good hands.

Dr. Cardinal suggests that we move to a larger conference room for the family meeting. He begins by asking us to introduce ourselves, asking each of us about our relationship to Adam. He then asks us to tell him about our understanding of Adam's present medical condition. Suzanne speaks. She was the first family member at the hospital and led the all-night vigil at his bedside. We acknowledge the damage his brain suffered from the drowning, how critical his condition is. Dr. Cardinal nods in appreciation. He confirms that the situation is serious. Adam was underwater for probably twelve to fifteen minutes. There was no CPR until defibrillation, perhaps as long as thirty minutes after Adam's seizure. Dr. Cardinal explains that Adam's brain is the biggest challenge. Adam's prognosis is very uncertain. The medical staff want to re-evaluate his neurological function after the cooling has ended.

Saturday will be a day for waiting as the staff monitor Adam's response. Dr. Cardinal takes time to answer our questions. And again, he extends a hand and puts an arm around the parents as we leave.

*   *   *

Adam's Choir

A much larger vigil is happening for Adam on the floor. His friends are there. Word spread quickly that a friend had discovered him in the water. It had happened early on Friday night, when Adam's friends normally gather at their favourite club in the Ottawa Market. Many come to the hospital instead. And the number of friends grows as news of Adam's accident spreads.

> Adam is 😊 feeling grateful
> November 6, 2014
> Glad I got the family/ friends I need

Are there ten friends here now, this Saturday morning? The numbers will grow all day.

In the waiting room, I hug a few kids whom I recognize. They are all "kids" to me, although most, like Adam, are now adults. I shake hands or hug others whose faces look familiar, mainly from Facebook. Their love for Adam fills the room. They are extremely upset.

They look a lot like my boy — the tattoos, the piercings, the tank tops, the ball caps on backwards, phones in their hands, the various styles of dress and occasional gender-guessing identities. It's Adam's choir, serenading their love and solidarity to their friend. This is a group that might draw a few stares from some folks, and yet all I stare at now is their unconditional love for their buddy.

Throughout the day, they parade to Adam's bedside, growing more comfortable but still upset at seeing him in this bed, unable to speak or move. This is unreal: their friend attached to all these tubes. Their friend who, on so many occasions, has lit up their lives and laughed away their sorrows. Where is their happy friend? Where is his silly grin? They should be at Zaphod's with Adam partying, but instead they are beside their buddy's bed. And they are not going anywhere, now or soon, as we are to discover. New friends arrive. They find someone to take them to Adam. They touch him.

With a few cues from family members, they get more comfortable in this hospital setting.

Is it noon now? Around the bed, I slip out an F-bomb when a larger group surrounds Adam.

"These fucking tattoos," I say.

A few laugh or smile. I ask his friends to tell me the story behind every one of them.

Me, who silently screamed each time my kid broke the news on Facebook, posting a picture of another tattoo, more money blown and more budget worries, his bare skin fast becoming an endangered species. Each tattoo tells a story. And those kids know the stories. A few kids have the same tattoos on their bodies, in kindred spirit.

Adam

February 28, 2015

New tat!! Only got 1st session still have one more to finish guitar and add music notes and touch up flower but still for only one session so far it's amazing!! I love it can't wait to finish it!

Adam is with Ciarra White
June 17, 2014
Second part to tattoo ripped skin and robot inside with purple ribbon for epilepsy 💜 will be finished next session! :) can't wait love it so far!

Lip prints are on one shoulder. "Life goes on" is inked on his back. A jar of hearts is on his left shoulder blade. This tattoo followed a bad breakup when he felt vulnerable. He has a rose on his ankle. He has the chorus of the lyrics to "Only Human" by Christina Perri. The special lyrics spoke to Adam about what being human means. Adam told a friend that the song's chorus describes how he felt through his journey — that he's only human, he does make mistakes, but that he is okay with that because, well, "I was only human."

In recognition of his epilepsy, Adam has three branches with a purple ribbon wrapped around them on one arm. He has a skull with a tie on his wedding ring finger, a couple's way of expressing their commitment to each other because they couldn't afford a wedding or rings. Of course, he has a Batman logo with the Joker inside of it.

He has a Batman on his finger, too, while a girlfriend has a heart on hers, so together they made Heart Batman. He has a crown on his collarbone and it says "King" — King to his girlfriend's "Queen" tattoo, but also King because he's the baby for the Capital Kings in their performances. His crown also has a big skull with roses and a guitar. Music is his special love.

Adam
January 14, 2016
Batman forever 🦇
#batmanfan
#gotham #gothamcity
#batman #ftm
#brucewayne
#justchilling
#arkhamknight
#darkknight

He has the Cheshire Cat from *Alice's Adventures in Wonderland* on his elbow because of his love for the movie *Alice in Wonderland*, but also because the cat has the power to disappear. The cat is a favourite character. He has the word "Strength" on his arm because he wants to stay strong no matter what he faces.

Strong, Adam, be strong now!

I want to rub the Cheshire Cat and disappear with my boy. At last, and late, I learn the meaning behind all those tattoos. Listening to these kids, I smile, recalling that Adam's first tattoo, as Rebecca, came on an epic trip to New York City six years earlier with a cousin, Claire, and her one-year-old son, Cruz. The highlight of the trip was the first tattoo. Rebecca got Mom's permission before the trip. The rose flower on his ankle is the New York tattoo.

I rub my own Murphy tattoo on my shoulder. Now, thanks to these kids, in this bizarre setting in the ICU unit, I know the stories of the other tattoos.

* * *

You sit, you stand, you walk and wait and think. And then you do it again. There is no program for these vigils, but there is a rhythm. Sitting in silence, holding a loved one's hand, rubbing a shoulder. I close my eyes and take in the room's noises: the humming of fans, the white noise from the orchestra of machines, the muted conversation of nurses at the window desk outside the room. There is little to do except love, the one chore the professionals leave to us, the job the loved ones shoulder instinctively, shoving aside any fears or barriers.

Adam, we are here to love you.

Alone with Adam, I drown in my powerlessness. "Batman, make it all right. Rise again, Adam, be the Dark Knight!" I pray, wanting to pull this kid back to us to be healthy again, or as healthy as the day I left for California.

Transitioning from a girl to a boy and eight-hour brain surgeries seem to have been a walk in the park for our son right now.

* * *

A Blessing

My sister Margie O'Connor and her husband, Jerry, arrive from London, Ontario, in the early afternoon. In Toronto, they picked up Claire Prashaw, my brother Marty's oldest daughter. Claire is my goddaughter as well as my niece. It helps to have my own family here to join me with Adam's other family. I will lean on them often in the next twenty-four hours.

Someone mentions the idea that Adam should receive the Catholic sacrament Anointing of the Sick. Adam has been baptized and has also received the sacraments of Reconciliation, First Communion, and Confirmation. The amusing text exchange a few weeks earlier flashes in my mind, the text in which Adam confirmed that he believes in God, but it is his dad who strains his understanding.

The ICU nurses tell us that they will find a chaplain. The anointing is a powerful, healing experience that I know well, both as a minister and as a recipient when I was sick myself. To the older generation of Catholics, the sacrament was called the Last Rites and was reserved for the dying. The arrival of the priest was seldom a good prognosis. Over the years, the Last Rites have evolved into the Anointing of the Sick. While the sacrament is still given to the dying, the emphasis is now on healing and forgiveness. The anointing may be received many times.

But this Saturday, in this hospital, looking at my son, Last Rites come to mind. Bad Rick/bad angel. The nurses identify a chaplain who is available. He will be here in the next hour. Hearing this news, a surprising anger wells up inside me.

In one of Adam's more serious chains of big seizures in 2013, we decided to ask for the Anointing of the Sick at the Queensway Carleton Hospital, also in Ottawa. I had hesitated asking then because, well, it's complicated. On the one hand, I absolutely believed in the power of the sacrament and this anointing. It would help my kid. But I did not want hassles from any priest or chaplain over my child's attendance record at church or, worse, over her same-sex relationship. There are priests who bring grace. And there are priests I know who bring grief.

The Queensway staff summoned a priest. We chatted briefly. He seemed pleasant enough. We left him alone to talk to Rebecca. She never told me what happened. She either didn't understand or was not saying. One of her sisters, though, was upset. It seems that the priest refused Rebecca the Anointing of the Sick — a rare decision that, according to Catholic teaching, should be done only in the gravest circumstances and only with those people for whom it might cause scandal if the sacrament is given: a Mafia don executing a family and then getting on his knees for absolution, for example. That degree of scandalous. My kid was a kid, and sick, and in need of God's love and the Church's blessing. This priest took it upon himself to rain his perverted (and wrong) ideas of God's judgment on Rebecca. He prayed with her but withheld the sacrament.

I was furious when I found out. Later, I dropped by the chapel area and met with another chaplain and told her what had happened, noting my theological training and priestly ministry. I wanted a follow-up to this incident, hoping others would be spared this man's warped judgment. She wouldn't break confidentiality, but it was apparent that I was not the first one to complain.

If this same priest were to walk into our hospital room, even now, over two years later, I fear I would punch him in the face.

I share with Margie my *Rocky* feeling. I speak to the nurses and tell them pieces of the previous, bad chaplain experience. The nurses are confident that the chaplain coming is not my 2013 priest.

In fact, a lay chaplain named Doug, a United Church minister, arrives soon after. His calm, peace, and faith are evident. Joining the family are my friends Janine Bertolo, a work colleague, and her partner, David White, a United Church minister; they happened to be visiting at the time. The chaplain prays for Adam with us. He touches my son. There are readings from Scripture. He invites family members to say what is in our hearts. Prayers, memories, and love spill out. The chaplain prays for Adam, and together we recite the Lord's Prayer. Adam is surrounded by love, God's and ours. This is all good.

Adam
July 25, 2015
Thunderstorm!!!
Love'em!

*   *   *

Mind and heart jump all over the place. Much like on the flight home, I alternate between being optimistic and pessimistic on Adam's chances for recovery. And, regardless, I can't block the bad thoughts seeping into my thinking. Pati's words at the San Luis Obispo Airport creep back into my consciousness.

"I am sure he wants others to have this gift from him." His organs. It is early Saturday afternoon, perhaps — my memory isn't clear — when I whisper the words "organ donation" to Suzanne. She holds up her hands firmly, indicating that this is not the time to have this conversation. That's okay. We have a long day ahead of us. And, at the time, I'm unaware of critical information that she has.

On the same afternoon, I mention the possibility of organ donation to a nurse, Julie, and again with Dr. Cardinal when I bump into him in the hallway. These are brief conversations. I tell them that we still have yet to talk, but we might be open to Adam's organs being donated, aware of his generous spirit. We will need a final report, too, on his condition. Where will this end? I am still praying for a miracle. The nurse did refer to damage that has been done to Adam's organs. Brain damage for sure. Other organs? This might well affect the decisions that are made if Adam dies and the family gives the okay to taking his organs. Still, the doctor and nurse express their gratitude for the heads-up.

The good Rick/bad Rick tension is haunting me. Adam seems to be on life support, the machines keeping him alive, waiting for the final word that he is not going to make it. But there's the extraordinary care, compassion, and medical help that he is getting. Could it pull him back from this precipice? I believe in miracles. I have witnessed a few. I am not thinking straight or thinking much at all this Saturday afternoon and evening. Good angel goes for the miracle. Bad angel sneaks up to death and dying.

* * *

Saturday Night

I almost miss my chum Alexie Steedman-Lalonde, who brings supper and baked goodies to the ICU waiting room. Others send food over. We are thirty or forty now, with all of Adam's friends. Few are leaving. More and more of his friends are arriving.

Early Saturday night, my sister Margie is chatting with Adam's friends. Before her retirement, she was a pioneer lay chaplain in the

London Catholic School Board. She was, literally, a godsend to the staff and students there who were in the midst of personal or family tragedies, weaving innovative faith rituals for people who were often alienated or distant from their churches or their own faith traditions.

She is tending to Adam's friends now, asking them to tell her their stories. Who is Adam to them? What does being trans mean?

Are we putting in time waiting for a final medical verdict? Watching Margie with the kids, does she know? I let her be with Adam's choir — except I whisper to her after one particularly long parade of Adam's friends to his bedside that the family will need time to be alone with him soon. She summons the kids around her. In her best schoolteacher voice, laced with love and gratitude, she makes it clear that they should go in one last time to say goodbye to Adam, and then tomorrow, Sunday morning, we, the family, will be alone with him.

Brittney Palmer thanks Margie and basically repeats her message. She then adds matter-of-factly that they will all be back tomorrow morning anyway to wait in the visitors' room. Ha! I love these kids. They are not going away. They are Adam's family, too. In so many ways, they are our spirit guides, taking us through this weekend.

Adam shared a photo — with Ashley Mary-Lynn.
July 4, 2015
Best friends are the people in your life who make you laugh louder, smile brighter and live better. What is a friend? A single soul dwelling in two bodies, and with you that single soul we put together is amazing, hilarious, and always smiles and laughs when together

As the family settles in to the long Saturday night, Lauren's partner, Don Bowser, has a laptop computer open, watching Lauren's team's curling playoffs. This short respite of "normal" helps. Life goes on beyond these hospital walls. Lauren's rink has won their semifinal match. Short a player for the finals, there will be no miracle on ice for Lauren or her rink tonight. They lose the final. We will not be booking flights to Grande Prairie, Alberta, for a repeat of the magical time last year in Moose Jaw, Saskatchewan, cheering on Lauren's team Quebec at the Scotties. There seems to be a shortage of miracles all around.

*   *   *

Saturday Night

After a long, long day, we are around Adam's bed. We are remembering Adam and Rebecca adventures. Mike mentions Rebecca's wedding.

"Crazy fun wedding," he said. "What a good time."

There are smiles and laughter in the room. This kid sure has crammed plenty into his twenty-two years.

I have always put the "wedding" in quotes and have told the story many times with much affection. Honestly though, there was far less affection when Rebecca first broke the news.

Ciarra was Rebecca's first long-term companion. They had lived together over a year, first in that apartment Rebecca moved herself into on Ciarra's moving day and then in a bachelor apartment on Elgin Street. I grew to appreciate Ciarra. She is a good person, a good soul. I enjoyed a Christmas meal in 2014 with "the kids" at Ciarra's mother and her partner's place. Ciarra helped me "let go" of dad duties and at least some of my worries about Rebecca. I recall one late weekend night when she used Rebecca's phone at the hospital to tell me that Rebecca had had a seizure and that they were at a crowded Emergency ward waiting for hours to see a doctor. Initially upset at the seizure news, I was also relieved to realize that I could stay in Kanata, in my warm bed. Rebecca had Ciarra to look after her. She was in good hands.

> Bekkaa
> April 29, 2014
> ********Happy 11 months anniversary to my amazing, beautiful, best friend/fiance Cee Prashaw! :) exactly 1 month & 2 days until our wedding <3 love you so much been great times together so far

Rebecca and Ciarra had been together a year when Facebook posts appeared referring to a marriage.

Shit. She can't! I thought. *She won't! Of course, she will!* I didn't know if her mother knew their plans, but this was why I was my kid's friend on Facebook: to learn of small matters, like wedding announcements!

The two of them had decided that they wanted to seal the relationship with a ceremony pledging their commitment to each other.

I was apoplectic, vowing to talk to them, to end this madness. Rebecca was twenty. Ciarra was a year older. They were too young, had no money, and hadn't been together that long. Getting married at twenty seemed among my kid's rasher acts — quite the feat, soaring to the top of the charts of crazy deeds.

They got engaged around Christmas in 2013.

Nothing I said to Rebecca persuaded her to postpone the wedding. This wedding train had left the station, picking up steam with the news that Ciarra's stepmom, Sheila, a second mother to her for many years, had been diagnosed with inoperable cancer. Ciarra and Rebecca resolved to be married before Sheila died.

I pleaded with them, noting that in previous generations, there would be an engagement, then a betrothal ceremony first. Couples would exchange vows. The bride would wear a wedding dress.

This all fell on deaf ears. They were having too much fun and were in too deep to stop now.

Bekkaa

May 31, 2014

Truly the most beautiful day and night thanks to our friends and family the wedding itself was beautiful and the partying was awesome ;) never going to forget such a glorious day for me and ciarra!

Once it was evident that there was no turning back, I jumped on the wedding train. I was not going to miss my kid's wedding day.

It was a beautiful day, one we all enjoyed. The wedding was in Petawawa in a community park, at a town gazebo beside the Petawawa River with its surging, spring-fed rapids. Rebecca wore a smart tuxedo, white shirt, suspenders, and black pants. Lauren joined Rebecca's friends in the wedding party. I was grateful that a few members of my family attended — my brother Jon and his wife, Nancy; their kids, Lindsay and Marci; and my niece, Claire. Ciarra's dad, Francis White; her stepmom, Sheila; and her mother, Debbie Speirs, beamed their love, too.

When Rebecca and Ciarra exchanged vows and the ceremony ended, they left for photographs at the river. As a priest, I had

Rebecca and Ciarra, the "wedding," Petawawa, Ontario.

Rebecca with her parents at her and Ciarra's wedding.

witnessed several hundred weddings. I went over to the registry that they had just signed. Something was not right. Where was the wedding licence? The kids had signed the officiant's rainbow book. There was no licence in sight.

For the rest of the day, I was swept away by the precious celebration of Ciarra and Rebecca's love: the standard wedding fare of food, fun, stories, dancing, and drink. As Mike says, "crazy fun." The friends of the couple squealed at Suzanne and my telling different parts of the story of Rebecca having Adam in his name right from birth, hell, right from the womb. They delighted in looking at Rebecca's hockey pictures as a goalie. I danced with my daughter, who looked handsome, in her shirt, suspenders, and pants.

> Adam is with Ciarra White
> July 8, 2014
> I have such an amazing wife :) came to my work to help me with inventory when I know shit all how to do it and am pretty well forced to do it now... and especially after this weekend it wasn't best time for thinking... and also brought me deodorant for after work cause she knew we would go out and id know id stink and want to smell good lol and bought me food, did dishes for me so i didnt have to! Lol you are truly special

The memories are sweet. As my tomboy girl, this kid promised to wear a dress three times in her life. Well, here was "the wedding," and my kid was in a tux.

A few weeks later, at the Elgin Street Diner with Rebecca Adam, we told stories from the wedding.

I looked at her.

"That wasn't a wedding, right?"

"Yeah, no, it wasn't."

I got Rebecca to tell the story. The officiant discovered too late that her Nunavut wedding licence was not recognized in the Province of Ontario. They had tried for a judge but were too late. It turned out that the legal part didn't matter. They would visit the courthouse in the fall. They went ahead with their "wedding."

Kind of like a betrothal.

I was relieved and, for once, smart enough to mute my "I told you so."

We are deeply grateful for Ciarra and Rebecca's love. Over their sixteen-month relationship, beginning in late 2013, my kid discovered the strength and support to begin his journey to Adam. Ciarra's love was very much the catalyst. Their relationship ended seven months after the ceremony. Sheila outlived the "marriage," dying in June 2015, nine months past their breakup.

Rest in peace, Sheila. Blessings, Ciarra. It was indeed a "crazy fun wedding."

* * *

We are all settling into the long Saturday night here in Adam's room, I-28, and the visitors' lounge. Suzanne and I agree that we will talk later tonight.

Visiting Adam now, my helplessness crushes me. I want to remove all those tubes, pick him up, and take him away to a safe place. There is no way.

I fail at being his superhero.

There is this acute helplessness. I couldn't protect him. I can't save him. Whose script is this that we are living, anyway? Who is directing this drama that we can't rewrite? Adam has exceptional health care all around him. The doctors, nurses, and technicians are completely dedicated to my son.

But I sense that there are other issues at play. All the power in the world cannot bring him back.

As a dad, as a parent, my job is to keep him safe. It's a parent's first duty.

I tiptoed into the bedroom when Rebecca was an infant, checking on her, making sure she was still breathing — crazy stuff we do as parents.

I checked the temperature of the water before the bath.

I tasted the food that she ate.

I triple-checked the seat belts, got her to look both ways before she crossed the street, knew the depth of the water before she dove into it, gave her the talk on cars and on whom she should trust, running various, scary "stranger scenarios" past my child. Molly, our Aussie cattle dog, used to quarter our yard, corralling, herding, protecting anyone who needed it. Are not parents the first herders?

Whenever our child got sick, Suzanne and I went to the ends of the earth for the right medicine, the cure, the end to the suffering. Parents suffer alongside the child.

And I never imagined not protecting him. There wasn't a time I entered an Emergency ward for a seizure that I doubted for one second that we would be leaving with my kid okay, on the road to recovery. I had exactly the same attitude after those two major brain surgeries in Montreal.

I spent many a night on my pillow asking God, my mom and dad, the angels and saints, to watch over my kid. It didn't matter the age. I did it for Becca as a baby. I do it for Adam in his twenties. I know other parents who do this.

I wish that I had pushed him harder to come to California. I failed at being his guardian angel in the hot tub yesterday. Where is his guardian angel now? Adam posted on Facebook, only a week ago, on January 15, a funny picture of a guardian angel with his head shaking in his hands, along with the caption, "I have a feeling that my guardian angel often looks like this." Adam's guardian angel for SNAFU moments. Undoubtedly, Adam keeps his angel busy.

Will the angels pull him out of a mess one more time?

Helpless, helpless.

*   *   *

There is talk this Saturday night of the selfie that Adam posted late Friday afternoon, just yesterday. This might turn out to be Adam's last selfie and last Instagram post.[1] He is in the hot tub. The time on the post is 3:52 p.m. He either has a shirt off or his top down. A brilliant shaft of light from the window solarium lands on his head.

Adam D. Prashaw
January 22, 2016
Hot tub time 😎 😴 #hottubtime #confidence #goodtimes #ftm #presurgery #timewillcome #transgender

A few have this picture up on their phones. It's an uncanny photo. Adam must have taken it minutes or seconds before his seizure in the hot tub.

*   *   *

I curl up on a couch in a waiting room for a few hours of sleep. Others spend time with Adam and will sleep later.

Adam is always with family. I know that he is in good company. From my ministry days, from talking with patients who recovered,

1. An online mobile photo-sharing, video-sharing, and social-networking service that enables its users to take pictures and videos and share them either publicly or privately.

I believe that Adam is aware of those who are in the room with him. Again, I crave the time to be alone with Adam. I reminded his friends earlier today what the research, literature, and experience testify about how a person who is in a coma or is unresponsive still hears the conversations in the room; how we can whisper important messages to them and they will hear, even if they cannot acknowledge hearing those words. Again, people have come back from near-death to confirm this was their experience. I have heard this personally from patients.

I find that private time with Adam. I whisper my love to my son, gratitude for all he was and is. Present tense. I can't use the past tense. I cry. And out of me pours a treasury of memories to remind him how special he is, how proud I am for all he is and all he has done, the challenges that he met squarely and beat, the health scares he survived, the astonishing and (at times) surprising success in school, aided by those Individual Education Plans set up through the high school resource centre. He is so brave.

Eve Joseph, a hospice worker and poet, recounts listening to an ICU intensivist talk to a family whose mother is in a coma:

> "Can she hear us?" they asked.
> "Yes," she replied. "She hears you the way a newborn hears the sound of its mother's voice."[1]

Joseph liked this. So do I. Womb to tomb, linked by a mother's voice. We hear our mother's voice in utero. We hear them when we're lying in our cradles and buggies, before comprehension. Adam heard his name in his mother's belly. Even more important than the words is our presence, the love, the touch that Adam is receiving — all of this now from his mom, his dad, stepdad, brother and sisters and other family, and those extraordinary friends.

Ten days ago, he posted a message wondering, if he were ever in a hospital bed, who would show up to see him. Imagine! He wrote this *ten days ago*. The "hospital bed visitor" question elicited many replies, his

---

1. Eve Joseph, *In the Slender Margin: The Intimate Strangeness of Death and Dying* (New York: Harper Perennial, 2015), 59.

buddies telling him that they would be there. And they are. I want Adam to know who has come to his bed, this day, this night. He had no need to worry about who would be here. This kid who wondered what others think of him — who feared how they would react if he told them who he was — is finding out now for himself. *All's good on that count, Adam.*

*   *   *

Our hockey goalie. Is there one more save in you?

Rebecca shone in the goalie crease during those hockey years from 2003 to 2011. No matter the level she played, Rebecca brought this fierce, competitive character to the ice. She thrived on the pressure — to play well, to not let her teammates down. For her, the only thing better than facing thirty shots a game from her opponents was facing forty shots. She enjoyed having the puck in her team's end; the more shots at her, the better. The best nights for her were when one of the teams playing next was short a goalie and she was drafted for a second round of netminding. The goalie crease taught my kid well. There's a physical toughness necessary to haul those heavy pads to and from the arena. I recognized, too, the mental toughness of the goalie. The goalie is the natural leader, the anchor for the team. The crease comes with pressure. Was it in the goalie crease my kid honed this true grit that has enabled him to stop life's brutal shots, to rebound from so many seizures and those two surgeries, to block the judgments and discrimination in the journey to manhood? He is incredibly resilient.

*   *   *

At night, in the still quiet of the room, with fewer interruptions from medical or family visitors, the reality sets in. There are no veils here to cover the prognosis. Adam's pupils are dilated, fixed. There is no response to any stimuli. No cough. The pulse is weak; the breathing light. He cannot breathe without the mechanical ventilation.

The doctors talk of anoxic brain injury, about what the lack of oxygen did to his brain.

I ask questions of the nurses. Julie, Hanna, and Danielle translate the medical jargon into plain English — the transfusion medicine, cardiopulmonary diagnostics, respiratory therapy, hematology, biochemistry; the checking of glucose, creatinine, hemoglobin, ionized calcium; the microbiology and pathology reports; the CT scan, neuro assessment, baseline skin assessment, blood work, phosphate levels, the enteral feeding tube.

It means so much, but not so much anymore.

What *does* mean the world to me is that the nurses and doctors and respiratory specialists slip into the room over and over again. I watch the nurses show professional, compassionate care. They weave their way around us, around the wires and tubes, to take care of my son. Family can stay. Family can cry. Family can be invisible. They don't ask us to move. They answer all our questions. They go quietly about their work. They adjust my son's blanket to keep him warm. They are so careful not to hurt him with their needles. They listen to our stories and look at our pictures.

* * *

What to tell your son at a time like this: tell him about his beauty, your love of him, the stories, the memories, who is here in the room for him, the love that his family and friends have for him, how they won't leave him alone.

Other family members are having their own privileged conversations.

Do I give him permission to go now? *Adam, do you realize how much you are loved? Are you taking it all in?*

* * *

That night, after midnight, after some sleep, I find Suzanne in the room with Adam. She is going to take a break herself, but we agree that we will talk when she returns. I find myself alone with Adam and his brother, David. We are quiet but the company is good. My marriage to his mother ended when David was young, twelve or so. We came to talk, eventually. Long ago, after the separation, David and I travelled on a few trips together. We talk about the East Coast trip to Newfoundland, the drive up its west coast to L'Anse aux Meadows. David's good buddy from his days in Russell, Dan Vincelette, comes in with coffee. Dan handles the emergency 911 phones for the police. Apparently, he was working when the call for the Elgin Street apartment drowning came in. He knew the address. He knew Adam lived there.

When David leaves with Dan, Suzanne and I are alone.

It is time.

We are on either side of our Adam, who is lying in the hospital room hooked up to so many machines. It is a surreal scene. Again, Adam brings us together, much as he did through a variety of school, hockey, and health care adventures. He is a bridge now. He is twenty-two.

Damn, God.

He is becoming everything he wanted to be in life — an adult, independent, making it on his own. And he is our boy. We love him. And we love those years he was Rebecca. Rebecca Adam had been our child for almost eighteen of those twenty-two years.

I bring up the matter of organ donation first. I start to say what I suspect Adam wants. Suzanne stops me. She knows for a fact what Adam wants. At sixteen, unknown to me, when Rebecca's G1 licence came in the mail at Suzanne's house, she discussed the organ donation line with her mom. She gave her unequivocal yes to help anyone if she ever died in an accident. There was no hesitation from her then. There will be no hesitation now. His goodness and his courage have been evident for so long.

Adam, unable to drive since seventeen, is still in the driver's seat this dark night. We will give permission for the doctors to take any of his organs that might help others.

Next, I ask Suzanne if my sister Margie might prepare and preside at a service, working with both families. Suzanne graciously agrees. We are feeling our way through the order of things. This is all so unbelievable, unfair. Our child is between us on life support. Dying. There is nothing right in planning a funeral for your child, no matter the age.

We grapple with the order of things: a wake, a viewing, a celebration, cremation. Is there a church or a place for all of this? That seems enough for now. I sense Adam is certainly alive during this sacred moment. He is bringing us together for these decisions.

It is nearing dawn, Sunday. Any time I left I-28 briefly, my return reintroduces me to this vigil of love from family surrounding him. You put one foot in front of the other.

Somehow, a day passes. Things get done. There are countless acts of love. Of the many precious memories this final night, none surpass for me the moment Suzanne and I spend as parents with our son between us. But also precious are the periodic visits by Hanna, one of the nurses. Suzanne and Hanna talk as parents, as moms. I drift in and out of the conversation. I never got to say goodbye to Hanna. She did find Suzanne before she left her shift early Sunday morning, hugging her, saying she will not be back to work the next day. There are other special nurses those forty-eight hours. The nurses all weekend have been our own guardian angels. Hanna is a light on this darkest Saturday night.

* * *

Sunday, January 24, 2016

Dr. Cardinal convenes a second, final family conference.

He starts to go through a list of medical data on Adam when he notices that there are a few new people in the room: Adam's brother, David; Mike's son, Troy; and Adam's special friend, Aunt Sandy. He introduces himself to them. This is one special man. The time has come.

Dr. Cardinal announces that, soon, he will be joined by a few other doctors to conduct the necessary, final medical testing that should confirm Adam is dead, neurologically dead. The organs are better than they were, but Adam is beyond help. He is not certain himself when Adam died, although this will be the final medical, legal, and official pronouncement.

Before the meeting ends, Margie speaks. She wants to express gratitude for this doctor. She shares a story on the meaning of his surname. "The cardinal is the bird who wakes everyone up when it is still dark and beckons us into a new day … The bird he is named after, the greeter of dawn, the new day, new life."

The good doctor smiles. Margie continues: "The cardinal is the bird that gets up earliest in the morning when all the other birds are asleep and says, 'Good morning, neighbours, it's time to wake up.' All the other birds look at the poor cardinal as though it is crazy. 'Why isn't she content to sleep on like us,' they jeer. But she is the one insisting the light is on its way. This cardinal burst into our lives, unwelcome at first, but a genuine gift."

No jeering on this Sunday morning for this cardinal. We are so tired. Dr. Cardinal is announcing the inevitable. Sunday is a new day. This is a new morning.

At 10:00 a.m., we gather in Room I-28 North. Dr. Cardinal enters, introducing a few other doctors.

I don't need to hear every word. I lean against the back wall, in a second cluster behind others closer to the bed. I wonder when Adam did leave us. I believe it was sooner than Sunday morning.

Adam is pronounced dead at 10:45 a.m. We hug and kiss him. We hug one another.

We hug Dr. Cardinal and thank him.

A new vigil begins.

Bekkaa

March 20, 2013

These times are hard but they will pass, and soon become times of happiness 🖤

CHAPTER 10

Dead Enough

#beadonor

Sunday, January 24, 2016
Late morning

ANOTHER PHRASE BY Eve Joseph serves as a still photograph for what happens next at the hospital. Reflecting on her hospice work, her companionship with death and dying, Joseph writes on the blur between life and death with respect to organ donation.

Joseph witnessed many deaths. She observed how families hear the medical pronouncement of death. They see something different when looking at their loved one. There is still breathing, aided by the machines, rosy cheeks. They look alive but are dead. Joseph describes this as "dead enough," a phrase of bioethicist Stuart Youngner, the condition necessary to pronounce a legal death.[1]

Sitting in I-28, this is what we see as we mourn Adam after the doctors have gone. Colour in the skin and lips, the chest moving a bit. He doesn't look dead. But he is.

---

1. Joseph, *In the Slender Margin*, 56.

Divergent lines converge here on the second floor of the Ottawa General this forlorn January Sunday morning.

There's the line from the San Luis Obispo Airport parking lot, my conversation with Pati: sister and nurse. She sensed the critical condition in which I would find Adam in Ottawa; she will tell me later that on the entire drive from her home to the airport, she was thinking how to bring up such a sensitive subject as organ donation so soon after getting the awful news about my son. As a nurse, she has been in these hard places, groping for the fleeting and right moment to introduce the topic, when you feel that the family is ready to hear it. Of course, Pati didn't want to rob me of hope prematurely, but she also sensed that there would be no opportunity for this conversation once I got on the plane. Her words on Adam's healthy organs and generous spirit were seeds planted deep within me as the plane lifted off the tarmac.

Another, far more critical conversation connects with us now — our Rebecca Adam telling her mother her wishes when her driver's licence arrived in the mail and she signed the donor card. That's a seven-year line from the spring of 2009 to this morning.

Adam is busy drawing other lines for his organs. We cannot fathom yet where this will lead.

Saturday night and Sunday morning, we take the step to ensure that Adam's wishes are fulfilled. No health care professional at the Ottawa General Hospital initiated any of those discussions. I'd had those first side conversations earlier Saturday with Dr. Cardinal and a nurse. Suzanne and I consented to Adam's organ donation as we spoke, with our son lying between us, during the night. From my political work, I am aware of the chronic shortage of organs and tissue available for transplantation across Canada, the long waiting lists, the need outweighing availability. On its website, the Trillium Gift of Life Network (TGLN) tracks the number of people waiting for an organ. It shows about 1,500.[1] Adam is dead. He wants to be a donor, and we know his healthy organs will save lives.

At that final family conference with Dr. Cardinal an hour ago, we, as parents, brought up the matter of donating Adam's organs. We want

---

1. "Statistics," Trillium Gift of Life Network, 2018, giftoflife.on.ca/en/publicreporting. htm#waitinglistbyage.

the close family members and friends who are present to know that he is a registered organ donor and that he talked with his mother years ago about his wishes. In the event of an accident and his death, he wanted to donate his organs to help others. But I cannot use the past tense for my son. This is what he wants now. His parents will honour and respect Adam's wishes. Knowing Adam's wishes and that his parents agree with them might console everyone a bit at this difficult time. They recognize Adam's generosity in this decision.

I feel Adam's presence at this last family conference, much as I did last night as he lay hooked up to those machines, between his parents.

The Ottawa General health care team worked non-stop on Adam from the minute the ambulance brought him to the hospital late Friday afternoon. The prognosis after the drowning was grim. The damage to the brain was catastrophic. They waited to see how Adam would respond to the cooling of his body and other meds. All weekend, we waited for our miracle that was not to be. The doctors and nurses did everything they could. On Saturday, I thought I heard that his organs might not be in good enough shape to be transplanted, even if there was consent for their donation. By Sunday morning, the doctor confirmed that the organs were much better. This is astonishing work on the part of the health care team, their care for my son, his health. It is a testament to our young, resilient Adam. Organ damage and organ function are critical factors in the final decision on the suitability of a donor.

At some point on the weekend, the hospital notified TGLN, the not-for-profit agency of the Government of Ontario that plans, promotes, coordinates, and supports organ and tissue donation and transplantation across the province. Hospitals in Ontario are required to refer deaths or imminent deaths to TGLN. TGLN reviews each case to see if donation is possible. I learn later that if there is potential, a donation coordinator reaches out to the family about donation. The preferred practice is to have the TGLN donation coordinator approach the family, rather than the hospital's health care team, as they are specially trained and have more experience.

As I also discover later, the family of every potential organ donor in Ontario is approached, whether the potential donor is registered or not. Almost all families of registered donors honour their loved one's end-of-life wishes. However, given that the registration rate in Ontario is 32 percent, many potential donors are not registered, and their families must make the decision to give permission for donation. In these cases, families give consent for organ donation only about 50 percent of the time.[1]

Adam will have his way.

We are in a new vigil with Adam. We keep him company. We are all tired. It is an enormous comfort to be given that room and time with Adam, to see my son wrapped in the love of his parents, sisters, and brother — all loving him toward death and beyond. Suzanne and I leave Adam in that embrace of family. We have two meetings that are time sensitive.

> Bekkaa shared
> March 5, 2012
> Life's a climb... but
> the view is great

First, we meet with the TGLN donation co-ordinator, who is based in the hospital, regarding the final organ donation decision. They know that Adam is registered as an organ donor. They want the consent of the family, too, before proceeding.

Before we begin, the Trillium staff member kindly lets us tell her about our son, share pictures, including the remarkable, final picture of Adam in the hot tub minutes before the drowning, with that light from the heavens shining down on his head. His angels.

It is the picture that will be our northern star, guiding us through the days, weeks, and months ahead — the shaft of light coming through the solarium directly to his head. It will be weeks before I also notice that this shaft of light enters Adam's head where doctors identified the source of his seizures. The angels were there with him.

TGLN wants to do the necessary donor screening, testing, and suitability assessment to minimize the risk of disease transmission in transplantation. Along with laboratory testing of any organs, they need a extensive medical and social history from family members and/or others with detailed knowledge of the donor to confirm donor suitability. There is a lengthy, personal, and somewhat difficult questionnaire to determine his suitability as a donor. This is tough, but when I think about what Adam faced head-on in his life, I am not about to shrink from this task. Adam will light the way.

1. Trillium Gift of Life Network.

The TGLN questionnaire topics include general health, blood transfusions, infections, lifestyle, sexual history, and travel. Information obtained during the donor medical and social history questionnaire will also help inform what organs and tissues might be suitable for transplant. The questionnaire is a requirement of Health Canada, designed to protect organ and tissue recipients. It feels intrusive. How can it not be, by necessity, so soon after the actual death of Adam? There are personal questions on his drug history, sexual partners, and blood transfusions. They want to protect as much as possible the integrity of the transplant and the recipient of any organ.

Adam has been open with us about his life, his few girlfriends. We track down contact information for his tattoo artist.

We are done with the questionnaire. Without hearing anything definite, there is a real sense from the conversation that Adam's organs might be used for transplants. We head back to be with Adam.

Bekkaa shared
April 17, 2013
"When we least expect it, life sets us a challenge to test our courage and willingness to change; at such a moment, there is no point in pretending that nothing has happened or in saying that we are not yet ready. The challenge will not wait. Life does not look back. A week is more than enough time for us to decide whether or not to accept our destiny."
Paulo Coelho, The Devil and Miss Prym

CHAPTER 11

Tania

Sunday, January 24, 2016
Early afternoon

AFTER OUR GOODBYES to the Trillium staff, we wait for Tania Tack from Basic Funeral Services. Tania is our second "time urgent" meeting. She is a friend of Lindsay's, and she graciously wraps up a child's birthday party to head over to the hospital. I will learn later that her son's name is also Adam.

For other reasons, having Basic Funeral Services show up now seems more than a coincidence.

Two months earlier, my sister Pati sent me an online invitation to a *Death Expo* podcast, a series on death and dying well, or at least better than many do. At the time, I imagined that this was a dark joke from my playful sister. Perhaps she was reacting to my mild stroke in 2014 that had triggered my sending her dozens of health queries.

I was intrigued by the invitation, though. I am in my sixties. Friends and colleagues are dying, some younger than I. And the title, *Death*

Expo, interested me, including the titles of several talks — "Dying Well," "Confessions of a Funeral Director," "The Green Burial Council."

I registered, started the podcasts in Ottawa, and finished listening to them in California. They nudged me to think about my death, my funeral, and my choices — not a bad thing, I thought, at my stage in life and living in our death-denying culture. Now, I wonder if those *Death Expo* podcasts foreshadowed the preparation for another death: Adam's, not mine.

We must make choices that I never imagined making for our son.

Tania arrives. She is a gentle, kind, compassionate breeze, bringing in some air for our long, sad weekend. Tania puts flesh and bones on all the wisdom that I heard on the podcasts about developing trends in the death industry — simpler, less expensive services that accommodate family wishes. Basic Funeral Services will assist us as best as possible to keep the human and the natural in this awful tragedy. They will reduce traditional funeral fees, in part because they use existing service locations rather than own their own chapels or visitation spaces.

> Adam shared 9GAG's photo
> December 2, 2015
> I'm not crazy. My reality is just different than yours

There is much to sort out.

This being Sunday, we choose Wednesday for the wake and a Celebration of Life, a little unsure of the timing required for the transplant of organs, if that is happening, and also aware that a few relatives will be travelling to Ottawa.

There are no plans or notes to guide us here. We are feeling our way through these decisions. Suzanne wonders if Mike, a builder, might make the casket. The idea of a wood casket built by family feels right. Adam will be cool with this. Mike will invite David and Troy to help him. Basic Funeral Services has no problem with the family providing the casket.

I want to have Adam's body present for the wake at the church. Many friends and even a few family members did not make it to Ottawa or the hospital to see him these past few days. I believe that final, physical goodbyes can nudge us toward acceptance, grudging as it may be. Tania assures us that Basic Funeral Services will receive Adam's body after any organ transplants. We also decide that cremation will follow the viewing of the body and Celebration of Life.

We need to contact David White, the friend and pastor at Centretown United Church who, with his partner Janine, joined the family on Saturday for prayers with Adam. We want to confirm that his downtown church on Bank Street is available. I feel a special bond with his church because, for thirteen years, from 1991 to 2004, I worked on the second floor there for an NGO: the Church Council on Justice and Corrections. A downtown church should be ideal for many of Adam's friends and our work colleagues.

We think that we might contact Joel Frappier at the Nature Café to inquire about hosting a service and reception there. Basic Funeral Services will handle Adam's body after the wake at the church while we head the few blocks over to the Celebration of Life. Adam will be there in spirit!

We are done our second and final meeting at the hospital.

There is one last visit with Adam. I don't sense his presence here in this body as much. There are a few more words to say to him, promises to make, and vows to keep.

Leaving the hospital, I spot a few of Adam's friends sitting in the large entrance foyer to the hospital. They are still there, as promised, in small groups, chatting.

Bekkaa shared
October 12, 2011
side by side or miles apart, friends are forever, close to your heart

CHAPTER 12

Soar, Adam, Soar

Sunday, January 24, 2016
Evening

IT IS THE DEAD of winter in Ottawa, but a dense fog moves into our lives. I don't remember much of the rest of the day, the blur of phone calls, emails, social media posts, futile attempts to nap.

Adam's siblings and Suzanne are home with family.

My family is staying near the hospital at the home of family friends Peggy and Dick Bakker. They are away and have agreed to lend their house; it is a generous gift and an oasis for our grief. There is supper and quiet conversation, preparing for what lies ahead. Many more relatives will be on the road to Ottawa in the next few days.

Before bed, I want to post some news on my Facebook page. Many are asking. I know many have been praying for Adam and for us all weekend. Sitting at the computer, I feel drained, desperate to find a little spark to speak truth to what has happened. I ask Adam to guide me. This is what I post at 9:42 p.m. on Sunday night:

Rick
January 24, 2016
Soar, Adam, Soar!

Some family and friends know my son, Adam D. Prashaw. Some did not know the latest chapters of his life although they picked up hints of that story.

Back in 1993, when Suzanne cheered my heart with news that we were to have a baby — my first, her fourth — I was over the moon happy. I was forty years old, naive in baby ways. Suzanne, smarter than a lot of people I know, told me she was certain we were having a boy, given that she carried this baby like her last child, David, and so unlike her first two children, girls, Lindsay and Lauren.

So, we began to refer to this life in Suzanne as Adam. When the intern who caught the baby announced it was a girl, Suzanne, gobsmacked, sat up on the table and asked whether the doctor was sure. He said he was only an intern but in his limited experience he was certain that we had a baby girl. We named "her" Rebecca Danielle Adam Prashaw.

That is my child's legal name.

And boy, did "she" like the fact of having Adam in the name. Rebecca was a tomboy. I have few "girl in a dress" pictures.

In high school, she like all of us searched for who "she" was. She liked girls and came to believe she was lesbian.

It would take a few more years and more growth before she recognized the boy that was in her all along, the guy his mom and dad recognized and named twenty-two years ago.

Adam began his counselling, trans meds and legal name changes.

He was growing into all it meant to be Adam.

His epilepsy also lurked in the shadows, biting

so much at a normal, healthy life. But like every-thing in this kid's life, he coped, summoned his courage and soldiered on.

And like enough of our kids, he drove his par-ents crazy with a fierce, stubborn independence, a constant "I know, Dad" message.

Despite two courageous brain surgeries, the epilepsy snared him in the end.

He drowned in a hot tub this Friday night.

I am inconsolable at the loss of my Adam. His friends, including some in the trans commu-nity, have taught me so much the past forty-eight hours about love, faithfulness and solidarity. They help me enormously along with family, friend and Facebook love.

We are firming up the Celebration of Life for Adam and will post it all tomorrow on social media and the newspaper.

In the early years, Adam and I loved *Lion King* a lot. Mourning his death, we would point Lion King out in the stars at night.

There is a bright new star tonight. You, Adam.

I love you, Adam. I am so proud to be your Dad.

CHAPTER 13

Heart, Kidneys, Liver, and Saint Jesus School

Monday and Tuesday, January 25–26, 2016

IT IS MONDAY, the day after Adam died at the hospital, the first day of Adam being dead, a day like no day I ever knew before.

I don't want to get out of bed.

I grope for the right words to describe the seventy-two hours since I boarded the plane in California. I feel like a dead man walking. Family and friends see me through this nightmare, a long line of love literally passing through me from hug to hug to hug. I know others are doing the same for Adam's mom and family. Today and tomorrow will be no different.

But I don't want to throw back this warm comforter.

My first conscious thoughts go to Adam, alive not dead, and his organs. What happened? When we left the hospital late Sunday afternoon, after completing the interview with the TGLN staff and saying our final goodbyes to Adam, my understanding, foggy for sure, was that the organs might be healthy enough to be used. The extraordinary work by the health care team for possible recovery for organ transplants seem to have made a difference. Honestly, I am unsure of what I heard about the timing of any organ news. If anything, I think Suzanne told me that she expected to get a call Sunday night with news on whether any organs were taken and transplanted.

Monday, up at last, I check in with Suzanne. No call. No news. I am raw with emotion and a bit upset not knowing. My son may be dead, but I still want to protect him. Right now, I don't feel that I am doing a very good job.

I put in a call to the TGLN number. A staff member notes my questions and urgent need for information and promises to have someone call back soon. Within a few minutes, a TGLN staffer from Toronto is on the phone. Yes, Adam donated four organs: his heart, his two kidneys, and his liver. I didn't think there were any more tears to cry but they come instantly, a flood of tears as I listen to this extraordinary news.

Four healthy young organs. Adam's heart, Adam's two kidneys, and Adam's liver are going to save lives. Our boy, generous and good. *Well done, Adam.*

While the organs appear healthy, suitable for transplanting, the TGLN staff says that there is no further information yet. They promise to get back to us as soon as there is more news to share. It will be weeks before I learn that, at the very moment I was talking to the TGLN staff on Monday morning, doctors in Toronto were placing Adam's heart in a patient.

I cry on the phone with the TGLN staff, cry when I tell my family members in the house, and cry when I tell Suzanne a few minutes later. It is becoming more clear what Adam's gift of life means.

TGLN expresses gratitude for the generous gift from our family. Well, as I will say over and over again in the weeks and months ahead, Adam is the generous one, the hero in this story. Quite simply, we honoured his wishes. There was no second guessing, no uncertainty in this otherwise tragic weekend, the worst possible weekend to be making a decision of that magnitude. It is hard to think straight and to make the right choices when grieving. On an awful weekend, this was one of the easier decisions to make.

As tragic as Adam's death is, this news is a glowing silver lining to begin this week. It is a silver lining that will burst back into our lives over and over again in the months ahead as we learn of the lives Adam saved. We cannot dream what lies ahead of us.

We ask TGLN what we might announce publicly, thinking ahead to the Celebration of Life that we are planning for Wednesday. TGLN gives us the wording: "Thanks to Adam's generosity and the generosity of his family, there are four people who will be able to live now." Four people no longer waiting. We cannot say more. We don't know any details of the transplants.

So, we now know what has happened to Adam's organs.

I assume that Adam's body is in the care of Tania and the staff at Basic Funeral Services. She has told us that this is the normal procedure. I assumed incorrectly. My kid does not do normal. In fact, Basic Funeral Services is waiting for Adam because the coroner has ordered an autopsy, a routine procedure for deaths that happen outside of hospitals or homes. It seems that I am having as much trouble tracking Adam's whereabouts dead as I did some days when he roamed around Ottawa.

* * *

There are chores to do today and Tuesday, long lists to work through, again with family passing me down that line of love. Grieving families know the routine — telling other family members, greeting them as they arrive, making phone calls and writing social media posts, writing the obituary, selecting organizations to receive memorial donations, searching for and sorting photos and mementos for the Celebration of Life, answering questions about the service that is being prepared.

A few family hugs, some literal hugs, some thrown virtually, stand out as they will enhance Adam's Celebration of Life. My older brother, Marty, and his wife, Maggie, are grounded in Collingwood because of recent health episodes. Marty was hiking on Blue Mountain earlier in January when he began to suffer chest pains. He is now recovering from a stent implant in his heart. Maggie is recovering from a hip transplant.

They hear a need for prayers to be written for the Celebration ritual and jump all over that request. Then there is my niece Jules O'Connor, a five-foot-one mighty mite who corrals me at a computer to record what I want to say about my son at the service. All Monday, she tolerates my "I will do that soon" promise to find a quiet place to think about my remarks. On Tuesday morning, Jules picks up my coffee and marches me to the computer, asking me for my thoughts and writing them down. Do not mess with Jules!

As I am certain is Suzanne's experience on her side, at her home, family becomes the anchor of love and support in these forty-eight hours. There is no way to survive, otherwise.

Adam seems to be pitching in as well, continuing to work his magic to bring the two separated families together in grief.

Now Margie sensitively navigates between homes and on the telephone to cobble together a service that will honour our one child with two stories: "his" and "hers." Margie has this extraordinary gift of honouring people in a funeral ritual that is truly a celebration of life. Any time in these two days that I spot Margie, she is either on the telephone gathering information or busy writing. She talks with family members. She speaks with Adam's friends: Who is he for them? What is he like? What did they do together? She listens. She looks online for any helpful ritual for transgender people, but cannot find any. She invites Adam's friends to participate as gift bearers in the service on Wednesday. Suzanne works with Mike, Adam's siblings, and Aunt Sandy and her partner, Kevin Leahy. Lindsay and Sylvie Paul-Hus, Suzanne's colleague and friend, generate a beautiful memorial prayer card; others there work on photo and music video collages, and, yes, a funeral casket, and more.

Adam's friends continue to envelop us in love, too. I spend much time on Facebook reading comments on my "Soar, Adam, Soar" post and liking what they have posted in their own profound shock and grief. No one can believe that Adam is dead. This is the kid who was the life of the party, who time and time again shook them free of sadness to laugh and carry on. As they had done at the hospital, so they continue online, joined by other grieving friends. Facebook gives me a refuge in the brewing storm of sorrow that is slipping into our lives.

A few of Adam's friends have a barrage of questions about the Wednesday Celebration of Life. Bizarre questions, or so they seem. Can they come to the Celebration? Can they bring their same-sex partner? Can they stay for the entire wake in the church?

I am puzzled at first. They are Adam's friends. Why wouldn't they and their partners be welcome? And then it hits me: They ask these questions not necessarily because they are young. They ask these questions because the church setting for the wake is a real concern.

For many in the LGBTQ world, churches are not often places of genuine worship or welcome. Churches can curse rather than bless who they are and who they love. No doubt there are shining exceptions to this prevalent condemnation, some right here in Ottawa, but I sense that it is the fact of the wake being held in the church that prompts these odd first questions. It may even be more than the church setting. Gender and sexual minorities seem routinely locked out of mainstream ritual. They can end up more as spectacles than participants at weddings and funerals, graduation ceremonies, Christmas carolling, and more.

One by one, I answer them. Of course, they are welcome. So are their same-sex partners. Adam and his family invite you. The United Church of Canada in its teaching and practice welcomes you. I know this and am even more confident in the hospitality and kindness of Rev. David White and Centretown United Church.

* * *

I draft the obituary to honour Adam's life and story. Lindsay and Suzanne edit it.

Adam Prashaw April 22, 1993–January 24, 2016

Adam Daniel Prashaw (born Rebecca Danielle Adam Prashaw) died Sunday, January 24, 2016 after a seizure-related drowning. He was twenty-two years old.

Suzanne Corbeil and Rick Prashaw are his proud parents. Adam is also survived and surrounded by

Adam D. Prashaw wearing his favourite red plaid shirt.

the love of Suzanne's husband, Mike Robinson, sisters Lindsay and Lauren Mann, their partners, Stefan Janichen and Don Bowser, brother David Mann, grandparents Dan and Jeannine Corbeil of Bonfield, stepsister Tarah, niece Jhade Robinson, stepbrother Troy Robinson, his special friend Aunt Sandy Corbeil, and many other aunts, uncles, cousins, and an amazing community of friends.

Adam was a proud and outspoken member of the transgender community. He lived on Facebook, was a Batman aficionado, adored Carey Price and the Montreal Canadiens. Throughout high school Adam was an excellent goalie within the Kanata Girls' Hockey Association. He studied at Holy Trinity High School and later at Algonquin College. More recently, Adam was proud to be living as an independent adult, working at the Canadian Museum of Nature Café.

A wake service will be held Wednesday, January 27, 2016 at 3:00 p.m. at Centretown United Church, 507 Bank St. at Argyle. A Celebration of Life will follow at 4:30 p.m. at the Canadian Museum of Nature, 240 McLeod St.

In lieu of flowers, the family appreciates donations to Epilepsy Ottawa, www.epilepsyottawa.ca, the Montreal Neurological Institute, www.mcgill.ca/neuro/donate, or Gender Mosaic, http://www.gendermosaic.com.

The family is deeply grateful for the compassionate medical staff of doctors, nurses and chaplain at the Ottawa General Hospital. We treasure Adam's many companions in his journey, especially Dr. B. Wallace Archibald of Russell, ON, Dr. André Olivier, McGill Neurology Hospital, Montreal, QC, Dr. Rajendra Kale, Ottawa, ON, and the Centretown Community Health Centre.

We suggest memorial donations to Epilepsy Ottawa and the Montreal Neurological Hospital and Institute for obvious reasons. A few further enquiries also identify Gender Mosaic, an Ottawa-based organization that "offers a safe, fun, supportive and non-judgemental environment where Trans and Cross-Gender people of all ages are free to express their gender identity."

Lindsay helps design a beautiful prayer card with a perfect cover picture of Adam in a tank top, with his ball cap on backwards, the rose tattoo showing on one shoulder, his lip and eyebrow piercing visible, and with the slight, sure, sunny smile that I typically saw as he bounced out of his Elgin Street apartment.

* * *

Monday is a down day in all ways, physical and emotional.

Tuesday is the day to run errands around town, comforted by the companionship of Claire and the arrival of more family.

Adam keeps us company. We need to find appropriate cards — one for a final letter to Adam that I will place in his casket, other thank-you cards for special people. I can't think of where to go, so I ask Adam for inspiration. His Venus Envy shop immediately pops into my head. Venus is in Ottawa's Bank Street Village area near Parliament Hill. I call it the sex shop, but there are books, gifts, and much more there. Adam laughed on the phone once when I called from Venus looking for a birthday card. Adam also brought me to Venus to buy binders to flatten his breasts. Claire easily finds the right cards and buys a children's book, *Backwards Day*,[1] for her son, Cruz. *Backwards Day* tells the story of a girl, Andrea, who wants to be a boy. Cruz will use this book a few months later to resurrect Adam in a powerful way.

Next door to Venus is a comic book store that Claire enters to buy Batman swag. I wonder how many times Adam went next door from Venus to do the same.

We stop at Suzanne's house. She shows us what she has collected for a memorial table that will be set up at the Museum of Nature tomorrow. At the top of the pile is a letter from Rebecca that we are told will not be for public display. Suzanne invites Claire and me to read it, though. It is an angry letter that Rebecca wrote to her mom. It is a run of sentences full of F-bombs, likely written when she was a young adolescent. There is no indication of what particular incident triggered Rebecca's note, but it is definitely the result of some mother-daughter spat. I comment on Rebecca's fine handwriting and how surprising that is, given how angry Rebecca must have been writing it. We smile reading the letter. I never got such a letter in all my years! Suzanne assures me that it is the lot of mothers to receive them. After dropping F-bombs all over her mother, Rebecca signed the letter, "Love Rebecca." This fiery, feisty kid is still speaking to us from the other side.

> Adam shared
> Oct. 3, 2015
> Notice: How to be Skinny
> 1. Notice your body is covered in skin
> 2. Say, boy am I skinny. Congratulations. You are now skinny.

---

1. Bear Bergman, illustrated by K.D. Diamond, *Backwards Day* (Toronto: Flamingo Rampant, 2012).

Adam graduating with his Algonquin College Community Studies diploma, Alleluia!

Next, Suzanne shares another Rebecca gem, a hilarious report card that she clearly wrote for herself. On the cover, at the top, is the name of the school, Saint Jesus School, and a drawing of the school. Inside are her marks, all excellent, top grades, along with glowing teachers' and principals' comments she invented, spelling mistakes and all.

> Picipal Comment
> "She is doing very well in schol. She the best studinty
> in the class
> I hope I can see her again"
> Teacher
> "Rebecca is a very good studint she must like running
> a lot"

Marks
1 excellent
2 Good
3 O.K.
4 Can do better
5 needs to do better

Math 2
Gim 1
ART 1
Listening 2
Colours 1
Shapes 1
Couting 2

I wonder if she wrote this fictitious report card in her bedroom the same night she reluctantly brought home another actual report card with far lower grades and less glowing remarks. I decide then and there that this will be my Adam's final report card, the child's eternal, true marks and personal evaluation. He passes, with honours.

Suzanne brings us down to the basement to see the maple and oak casket that Mike, David, and Troy are building. It is natural wood, oak, so simple yet so magnificent — beautiful craftsmanship. I lean over to smell the wood. I expect to cry but strangely do not. It is one of many times in the days and weeks ahead when I realize that my emotions will rule me. I can't boss them. The funeral casket brushes the ache inside.

Adam

January 22, 2015

Was good day at work to begin with then went all crazy but finally back to quiet and calm and going home relax until another crazy amazing night with couple my best of friends @Ashley @Mary-Lynn & @Chris Schnobb at Skyzone!

CHAPTER 14

Celebration of Life

Adam

January 22, 2016

My thoughts are stars I cannot fathom into constellations

[— John Green, *The Fault in Our Stars*]

* * *

Wednesday, January 27, 2016

At last, it is the day to come together to say goodbye to Adam, to celebrate his life.

Personally, I vow not to say goodbye. A strong mix of faith, Gaelic stubbornness, and a dash of denial will see me through this day.

The wake is scheduled to start at 3:00 p.m., with a private family viewing scheduled before the church doors open to the public. Adam's Celebration of Life will begin at 4:00 p.m.

There is much, though, to celebrate, much gratitude to grope for while deep in sorrow, much pride in Adam to share. All twenty-two years, nineteen or so with the name and identity of Rebecca Adam and three as Adam. Or, is it not, in fact, that the entire twenty-two years were spent as Adam, while the body began to catch up to the boy he always was? Adam had been his name months before his birth, too.

We know that people are coming from many different places. There are many relations, with various family connections. Some only know our kid as Adam, some know only Rebecca, some know both, and some have never met him. There are friends and work colleagues of parents and siblings.

*　*　*

I am still in bed. It feels safe, like nowhere else does right now. Here my mourning feels a bit on pause. I smell the coffee in the Bakkers' kitchen; family has now filled up every corner of this home away from home. I am not sure how I will get through this day. Once again, I underestimate family and Adam.

Up at last, and in the kitchen, the love begins to flow. My nephew Brian O'Connor is a splendid stonemason. Along with the strong coffee and family chatter, Brian offers his hard, well-worn fingers to massage my rock-hard shoulder and neck muscles. My niece Natalie is a Traditional Chinese Medicine (TCM) practitioner in Sudbury, Ontario. She takes me to the basement for acupuncture and reiki.

It is at some point during this treatment that I start to sob, the first real release of the catastrophic loss I feel. It's been surreal, from the red-eye flight out of California to the weekend at the Ottawa General ICU unit. That vigil and these early days of mourning have had me locked on automatic; it has all felt like a script that has to play itself out. I shed tears in the hospital but the sadness seemed to leak out ever so slowly. Now, with the TCM treatment, the sorrow cascades down my cheeks.

Natalie's acupuncture and reiki cleanse me. I am different coming up those stairs. I can't explain it, but I know that Adam is with me.

Earlier, in bed, I asked Adam to help me through this day. Asking Adam for a favour, the parent leaning on the child. This is new.

I think ahead to the service that Margie has prepared. Suzanne had commented at some point, somewhere, that there is a difference between letting Adam go and letting Rebecca go. I get that as the dad. We loved Adam to the moon and back unconditionally, but there were many more moons with this child we knew as Rebecca; Becca needs a special goodbye, too. I hope that Margie has grasped all of this, listening those forty-eight hours as she sculpted the Celebration of Life that will cap the five long days since the news of the drowning. We must say goodbye to our Adam in a way that includes his Rebecca years.

This will not be easy for everyone. Many of his current friends know him only as Adam. They are fiercely loyal, knowing what the name Adam means to him. Their buddy stood up for their right to be themselves and now they have his back. It is special to see this. Indeed, Facebook fireworks flared up the night before. A boy who long ago played with Rebecca when she would come to stay with me at my Brittany Street apartment in Ottawa, after the separation, paid his respects on Facebook, referring to Adam as "she." Boy, did I know that pronoun mistake! This exchange then happened:

Chelsey It's he. He was my boyfriend. He wouldnt want people to remember him as Rebecca. He went through a lot to become the man he was.

Sebastien I only knew Rebecca from childhood as she moved far away and we lost contact, unfortunately I didn't know her when she went through changes. Which is why I referred her as I knew her. That's all. I'm not having a debate on he/she just saying my goodbyes as I knew her. Wasn't meant to disrespect.

I intervened, one of the few times I've commented on his friends disagreeing publicly on Facebook. I knew in some way that they were both right. I thanked Sebastien for his friendship with Rebecca. I told him that those were good times. In my post that night, I told Sebastien I once worried that Adam might want to delete his "Rebecca" years, perhaps too young still to appreciate that, one day, they all would be part of the story he would proudly tell. I told Sebastien that I finally realized I did not have to worry about that. Adam treasured his girl hockey goalie pictures. He had come to love posting those early Russell pictures of the tomboy wearing the leather jacket and sitting on that rock in the Castor River. He was not going to delete or ignore the years he spent assigned with the girl's name and the girl identity.

Adam

January 7, 2016

[Accompanied by a picture of when he was Rebecca] Big step up for me to even share this… I hate to look back at these. But I'm kind of glad I still have some of the photos of old not yet real me. Shows how much I've grown and stepped up to be the REAL me. Adam. Thanks to old me I helped me realize sooner than later who I was truly meant to be. And I cant wait for my journey and being on T starts to show more changes. But so far I can already say what a Change it's been. And definitely for the better! 😄 💪 #steppingup #shy #gettingtoshowthechanges #therealme #finally happy #mytrueself #transgender #ftm #ilovemy friendsandfamilyforallthis #excitedformoretshow #myjourney

The old not yet real me. The real REAL me.

*   *   *

I will wear my rainbow tie to Adam's Celebration today. It is the tie that I bought at the Venus Envy store two years ago, for the "wedding."

Early in the afternoon, I walk into Centretown United Church, spotting my friends, the pastor, David White, and his partner, Janine Bertolo. We hug, the beginning of hundreds of hugs that will embrace family this day, passing us from friend to friend in this community.

I want to slip into the front of the church and the sanctuary, where Adam is.

Is it not strange to say that a dead person looks good?

Adam does look good, in the red-and-black plaid shirt that he's been wearing a lot lately — to a Redblacks football game with me, to pépère and mémère's early Christmas celebration last month, to Montreal on January 4 to visit the Neuro and snap another picture with Dr. Olivier and Monica Malecka, his staffer. It is the same shirt that I texted him about, commenting on how he looked so like Adam, and to which he replied that it was so because "I am Adam!"

I love Adam wearing this shirt. He's handsome. He's a boy.

The sleeves are rolled back to show off a few tattoos. There's a Batman pillow resting above him and a magnificent rainbow chrysanthemum floral arrangement from Montreal in front of the casket, courtesy of Silver Rose florist Gerry Arial. It is bright, bold, and beautiful.

I thank Tania, Patrick, and the others from Basic Funeral Services. They confirm what I had heard about the autopsy. They had received Adam's body from the coroner only twelve hours earlier.

The magnificent wooden casket is indeed special and perfect. I will lean over Adam several times in the next few hours. Is this strange, or does the strong smell of natural wood act as smelling salts for my mourning?

My sister Jude arrived Tuesday from Virginia, bringing her painting of that final Instagram post, the selfie of Adam in the hot tub.

Jude did the painting on the weekend, meditating on Adam's journey between two worlds. She calls it *Sail to the Light*. She tells me that she added Adam's stud near the eyebrow as she finished her painting. We position it on the altar right behind Adam.

He looks so handsome. And yet so dead.

I go back to the entrance of the church to find young Cruz to bring him to Adam. He comes, hesitatingly, keeping his distance, but near the casket. As the family come forward, as people talk, cry, and laugh, Cruz inches himself closer to Adam. It is not long after that I

Jude Prashaw's painting of Adam's final selfie.

see Cruz touch him. And not long after that, he is drawing Batman on the casket, his wings outstretched. He prints his name, Cruz, on the Batman figure.

Yeah, CRAYONS, Adam!

Margie suggested that crayons be left around the casket to allow anyone to write a message or draw a farewell to Adam on the wood. She borrowed the idea from a farewell celebration for her close neighbour, Anna Douthwright. The London, Ontario, community they live in used the coloured markers to celebrate her life; Margie witnessed then the healing powers of art and the consoling colours of those crayons. We will witness the same in the next two hours.

We learn that there is already a long line-up forming outside on this beautiful, sunny January winter day. Adam loved those sunny

Adam D. Prashaw
November 17, 2014
In my batman briefs
and onesie, watching
batman animated series
on netflix while Gotham
loads on primewire! lol
it's a batman night ;)

Close-up of Adam's casket showing some of the messages written to him by his friends, and, of course, a Batman emblem.

winter days. They were the best days to skate the Rideau Canal and eat those BeaverTails. The brilliant sunshine through the church windows bathes us all afternoon.

As we gather at the front and to the side of Adam, people start coming in to pay their respects. And the long line doesn't shrink for the next ninety minutes. Is it three hundred people who file by? Four hundred? I hear those numbers later. I hear over seven-hundred and fifty when we add those who join us at the museum for the Celebration of Life.

We are overwhelmed. There are parents, family, and work friends streaming in. Among the visitors from my New Democratic Party Parliament Hill work are members of Parliament Charlie Angus and Carol Hughes. Former MP and friend Megan Leslie is there. On Suzanne's side, there are many from her work for the U15 university research group, including former University of Ottawa chancellor and cabinet minister Allan Rock.

Not bad, Adam. Not bad. This ordinary twenty-two-year-old kid is soaring in fine company.

But as precious as family and all these people are, I keep my eyes focused on the large turnout of his friends, many like him with their plaid shirts, tank tops, ball caps, body piercings, and tattoos. They wrap him in their love. They anoint him with their tears and touches. They kiss him. They stroke his hair, as they did at the hospital. One friend, on behalf of five others, puts a "forever" bracelet on his wrist that matches one that they will each wear.

And they pick up those crayons to draw rainbows, Batman, and hearts, and scribble love or farewell notes that fill all the sides of the casket:

"Rest easy, Adam. You were my light to Infinity and beyond."

"Always loved, You will always be a rockstar."

"You're the most handsome, caring man I've had the pleasure of knowing. I love you, Batman."

"Until we meet again."

"Earth is extinguishing the lamp because the dawn has come, Tagore."

"Rest easy, handsome."

"You are an amazing soul."

"Live in love."

"I will never forget you."

"Shine bright upon us."

"You followed your star ever so courageously."

"I will never forget your contagious laughter."

"Bromance."

"I will miss you and our talking every day."

"May your positive stay with us always."

"You always knew how to light up the room."

"Thank you for teaching me how to be a man, be vulnerable, have compassion and care."

"May our wings open wide."

Love notes for the beyond. The casket now contains not only my Adam but the love of his family and friends.

Looking at this entire spectacle, Henri Nouwen's book *Clowning in Rome* comes to mind. It is a favourite book of mine. A well-known Catholic writer, Nouwen was inspired by those people who live on the edges of St. Peter's Square in the Eternal City — the carnival buskers, the sellers of Catholic statues and rosaries, the hustlers, the beggars, the ordinary and scandalous folk who, as Jesus taught, have a special place in the kingdom of God, a point that the self-righteous religious tend to forget.

I make the sign of the cross on Adam's forehead.

"Blessed are the poor. For theirs is the kingdom of God" (Matthew 5:3).

I preached this. I believe it. I am consoled that Adam is surrounded by these real, ordinary people. Adam is one of them. Adam is at home.

During the wake, I look at the long line to the back of the church and notice three young women, all with tiny babies hanging down their fronts. Am I seeing triple? I peek at them a few more times as they get closer. After they pay their respects to Adam and come up to offer me their hands, I hug them and ask the last one what their connection is to my boy. They met Adam at the parenting classes he went to with Chelsey. They were all in the same class. Six moms from that class were in the church that day. They tell me that Adam stood out as a good dad, how special he was with Landon and with the other kids there. They say that they wish that they had "Adams" in their lives. *I am proud of you, Adam.*

As hundreds file into the church, many choose to stay, standing around or sitting in the pews. There's conversation, laughter mixed with tears, and plenty of loud noise. Among them are probably those who asked if they could come to the service. David White tells me later that kids did approach him directly once they learned that he was the pastor. They wanted to know if they could stay. David reassured them that they were welcome for as long as they liked. It comforts me to see these kids in this church with Adam. They enjoyed so many good times together. This is their day, too.

Bekkaa
October 13, 2013
off to family thanksgiving
supper my sister Lindsay
Mann's place

The wake is ending. All afternoon, a close friend and former colleague from the diocese of Sault Ste. Marie, Father Peter Moher, has been playing the piano in the sanctuary — soothing, sweet music. Peter's favourite Beatles songs, including "Yesterday," Elton John's "Your Song," Leonard Cohen's "Hallelujah," and spiritual music as well: "On Eagle's Wings,"

Adam and me on the Rideau Canal — skating followed by BeaverTails.

"Morning Has Broken," and more. The music carries us through the afternoon. We are ready to head over to the museum for the Celebration of Life.

Jerry O'Connor, my brother-in-law, goes to the pulpit to invite people to sing "Be Not Afraid," a family favourite hymn, and a favourite from my ministry days. The words *Be Not Afraid* are on my dad's tombstone in North Bay.

"Be not afraid. I go before you always. Come follow me, and I will give you rest. If you pass through raging waters in the sea, you shall not drown."

Rest, Adam. Go, Adam. You shall drown no more.

"Blessed are your poor, for the kingdom shall be theirs. Blessed are you that weep and mourn, for one day you shall laugh."

The family are left alone a few moments to say a private goodbye to Adam. Basic Funeral Services will care for his body afterward. I kiss my son and again whisper my promises to him. I will not say goodbye.

Outside, the cold weather rejuvenates me. It is good to clear the head on the short winter walk over to the Museum of Nature. Walking into the atrium, I am speechless. Hundreds fill the room. Joel Frappier, Adam's boss, is swirling through the large room, choreographing the Celebration.

He's our Peter Pan, throwing magic dust everywhere. The natural light, the flowers, the food, the drink, the display of Adam and Rebecca's pictures and mementos are a work of art. Lauren, cousin Jules, Joel and his staff, Adam's colleagues, have all contributed. *Enjoy, Adam!* We had told Joel that we could not estimate how many might come but suggested he be ready for as many as 150 people. Joel tells us later there are 450 in the atrium. I wince, though, remembering Adam's excitement after meeting Joel the week before, eager to return to work this week. That was supposed to happen on Monday, two days ago. This will be Adam's final shift.

*   *   *

The young people are invited to the second-floor balcony in the atrium. It is the best view, and their solidarity will wrap comforting arms around the gathering below.

Near the beginning of the ceremony, Suzanne and I light a candle to recall Adam's baptism.

There are sacred and secular readings. My sister Jude reads from the Gospel of John: "Do not let your hearts be troubled.... There are many rooms in my Father's house" (14:1–3).

A Scripture shout-out for diversity. *Adam, are you living this now? I suspect that wherever you are now and whatever its name is, it has many rooms and is so blessed, bigger than many can imagine.*

Lindsay reads from Hope Bradford's *Oracle of Compassion: The Living Word of Kuan Yin*:

> Death is like giving birth. Birth can be painful. Sometimes women die from giving birth. However, when the baby is born, all that pain (that was endured) vanishes in an instant. Love for that tiny baby makes one forget the pain, the fear. And as I've said before, love between mother and child is the highest experience, the closest to divine love.

You might wonder about the parallel I'm making between birth and death. But I say to you, the fear and pain accompanying an awful death is over quickly. Beyond that portal one is suddenly in the light, in oneness and bliss.... Just as a woman heals rapidly after childbirth and then is able to fall in love with her baby, those who pass over also are able to fall in love with a new life.

Another birth for you, Adam, this time as Adam.
Falling in love. Adam enjoyed every one of his falls.

Margie invites a group of Adam's friends to bring up gifts that represent him. Kendra Borthwick parades in the LGBTQ rainbow flag. Chris Schnobb brings up a photo of Adam with his beloved dog, Dallas. Brittney Palmer carries the Batman pillow. Simone Dominique Levesque brings a picture of one of Adam's tattoos. Ashley Deschamps delivers Smartfood popcorn (Adam loved food 24/7). Jak Lavergne carries music that was always playing at the apartment.

Bekkaa
April 26, 2014
I just want congratulate my amazing big brother on graduating from his helicopter/pilot college today! Ceremony will be amazing sorry I couldn't be there but I will be thinking of you today! So proud of you and miss you and can't wait to see you soon! ♥ ♥ love you @David Mann :)

Margie shares what the kids have told her about Adam: "Big-hearted, amazing, accepting, forgiving, trustworthy, funny, weirdo, cool, silly faces, smart, determined, stubborn, full of life, adventurous, brave, inclusive, never judged, a true fighter facing epilepsy."

"WOW," Margie comments. "So many beautiful tributes to Adam."

Bekkaa
June 16, 2013
Happy fathers day to my amazing dad! Hope you have a great day

Aunt Sandy, with her partner, Kevin Leahy, created two photo collages that are now played on the atrium screen. One is dedicated to Rebecca, the second to Adam.

Suzanne has selected two songs to go with the photo collages. First, Sarah McLachlan's "Beautiful Girl" plays through the pictures of our tomboy, Rebecca. The lyrics serenade the mourners through the bitter breezes.

For the pictures of Adam, we listen to Carole King's "Child of Mine."

The songs take my breath away. The pictures rush us through a lifetime.

As I watch all those Rebecca pictures go up on the screen — the tomboy, the haircuts, the clothing — I smile a little. Our Adam was indeed trying to tell us something all those years. And I guess when we didn't pick up on those somewhat subtle messages, well, his "Adam" dominated his behaviour and looks, anyway.

Adam
May 10, 2015
Happy Mothers Day Mom!!
😄 you're truly one of the best mother anyone could possibly ask for! And I couldn't tell you more how much you've done for me and how much I love you! Have a good mother's day!

Nobody will kill Adam's dreams now.

The Prayers of the Faithful, or intercessions, are next. They are a lens to Adam's life and what he teaches us now:

Adam, you personally stood up and were counted and thus made a difference for all of us today. We remember you.

Adam, whether by combating an ugly word against another or through the personal act of coming out, we remember you.

Whether it be Adam's activism in challenging the system or by changing it from within, we remember you.

Adam, by actively sharing your ideas with others or by quietly affecting individuals one at a time, you made a difference. We remember you.

Adam, whether by looking outward to help others understand the trans community or by standing tall as a proud member of this beautiful community, Adam, we remember you.

Adam, through your courage, through your actions, through your bravery, through your love, you moved us forward. We remember you.

Despite the burden of seizures and surgeries, the hate and hurt of bullying, you braved it all, our fearless warrior. Your clever words. Your generous heart. Your impulsive nature. Your infectious smile. Your spirit moved us all a little closer to a world that more fully celebrates love. We remember you.

May we work to build a community where LGBTQ people are celebrated as full and equal members, recognizing their many gifts. Where sexual and gender diversity is seen as a blessing that enriches us all. Hear our prayer.

We pray for our young people, that their concerns, struggles, and ideas are validated and that their energy and enthusiasm is encouraged. Hear our prayer.

We pray for all those who work tirelessly in the medical profession, who work in a publicly funded health care system, especially those doctors and nurses in the ICU at Ottawa General Hospital who cared for Adam. We are grateful for their care and compassion. Hear our prayer.

We pray for the acceleration of legislation and services that will support the trans community in their struggles for equality and acceptance. Hear our prayer.

At least four families in Ontario received the gift of Adam's heart, liver, and kidneys. Even in Adam's death, he continues to give. May all be as generous as Adam and go home and sign our donor cards and register online today. Hear our prayer.

> Adam
> April 19, 2015
> This is why I love my family. Lmao my aunt gave me my gift who ended being for Dallas and not daddy aha but that's a great gift for how much I love her lol but last gift was best got four cans of spray and we all took one and attacked each other lol 😄 love love love my family xo
> @Sandra Corbeil

At the hospital, Margie had asked Adam's beloved Capital Kings to perform an "appropriate" song and dance for this service. I grinned at the word *appropriate*, remembering a few of their performances that I caught on Facebook. Talking to them, Margie again mustered her best schoolteacher voice and noted that there were going to be members of Parliament and other important dignitaries present. She asked that they be sure to pick something that wouldn't be too outrageously shocking, as they needed these politicians as allies in the fight to seek recognition of their rights. After Margie finished, Brittney said, "So you want something politically correct? Okay. We can do that."

Adam
October 2, 2015
At work for now, then I'm off to a nice weekend away in North Bay at my memere and peperes for their 60th anniversary party and family reunion. Excited to see them

They perform Justin Bieber's "All Around the World." But first, they tell us what Adam meant to them:

Adam was there to cheer us on, and came to every show and called himself our biggest fan. He volunteered so much of his time to help us out, handing out flyers, advertising our performances, posting photos and videos, and even braved the stage to perform alongside us. He was always able to make us laugh by finding the humour in a tense situation. He loved when we performed pop songs and this song was one of his favourites, so we'd like to dedicate this to him. This is for you, buddy.

The Celebration is drawing to a close. It is time for the parents to speak.

I ask Adam to meet me at the podium. And I am relieved to see Suzanne making her way there, too. She had warned me earlier that it would be a last-minute decision whether she could.

Suzanne tells the story of Adam's birth and his name, Rebecca Danielle Adam Prashaw. I tell the story of the Saint Jesus School report card. We share memories of our child. I mention the Ph.D. in parenting studies that this kid immersed me in — the worrying, wishing, hoping, wondering, pushing, teaching, and then stepping back to give space so that he might find himself and his place in this world. I thank my teacher of pronouns, reminding those present why they matter — to him and to others. I try to thank everyone for their walk with Adam, especially Suzanne, Mike, Lindsay, Lauren, David, the grandparents, and other family.

My final words are to Adam's friends, what they mean to me, the hope that they give me.

I say that I might be able to accept Adam's death, as tragic and wrong as it is, if the young people present find the love, the acceptance, and the justice that they deserve, that are their rights. Adam's death will be bearable for us if our community can become a more accepting place for our young people, so that they will be able to be who they are, to love who they love.

I want Adam to have the final word, so I repeat the words chosen for Adam's prayer card from a Facebook post nine months earlier:

Adam
September 10, 2015
If only people could see through another's eyes and truly understand what they go through, think and see. It's not always as easy as it seems. We all need help, love and support. No judgement.

We are done. Adam, we love you. We accept you. Be who you want to be.

At the reception afterward, besides the new stories I hear, I particularly remember hugs from a few older men, strangers, hugs that lasted longer than usual. They whisper words that suggest they have work to do. Is it work as parents? Is it work as parents of LGBTQ kids? I suspect so. This is good. Adam seems at work here.

Among the people in the room whom I do not know is Kate Hewitt, who I will have coffee with later. Kate is a trans woman.

Kate will write me a note soon after the Celebration: "I left the service feeling sadness, yes, but also feeling energized and inspired with a renewed commitment to living life and working to make the world a better place."

Amen to that.

Margie's ritual did justice because, well, I sensed Adam did justice to himself, in his own, intimate SNAFU way.

"Even though we walk in the valley of death, we shall fear no evil" (Psalm 23). We are living in the valley of death. This is a time and place where you don't understand how you are still standing. Friends, family, community literally carry you. The Psalms happen to be my favourite biblical verses. Poetry, bald prose for the human condition, bloody, gritty, screaming shouts, full of people's hopes and lamentations. They offer the real, frank talk with the deities that I will need shortly.

Suzanne heads home with family. I head to our home away from home. There is more food to eat, more stories to tell, drinks, and healing laughter as we revisit Adam's more monumental escapades, including another requested retelling of the story of that "crazy fun" wedding.

Adam

September 21, 2014

People usually say amazing day because of something big or important or whatever happened but I had an amazing day yesterday just from chilling and relaxing at dog park with my puppies, walking all over downtown with Kendra Borthwick and came back and watched pitch perfect and had pizza lol then bday drinks at The Lieutenants and then kendra and me met up with Kelsey and Stef for a hello after their burlesque event they went to. Busy day of running all over but every moment was amazing for me :)

CHAPTER 15

Angels in the Snow

January 28–29, 2016

THE DAY AFTER Adam's Celebration of Life, I wake up to the sound of people cleaning, packing, whispering, and leaving.

It is a day I dread.

A few out-of-town family members offer to stay on a day or two. I push them away, resigned to being alone, hoping my exhaustion will at least let me sleep for several days. Sleep should mask the emptiness I feel, delay the brewing grief. I know but don't know what lies ahead, including further unimaginable news about one of the organ recipients.

Where to begin. Is it almost a week since my brother Jon's call in California? My brothers and sisters, nephews and nieces are heading back to their homes today, and back to their lives. I am at the Kanata Hazeldean library in the afternoon, reading the *Ottawa Citizen* online obituary guest book for Adam. There are many messages: from Sudbury, North Bay, Ottawa, and from friends from my former parish and Church Council on Justice and Corrections days.

It is good to read the note from Dr. Wallace Archibald in Russell. He was Adam's family doctor his entire life. He comments on that twenty-two-year relationship with Adam, noting his strength, courage, and smile.

*   *   *

Friday is Adam's cremation. The family is meeting at Hope Cemetery in south Ottawa. There is blowing snow, another favourite kind of winter day for Adam. Basic Funeral Services tells us that we may want to sit indoors in the warm chapel and watch from a distance. We don't like any distance from Adam right now. Instead, we drive to the back of the cemetery where the crematorium is located. We can't go inside, of course. But we do want to keep Adam company outside. Adam's special friend, Aunt Sandy, is the first to lie down on the ground to make a snow angel. Suzanne and I follow Sandy. There are now a mom angel, dad angel, and aunt angel for our SNAFU angel.

> Adam
> November 14, 2014
> Holy sudden snow fall! lol

Angels in the snow, at the cemetery, during my son's cremation. We try to tame a terrible day. I suspect that Adam loves this craziness.

We are in several cars. We drive the half-hour to Russell and the Russell Restaurant, where Adam ate dozens and dozens of family meals. Adam always or-

> Bekkaa shared
> May 22, 2011
> Laugh when you can, apologize when you should, and let go of what you can't change. Life's too short to be anything... but happy (unknown)(<3)

dered chicken sandwiches there. Many make that their order today. We share forkfuls of a piece of rich coconut cream pie. We then drive past our old family house and head into the woods to the Castor River and the rock that Rebecca sat on for her picture when she was three and that Adam sat on last fall when he was twenty-two. Suzanne places a rainbow flower there. I close my eyes. I can see my tomboy in the leather jacket sitting on that rock, little Rebecca for a moment, who slips into the young man, Adam. They are both on the rock like beautiful sirens tempting me to go into the river. I had better check the ice this time.

We end this melancholy day at Suzanne's house with some food, drinks, and card games of Hand and Foot (Canasta lite).

Jessica
January 24, 2016
@Adam D. Prashaw, it is so strange not to have you here tonight. It hasn't quite sit in yet… has been a quiet night without you to spice it up! You were such a bright light in our lives, always such a contagious smile on your face that you just can't help. A super duper party goer, amazing friend, and someone you could always count on to brighten your day with something silly! You will always be remembered as an awesome dude surrounded by loving people in an amazing world. May you rest in peace wherever you may be, know that you are free to be the you that you always wanted, and know that we are down here cheering you on through every step! Love you always Batman

CHAPTER 16

Give Sorrow Words

Give sorrow words. The grief that does not speak
Whispers the o'erfraught heart and bids it break.
— William Shakespeare, *Macbeth*, 4.3.246–247

January–July 2016

I AM NOW BACK in my Kanata condo in Ottawa.

Alone, but not for long. Grief moves in.

This messy, irrational, terrifying, unpredictable, and petty visitor is settling in.

More like barging in; unpacking, for the long haul.

My sister Jude offers to stay on for the first weekend after the wake and Celebration for Adam. I push her out the door, noting my exhaustion, telling her sleep will get me through the first few days. It is a lie. I close the windows, draw the drapes, and brace myself alone for the sure storm to come.

I'm thinking that I can do this gig in private. I certainly don't see the need to include a chapter here on my grief after Adam died. I want to shine a light on Adam, his story, his courage. This grief is mine, not his. I believe he is fine right now, in a good place. I am left behind. I have to manage.

Jude begs to differ. She reminds me that Adam didn't live or die in isolation: "You cannot remove yourself from this story. Remember, many struggle with these same painful, heart-wrenching circumstances. Your story is their story."

Damn you, Jude. And I might as well throw a damn my son's way, too. I sense my co-author Adam isn't done writing. He's never been good at relinquishing the driver's seat.

Strangely, and this makes little sense to me, I am not sure that I even want this visitor, grief, gone. As certain as Adam's epilepsy and transgender journeys were joined at the hip, my Adam and grief likewise appear to be inseparable. I want Adam's company, and I sense that means I must take the grief, too. I suspect my grief matters to Adam as well.

Apparently, Adam and grief are a package deal. I need to learn to live with this visitor. It will take much longer to recognize grief as my friend. I do so grudgingly, as I try feebly to befriend it, to accept any healing, understanding, and growth that it will bring.

It takes me a while to figure out that Adam has moved into my condo, has returned after that January weekend. Rebecca had lived here, in the second bedroom, for a good part of her high school years. Friends, hockey, school, and jobs were all Kanata attractions then. My condo put her closer to her high school universe. I saw a great deal of Rebecca in high school. I was over-the-moon happy for that family time.

That bedroom is where I write now. I feel my Adam's presence.

I described my kid's epilepsy as akin to a home invasion, a monstrous stranger stealing into my kid's body and our lives, refusing to leave, try as we did to evict it. For years, it was a permanent stranger in the home. I tried to ignore it, when it let me. Now, like the epilepsy, grief has broken into my home and my life. I imagine it is the same for others in Adam's family, for his friends — grief has broken into their own places, too. I can't evict grief, either — this grief that takes us to the cliff and beyond sometimes. I hope we can survive it.

I know this visitor. I was sixty-four when Adam drowned. Life had already dealt me some huge losses. I may have chosen to leave the active priesthood to marry, but I still grieved the loss of actively serving as a priest. It was meaningful, enjoyable work. I weathered the deaths of both of my parents, whom I dearly loved. First, there was the shock of my father's sudden death on New Year's Eve, December 31, 1984, when he suffered an abdominal aortic aneurysm. I had kissed him goodbye at the end of our Christmas holiday at our North Bay home that night, only to have the news of his death greet me ninety minutes later in Sudbury. Nineteen years later, my mom died at eighty-six. Her longer life seemed to double down the grief for my siblings and me.

The years of hospital and grief ministry acquainted me with sorrow. But nothing can inoculate me for this latest visit of an old acquaintance. This is my son. This is not supposed to happen.

What is supposed to happen is the African proverb: "May our children bury us, and we not bury them." That is the way life is meant to be.

What happened to my Adam was cruel, so Shakespearean cruel on every level. I recount everything that he endured — the courage he always mustered, the promise of the epilepsy surgeries, the periodic disappearance of the seizures, his tangible excitement for his transition to a boy.

I want Adam back. On so many levels, the tragedy on January 22 robbed us of so much.

* * *

Give sorrow words.

I sit in this grief, not knowing how to survive, not knowing if I want to survive.

Am I completely losing my sanity, to be strangely comforted by the few people speaking so honestly to me? My good friend Lorraine Berzins from my days at the Church Council on Justice and Corrections calls the drowning "cruel." The only word for it. My friend Alexie Steedman-Lalonde mentions that it might take five to seven years to find a rhythm of normal again. That feels about right. My former MP boss and friend Claude Gravelle emails me that one never gets over losing a child. NEVER. Yes, sir. It makes more sense to speak of a cruel tragedy that I will never get over than to hear well-meaning words about "moving on," or "time healing," or "closure." I don't expect any of that to be happening soon, even though I know that there are elements of truth in those words, too.

Ordinary acts of kindness from family, friends, and strangers help — deliveries of food, restaurant gift cards, condolence messages, donations to charities in Adam's memory. One day, Alexie brings her two young kids over, and we go for a walk to a nearby playground and then to lunch at Kathleen Edwards's Quitters Coffee in nearby Stittsville. That is a good morning. It is a pleasant surprise that contact with other people's children does not trigger more grief. I like the life that they bring. On Father's Day, Janine Bertolo and David White meet me for brunch, followed by a trip to an Ottawa Champions independent league baseball game. That is thoughtful. Others drop by to say hello. There's the normal, awkward discomfort — what can you say to someone who has lost a child?

These are respites from the monster in the home.

I am learning how to keep busy by taking short trips away to family or friends, sticking to some routine each day, finding the right company to duck grief. Grief vacations, I call them. Denial or at least the odd flight from grief are not bad things. I can't stay in denial long. Grief is at the front door waiting for my return. Sometimes it finds me on those trips.

Pickleball games at the Richcraft Recreation Complex in Kanata are a magical respite from grief, two sure hours on the court without a second of sadness. That is, until someone in the older generation inevitably gets asking about family, children, and grandchildren. I head to the water cooler then.

*   *   *

There is now further news on Adam's organs, the people he saved. Three weeks or so after his death, I receive a message from Suzanne. I'm in Picton, Ontario — yes, a grief vacation to visit my nephew Brendan O'Connor and his girlfriend, Stacey Croucher. Trillium Gift of Life Network sent the family a letter telling us more about the organ recipients:

An adult female with extensive liver damage received Adam's liver.

Two adult women with end-stage renal disease got his kidneys.

An adult male with irreversible heart disease received a life-saving heart transplant, providing him/her a second chance at life.

I am in their upstairs bathroom reading this, crying. Adam's act of love seems more real, more alive now; here are flesh-and-blood people he has helped. Three women and a man. I don't know their names but I can picture actual people now. I am so proud of Adam.

I read the letter to Brendan and Stacey. It is Jude, however, who catches the odd "him/her" wording in the reference to the heart transplant recipient. I assume that it is a clerical error. Likely a staff member simply forgot to adapt the generic letter they use, not putting in the right pronoun to identify the heart recipient as a man, as they did for the other organ recipients. Jude, however, suspects Adam's mischief is at play. Given Adam's transition, his Adam and Rebecca years, a his/her reference for a recipient is perfect! We surely stumbled over the pronouns in Adam's adventures. The pronoun miscues continue.

And I break into a wide grin when I read that Adam's heart is in a man. This seems, well, providential. My son has to be pleased.

On February 22, Family Day in Ontario, I post on Facebook these new details on the people Adam helped:

Rick
February 22, 2016
I cannot think of a better Family Day message than the letter we got from the Gift of Life Trillium network confirming that the organs of our Adam saved four people in terminal stages of heart, liver and kidney failure. I hope you can read ok the copied letter below. Adam drove a car only for one year, when sixteen. They thank us for our generosity in

our grief but in truth this happened because Adam
as Rebecca signed an organ donor card at sixteen,
the one year she was driving, before bigger seizures surfaced. She sat down with her mom, wanting to do that. We knew her wishes then and knew
this honoured Adam's spirit of generosity. And it
gives us enormous consolation in our grief. (That
Adam's heart is in a man puts an extra smile on my
soul). Have you signed your donor card or registered? It takes two minutes #TrilliumGiftofLife
BeADonor https://beadonor.ca

Dozens of messages flood my Facebook page, each one a balm to a
gaping sore. Again, the reaction online — the love, likes, and commen-
tary — carries me a few more days. Facebook may feel like a drive-by
hello at times, but it provides contact and offers messages to read, react
to, and return to frequently. It also helps now to hear the perspectives
of family and friends of organ recipients or others who are in similar
circumstances, on both sides of this transplant experience. I am buoyed
to read that, since Adam's death, several people have registered to be
organ donors or renewed their cards.[1] His friend Kendra posted that he
hopes the heart recipient knows how big this heart is. Three relatives
of organ recipients reiterated their gratitude and acknowledged the on-
going prayers for the donors. "There is no greater gift than to give one's
organs," wrote Carol Muncaster Simon. "My niece who was dying with
CF received a double lung transplant, and to watch her come alive was
beyond words. The gratitude cannot be measured. Adam truly lives on
in four lives and loves."

The Facebook love is genuine, and it helps; however, it is still the
TGLN organ donor letter that I go to for consolation. I am proud of
what Adam did. The organ news helps a bit, but it still will not keep
the grief from the door. My son is dead. The anonymous people who he

1. Donor cards are now obsolete in Ontario. Check your jurisdiction on the procedure to
register: canada.ca/en/public-health/services/healthy-living/blood-organ-tissue-donation.
html#a2. To be a donor in Ontario, Trillium Gift of Life Network asks everyone to register
online at beadonor.ca or giftoflife.on.ca or at a Service Canada kiosk. Even if you still have
an old card, you need to do the registration online. It only takes a few minutes.

saved have given me a lifeline to my son, to my love for him. But it cannot bring Adam back. These anonymous organ recipients are not Adam.

There is a period in February and March during which the rock band Coldplay saves my sanity. Lindsay posts on Adam's still-active Facebook page these comments on a song called "Everglow" by Coldplay and its lead singer Chris Martin.

> This song. I swear it was written for you. It's more perfect than it should be. The lyrics are exactly what I feel and want you to know... my sister, a goddess; my brother, a lion; eagle to the world, sharing hope and equality.

I start listening to "Everglow" every night before bed.

I can't imagine a world without music. It's my eternal medicine, better than a lot of the pills I have in the medicine cabinet. Coldplay's melancholy music releases many feelings that I have pushed deep below the surface since the phone call in California. It's good music in and of itself, but I appreciate that it is playing to my soul and broken spirit.

Adam's friends again become a temporary, precious refuge from grief. Like at the hospital, the wake, and Celebration, they join me on this journey.

* * *

On Adam's birthday, April 22, the family is invited to a crazy Chick Magnet competition at Zaphod's. Adam himself performed one year, for fun. Now, exactly three months after he drowned, on what would have been his twenty-third birthday, I wear Adam's Carey Price Montreal Canadiens jersey on stage with his mother. No, I am not a contestant! But I do tell them that I can't wait to brag to my brother, Jon, that I am on stage for the Chick Magnet contest. The kids laugh when I tell them that I still hate my son's hockey team but I wear the jersey because I love him more. And "hate" may now be too strong a word for the Habs. I am warming up to Carey Price, who stands in

Adam's goalie crease. It's just that Montreal induced much suffering when I was growing up and cheered for the Boston Bruins.

The kids raise $598.25 to split between Gender Mosaic and Epilepsy Ontario. We learn later that Gender Mosaic will give some of their Adam Fund to assist Rex Emerson Jackson, a young Hamilton actor who is launching a musical, *Twenty*, to tell the story of "who people really are" and of his own transition from Jenny to Rex.

Bekkaa
April 22, 2010
HAPPY BIRTHDAY TO MEEEEE

I return to Zaphod's in August for the party to launch Pride weekend. I brace for the inevitable pain of those nights and those contacts; still, Adam's friends are a tonic, as all of us have been touched by Adam's life and death. They appreciate seeing Adam's family. I soak up more of what these clubs mean to these kids, what they meant to my Adam.

The media learn of Adam's story. A few interviews allow me to tell others about Adam's exceptional epilepsy, transgender, and organ donor journey; as I talk about Adam, he seems alive. Those media interviews are "good pain." The time immediately after those interviews brings back the sadness, but the trade-off seems well worth it for touching Adam again.

All these occasions — being on Facebook, the news of the organ recipients, the time with Adam's friends, the media shining a light on Adam's story — appear like safe bays in the raging storm.

But always, always, the grief is waiting for me; the refuge can even be bittersweet, at times compounding the grief.

Still fresh in my mourning, I receive a post from my niece, Claire, a reflection on grief. It's gone "viral," as they say, its older author unknown. Ironically, its terrifyingly honest yet loving prose becomes a lifeline for me. Its shipwreck metaphor will define my life for a long time after Adam is gone.

I'm old. What that means is that I've survived (so far) and a lot of people I've known and loved did not.

I've lost friends, best friends, acquaintances, co-workers, grandparents, mom, relatives, teachers, mentors, students, neighbors, and a host of other folks. I have no children, and I can't imagine the pain it must be to lose a child. But here's my two cents …

I wish I could say you get used to people dying. But I never did. I don't want to. It tears a hole through me whenever somebody I love dies, no matter the circumstances. But I don't want it to "not matter." I don't want it to be something that passes. My scars are a testament to the love and the relationship that I had for and with that person. And if the scar is deep, so was the love. So be it.

Scars are a testament to life. Scars are a testament that I can love deeply and live deeply and be cut, or even gouged, and that I can heal and continue to live and continue to love. And the scar tissue is stronger than the original flesh ever was. Scars are a testament to life. As for grief, you'll find it comes in waves. When the ship is first wrecked, you're drowning, with wreckage all around you. Everything floating around you reminds you of the beauty and the magnificence of the ship that was, and is no more. And all you can do is float. You find some piece of the wreckage and you hang on for a while. Scars are only ugly to people who can't see. Maybe it's some physical thing. Maybe it's a happy memory or a photograph. Maybe it's a person who is floating. For a while, all you can do is float. Stay alive.

In the beginning, the waves are one hundred feet tall and crash over you without mercy. They come ten seconds apart and don't even give you time to catch your breath. All you can do is hang on and float. After a while, maybe weeks, maybe months, you'll find the waves are still one hundred feet tall, but they come further apart. When they come, they still crash all over you and wipe you out. But in between, you can breathe, you can function. You never know what's going to trigger the grief. It might be a song, a picture, a street intersection, the smell of a cup of coffee. It can be just about anything … and the wave comes crashing. But in between waves, there is life.

Somewhere down the line, and it's different for everybody, you find that the waves are only eighty feet tall. Or fifty feet tall. And while they still come, they come further apart. You can see them coming. An anniversary, a birthday, or Christmas, or landing at O'Hare. You can see it coming, for the most part, and prepare yourself. And when it washes over you, you know that somehow you will, again, come out the other side. Soaking wet, sputtering, still hanging on to some tiny piece of the wreckage, but you'll come out.

Take it from an old guy. The waves never stop coming, and somehow you don't really want them to. But you learn that you'll survive them. And other waves will come. And you'll survive them too.

If you're lucky, you'll have lots of scars from lots of loves. And lots of shipwrecks.[1]

I cannot speak for everyone who is on their own unique journey of grief, but for me, living with Adam's tragedy is indeed a calamitous shipwreck. My son drowned. I was on that ship. I cling to wreckage in a stormy sea, floating, bracing to survive those ninety- and one-hundred-foot waves in the storm. The waves never stop coming and somehow, now, just a bit, I understand that I may not want them to stop because they are my one, true connection to Adam. Every scar that I feel touches the love for my boy.

The shipwreck — the tossing in the sea — is the only thing making sense in the non-sense all around me. The crashing waves are making more sense than any talk of how time heals.

---

1. "When Asked for Advice on How to Deal with Grief, This Old Man Gave the Most Incredible Reply," Atchuup!, September 21, 2017, atchuup.com/advice-on-how-to-deal-with-grief.

I belong in this water with Adam.

This grief terrifies me, though. The madness that grief is, as Eve Joseph called it.[1] Crying in the shower; driving downtown avoiding Elgin Street where Adam lived — the neighbourhood where I had planned to move and be back in his downtown orbit; nights in the late winter and early spring, dreading going to bed, where there are no longer any distractions to veil the truth of how gone he is; nights of convulsive sobbing, holding on to the edges of the bed for dear life, wondering if I might make it to morning, wondering if I want to make it to morning.

For the first time that I can ever remember, my bedroom windows are closed as summer arrives. I shut my grief inside my wailing walls. More "Everglow."

At times, in those stormy waters, I want to let go of the plank. Join Adam. The deep, green calm beneath the stormy surface beckons, inviting me to let go. Darkness.

I recall a summer long ago in North Bay when I worked as a journalist at the *North Bay Nugget.* The city desk editor sent me to the city government dock to check out a police radio bulletin about a body. When I got there and found the police in a clump of bushes, I spotted him. A scrawny teen hanging from a tree above. They were waiting for the coroner before cutting him down. I went back to the newsroom and traced the boy to a Quebec family. I tried to find enough details, a name, a life, interests, anything that might shine a light on a kid who ended his life alone in the dark bush in a strange town in northern Ontario.

I have thought of that boy from time to time, more his lonely death than anything else. In my own pain, wanting to let go of the plank in those waters, I remember that lonely teen. I can see myself following his lead. I am not sure why I don't. The deep green below is so inviting. I want to join Adam. But my boy grabs the plank and hits me over the head with it. He knew my values. He knew what I had taught him. It was I who needed the reminder. Giving up seems reasonable but that's not me, not what I taught Adam. I laugh out loud. Adam knows how to get my attention. *Live, Dad!*

I can't stop thinking about Adam.

My grief is both predictable and equally so unpredictable.

---

1. Joseph, *In the Slender Margin,* 79.

There are the certain dates to brace for — Adam's birthday, April 22; Father's Day.

But grief has its own timetable, sneaking up in the strangest places to bite.

I am at the Queensway Carleton Hospital on a Saturday morning for a previously scheduled abdominal ultrasound, a few weeks after Adam died. It is 8:00 a.m. The intake staff is reviewing my information on record.

"Is Rebecca still your next of kin?"

Now, that wakes me up. In my head, I practise one answer. *No. Rebecca became Adam and then died.*

"Yes," I answer instead.

That lie will do for now and, hell, he still is my next of kin, although it might be difficult to contact him.

> Adam shared
> September 19, 2015
> Life is too short to argue and fight with the past. Count your blessings, value your loved ones and move on with your head held high

In March I am at the Brier, the national men's curling championship, when I discover again how sneaky grief can be. Sitting there with other curling fans for the Round 11 draw, I witness curling history. Apparently, for the first time, two pairs of fathers and sons are on the ice at the same time for the same rink. This happens with Ontario leading Prince Edward Island 9–4. The Ontario skip, Glenn Howard, taps his shoulder, signalling that he is bringing in nineteen-year-old Joey Hart to play lead. Joey's dad, Richard, sweeps his son's first Brier shot. The other sweeper is Howard's son, Scott. The curling is terrific, and I enjoy this special moment, too, for a bit.

Fathers and sons.

Then the tears start streaming down my cheeks. I flee the arena. Grief ever near.

Then in June, the second Neuro post-surgery appointment booked for Adam pops up on my screen. I wince. I forgot to delete it in my calendar. But I don't want to delete Adam.

I choose to touch and rub the scars that the old man cited, as they touch my Adam and so many memories.

Cruz helps me touch those scars and Adam, too, bringing him back to life in a powerful way. Cruz is the son of my goddaughter and niece,

Adam and cousin Cruz.

Claire. Cruz Ramirez Marley Prashaw. A lot of names, for a lot of boy. He was seven years old when his cousin Adam died. We holidayed with them in New York when Cruz was one. While Cruz doesn't remember that visit, he likes the pictures, and after the holiday, he and Adam visited between their homes in Toronto and Ottawa. They were buds.

Claire tells me that Cruz is still very upset by Adam's death.

I flash back to the moment I took him up to Adam's casket. Like other children, he was tentative at first. The more normally everyone acted, and the more Cruz heard the conversation and the laughter, and saw the hugs and the tears, the more comfortable he became. He circled Adam and kept him company. He finally picked up that crayon and drew Batman wings on the casket.

Now, a few months later, Claire calls for a favour. Cruz has to give his weekly show and tell presentation for his grade one class — five lines in French.

He wants to do his presentation on Adam. She asks if I will work with Cruz on this homework when they come up to visit that weekend.

Claire reminds me that she bought the book *Backwards Day* for Cruz on that Tuesday before Adam's funeral. In it, there is this super-cool planet named Tenalp where everything is backwards. Uphill is down, day starts at evening, the girls turn into boys, and the boys turn into girls.

While some football players have high voices, and there are hairy-chested ballerinas, a few of the children, much like Adam, don't look much different at all. Boyish girls and girlish boys look like they do every other day.

Andrea, the heroine, has to wait for the day after Backwards Day when she discovers that she has become a boy — and for the rest of her life. "At school, people were surprised to see Andy as a boy again. But it wasn't all that exciting (except to Andy). For everyone else, Andy-the-Boy was a lot like Andrea-the-Girl: a fast runner and a good friend, someone who loved peanut butter and hated peas. He told his friends to call him Andy now. And nobody seemed surprised."[1]

I take Cruz to the library to help him write what he wants to say. I ask him to tell me the story of Andrea and Backwards Day. After listening to his version of the story, I wrote five draft sentences in French and read them back to Cruz, a neat summary of the story of Andrea and Backwards Day.

"Is this what you want to say?"

"No," he shoots back right away. "I want to speak about Adam, not Andrea."

So, we work on his speech some more. The next week, Cruz stands in class:

> *Ceci est mon livre,* Le jour à l'envers.
>
> *Il est vraiment spécial pour moi parce que la personne dans le livre, Andrea, veut être un garçon, tout comme mon cousin Adam. Dans le livre,* Le jour à l'envers, *les filles deviennent des garçons et les garçons deviennent des filles.*

---

1. Bergman, *Backwards Day*, 12.

Andrea devient Andy comme ma cousine Rebecca est devenue Adam.

Adam est né Rebecca, mais vraiment elle était un garçon. Adam aimait Batman et était un gardien de but de Hockey.

This is my book, *Backwards Day*. It's special to me because the person in the book, Andrea, wants to be a boy, just like my cousin Adam. In the book, *Backwards Day*, girls become boys and boys become girls.

Andrea becomes Andy like my cousin Rebecca became Adam.

Adam was born Rebecca, but really, she was a boy. Adam loved Batman and was a hockey goalie.

Cruz throws me a shiny new life jacket in this stormy sea. Listening to him, I want to survive, beat this grief or befriend it. Cruz, Adam, many sightings of Batman, and others are seeing me through this storm. I grin, too, hearing Claire's account of Cruz's presentation, imagining the interesting conversations at the supper tables of his classmates' families in High Park–Roncesvalles in Toronto that night.

*   *   *

A Trillium Gift of Life Network letter arrives in April.

Each of us grieves in our own way and in our own time … [sharing] similar experiences, but uniquely different…. While the pain of your loss is still new, you may encounter others who have different expectations of you to "move on" or "get back to normal." It feels like trying to swim in black dense crude. Finding your "new normal" takes time. Physical effects are forgetfulness, inability to concentrate, difficulty in making decisions, appetite and sleep disturbances, confusion and lack of energy, among others. There are days you don't want to get up, days you don't get up, days you lie on the couch, don't answer the phone from friends or family checking in.

Yep, black, dense, drowning crude. In those ninety-foot waves. A proper image for me these days. Family call from time to time. I do not always pick up the phone. Days my arm aches, I swear I am having a heart attack. I can't breathe normally. I rewind and replay the hot tub drowning; I don't know how to turn off the voices playing in my head. It is exhausting trying to sleep. I take the sleeping pill and the grief still wins. I wake up tired.

I work to focus on the good. From time to time, I am grateful for the surprise of waking up on a better side, remembering a brighter memory for Adam. I ask Adam to help. I pray to God. I rail at God. I swear at God. I have gone beyond what I can bear. There's a condolence card on my windowsill that says God will never give me more than I can bear. Really?

Grief hangs around tender memories. But grief makes me seem so petty and so stupid at times.

The day after the Celebration of Life service, that Thursday, we were cleaning up at the Bakkers's, Claire's friends' home. That morning, I was too tired to think anything through sensibly. The simple task of sitting at their computer to remove or transfer my files proved too much. I asked for help. I was trying to deal with the computer stuff, but I also found myself bizarrely focused on a large bag of sour jujubes. I had bought them two days earlier, wanting Cruz to hand them out to people at the Celebration of Life. Adam loved sour jujubes, and many in my family hoard them, too. As a joke, I used to swing a bag out the car window when I drove up the hill to my sister's cabin in Vermont. The "only available in Canada" candy serves as my true passport to the property.

With all the activity during the wake at the church and the Celebration at the museum, I forgot the jujubes somewhere. I never found them to give to Cruz to hand out.

In that house, I fixated on those damn jujubes. I needed to know what happened and where they were. Nothing else mattered! I asked everyone and couldn't get a straight answer. Even with my bad hearing, I heard whispers — "poor Rick, the jujubes" — coming from family members in adjacent rooms. Finally, Jerry, my brother-in-law, stepped in to say that Joel, Adam's boss, had placed them on a table for the Celebration. That was their story and they were sticking to it.

I found the jujubes days later in a bag that was returned to the house. I obsessed over lost jujubes that Thursday morning, a petty obsession, pestering the same family members who, over the past several days, had delivered countless miracles, loving me through the ache of Adam's death.

There is a good ending to the jujubes story — visitors dropping by the condo in the next few weeks enjoyed them.

Petty, stupid grief. Grief has no brains. My brain was mush that morning.

I will revisit this silly, stupid grief again.

Not long after Adam's death, as a large number of messages pour in on the phone, on Facebook, in cards, or in online obituary condolence remarks, I wonder if my own New Democratic Party leader Tom Mulcair knows the news and, if so, why have I not heard from him? No matter how much love and support or how many prayers I am getting, Tom's silence keeps nipping at my thoughts.

He was a party leader whom I had grown to respect; like some others, I had weaned myself somewhat from the much-loved, late former leader Jack Layton. Now, given the party's Official Opposition status and the growing number of NDP Parliament Hill staff, we who worked for members of Parliament tended to have less contact with the leader. Nevertheless, Tom knows me, partly from my work with MP Claude Gravelle and partly because I accompanied him and Claude to the annual mega Prospectors and Developers Association of Canada (PDAC) Mining Convention in Toronto.

Tom also called me his "hockey guy," a shout-out for the yearly caucus outing to an Ottawa Senators game that I organized for MPs and staff. Once I saw how big a hockey fan Tom was, I made it a point to put him and any of his family in the best seats in the lowest row of the fourth-level Sens restaurant, The Ledge. The other MPs and staff might have been on their BlackBerries and talking politics, but Tom is a rabid fan who came to watch the game. Whenever I could, I picked a Montreal Canadiens–Ottawa Senators game for the caucus. Tom wears the Montreal colours, I my Sens jersey. One year, I brought Adam, who of course wore his Carey Price Montreal goalie sweater. I brought Adam over to meet the leader. Typical of Tom, he took time to chat with Adam, get the selfie, and then elbowed me hard when I confessed my obvious failing as a parent in raising my Ottawa kid to become a Montreal Canadiens fan. I can still feel that elbow.

It is a few weeks since Adam died, and I am on a bench outside the Kanata Hazeldean library. A friend gave me the heads-up that my phone's answering machine is no longer receiving messages because it is full. I discover several messages I had never heard. The very first message is from Mulcair. He had called the day after Adam's death. It is quite a lengthy, touching message on behalf of his wife, Catherine, and himself, expressing his shock, sadness, and, yes, a cheer for my "Soar, Adam, Soar" Facebook post.

Grief can make you miss much.

My grief catapults me to chaos and darkness, as dark as those mines I visited in the North, where, thousands of feet beneath the surface, you switch off the lamp on your hard hat and you cannot see anything, even right in front of your face.

You need to light a candle.

Even a flickering candle helps.

I start visiting Adam's Facebook page, a seven-year diary of Adam's life, loves, emotions, deeds, accomplishments, and more.

Adam
May 5, 2015
Best way to end the night! Thank you @Kendra SupraSwag Borthwick for introducing me to your ball hockey team and giving me the opportunity to play goalie again for your team for rest of the season! Been almost 4 years and I've truly missed playing! 😄 and it'll definitely help keep me fit and off my lazy butt! 😏 And first game & I'm apparently player of the game?? Haha sweet! 😄

A visit to his Facebook page becomes a daily ritual for me, a flickering candle, a refuge.

Adam lived on Facebook, we said. Well, he still does. Working myself back from January 22, his final selfie post, that beam of light from the heavens to his head, I spot in the posts from his last month several references to death, some surprising. Had there been no drowning, these posts would not have been remarkable.

At 1:50 p.m. on January 22, a few hours before the drowning, this: "What a slut time is. She screws everybody."[1]

At 2:22 a.m. on his last day, he posted about how relaxed he was. I don't remember him ever using that word on Facebook to describe himself.

In this last month of January, he posted a series of Rest in Peace shout-outs to three famous people — actors Alan Rickman and James Avery and singer David Bowie. On his Avery post, he comments, "Stop dying everybody."

On January 20, two days before his drowning, he shared, "Death is not the greatest loss in life. The greatest loss is what dies inside us while we live."

That post consoles me greatly, remembering that Adam definitely lived those twenty-two years. My philosopher prince is speaking great wisdom.

Astonishingly, on January 13, he posted an image of two people hugging in a hospital bed with the comment, "if I was dieing in a hospital bed, who'd be standing next to me?" Dear friends jumped all over that post to assure him that they would be there, as they in fact and incredibly were just nine and ten days later. Did Adam have some premonition? Was he preparing us?

Bekkaa shared Steve Aitchison's post
May 4, 2010
true love isn't finding someone else, it's finding the missing piece of yourself ♥ {i.l.y}

Did someone whisper to Adam that he would not have a long life? Did he sense from the epilepsy that he would not reach old age? My boy filled those short twenty-two years — his "wedding" with Ciarra, his dad relationship with Landon; his girlfriends, hockey career, friendships, and jobs; his courage and his unwavering and ultimate commitment to be who he was and to love who he loved, and to do it all with a troupe of friends and a sense of humour that either made me laugh or shake my head in dread.

---

1. Green, *The Fault in Our Stars*, 112.

* * *

In the spring, I order from Basic Funeral Services a neck chain with a silver and black cylinder that will carry a portion of Adam's ashes. It hangs from my neck right at my heart. I touch it from time to time for my Batman to appear. It is a comfort at night. Somehow, the touch connects me to my kid. I shouldn't be surprised. It is him. I have more of Adam's ashes in a clay urn that Jude fired up.

In early July, after some hesitation, I make a decision to head to British Columbia for my niece Katie O'Connor's wedding to Pete Golden. It is another brief grief vacation, a pass out of a private hell. Family — their elephantine energy, noise, and fun — is what the doctor orders. The wedding takes place on a mountain; it is exhilarating. One night before the trip, Adam inspires me to give my neck chain with its cylinder urn to his cousin-in-arms Mack Merdinger, who has come from California. Mack is six months older than Adam. Mack has a speech impediment that brings its own social challenges, and that bound him closely to Adam. They didn't need to see each other frequently; it was just special when it happened. Out West, I put the chain around Mack's neck, and his eyes instantly tell me all that I need to know. *Thank you, Adam.* Back home, I order another jewellery chain. It is a surprise how much I miss the chain in the few weeks that I am without it — the power of symbol and ritual we feel as human beings. I hadn't worn the cylinder for more than a few months, but I now feel a bit back in the sea and lost without it.

Adam shared Sean Kingston's photo
December 23, 2015
Hi Five my lips with your lips

This Facebook grief nudges me a little toward acceptance. Just a little. There are good memories there. And yet grief triggers more grief, going back to where I was months and months ago, year after year of Facebook posts.

How do I go on? How do I find Rick again?

There is a second Facebook page, Rebecca's page, this one for the years 2009 to 2012, with most of those posts capturing the "normal," healthy, preteen and early teen years before the more serious seizures erupted. She posts on hockey, passing tests (barely), parties, dances, sleepovers — the sweet, normal, crazy stuff of adolescence. The epilepsy clouded my memories of those good years. Now gentle waves creep up to the other monstrous walls of waves, gentle waves that remind me of Rebecca's silliness, her hockey years, her Holy Trinity High School friends and somehow miraculously passing exams, her Farm Boy cashier job, and her graduations from high school and the general Community Studies program at Algonquin College. These were monumental feats given the formidable challenges that she faced.

Scars leading to love, circling to grief. They are good years, good times, to unpack now.

Bekkaa
March 30, 2013
"some things last forever"

CHAPTER 17

The Brave Heart

FROM TIME TO TIME, I think about the people who have Adam's organs — the three women and the man. I pray for them. It's hard to explain exactly why I am curious. Do I want to meet them? I am not sure. Do I just want to know more about them, their names, where they live, their families, any details that might make this more real? I treasure what they have. Perhaps I just want to cling to any remnant of Adam, any news that reconnects me to my son. Without knowing the reasons for its policy, I am aware that the Trillium Gift of Life Network does not introduce the donor families and recipients to one another. Anonymous letters can be exchanged, letters that do not include any personal or identifying information. TGLN vets the donor family and recipient letters before forwarding them. As well, there is a cover page to any letter forwarded from TGLN reminding both the donor and recipient families that there is no obligation to read or respond to any communication.

Well, I have to wonder no longer.

Again, it is Suzanne, TGLN's first contact, who reports the incredible news in early March that the heart recipient has written us a beautiful, lengthy letter of profound gratitude for what Adam and we did. His letter runs three pages. Amazingly, he wrote while still in early recovery, only weeks after he received Adam's heart. He tells us his own story about his three-year struggle with heart disease, his long wait to be identified as a suitable candidate for a transplant, and his impressive recovery as he beat every medical timeline set for him. Most important to us, we read of his overwhelming, passionate, "to the brim" joy, a commitment to live not only for himself but for his anonymous donor.

He writes:

Dearest Donor Family,

I'd like to share my story and tell you of the extraordinarily significant role you have played in my life.

I am (or was) a rather ordinary and lucky guy, living a pretty good life. I always took care to look after myself and keep well. I liked to run usually three to four times a week, whether outdoors or on a treadmill; I played golf once a week, as the weather allowed. I never smoked, never used any drugs of any kind, ate healthily, and while I certainly enjoyed a nice cold beer on occasion, overall I was pretty fit and healthy.

In March, 2013, everything changed. I experienced a seemingly mild heart attack. Complications arose quickly and I began experiencing Ventricular Tachycardia and rather severe bouts of Ventricular Fibrillation.... My Cardiologist advised I was at grave risk of sudden death and within days of my heart "event" I had a defibrillator implanted in my chest.

Upon further tests and procedures, including a six-hour ablation to measure and help correct the misfiring/miscommunication of the electrical currents in my heart, it was decided I needed to upgrade my defibrillator to a full pace-maker and defibrillator combination ... which kept my faulty heart ticking for the next three years.

Eventually, though, my team of cardiologists helped me come to the realization that my heart simply was not going to get any better and that I should seriously consider a transplant ... a scary proposition for me, to say the least.

After many months of reflection "soul-searching" and discussions with my family and coming to the realization that I couldn't continue to live much longer the way I was, the day came when I started to seriously think [a] transplant was indeed the best solution for me.

So, I shared my feelings with my wife, then had some discussions with my Cardiologist, who agreed "whole-heartedly" and by October, 2015 I was being worked up, tested and readied for possible surgery.

At approx. 12:45AM, on Jan 25th, I got the call I had been anticipating, but not expecting to come until the early next summer. I was the best match for an available heart transplant. And, so, by that morning I was in the hospital being taken to the operating room, and by that afternoon, my surgery was complete.

I won't be having much contact with people for the next couple of months, as I have to be extremely careful to avoid any bugs, due to the high doses of anti-rejection and immunosuppressant drugs [I] am on. Other than retaining some fluid, and the occasional feeling that someone has ripped my chest open and sewn it back up again (oh, I suppose that did happen, didn't it!?), I feel great! It's amazing to actually feel a strong heart beating in my chest again, a feeling I haven't had in three years!

I have had incredible caring and support from my family and my absolutely amazing and wonderful team of Cardiologists, Surgeons, Transplant Coordinators and Nurses, etc.

But, there is no one whose generosity, caring, thoughtfulness and compassion even remotely compares to that of your beloved family member ... my donor. Words cannot possibly explain the feelings of pure joy, love, respect and gratitude I have toward your family member and all of you.

How can simple words do justice to explain to anyone how their choice has given me the most significant, life-giving, perspective-changing gift of my life. You have given me my life back, and I am forever eternally grateful!

My solemn promise to you is that the man I was before my transplant is but a fraction of the man I will become! I will devote my life to making my life, and the lives of my family even better and stronger ... and much of my driving force from this day forward will be thinking of you and your lost family member, to make you all proud of your loved one's decision to be a donor.

Thank you, thank you, thank you, from the bottom of my amazing, healthy, love-filled heart!

Yours, with a heart full of love, peace and friendship,

Your heart transplant recipient

I read the letter many, many times that day. I read it over and over again in the weeks that follow. I undertake to write back, wanting to collaborate with Suzanne as Adam's parents. We are keen to reply in kind, astonished that so soon after the transplant and while still in recovery, this man wrote this fine letter, where we could feel his emotion and depth of gratitude. TGLN reminds us to leave out any identifying information and to forward our anonymous correspondence to them and it will be directed to the heart recipient.

Here is the letter Suzanne and I write:

To Our Son's Heart Recipient:

I am your donor's dad. I will begin this letter and his mom will finish it.

Just as nature outside nudges us to believe again in spring and new life, your letter arrived. We find ourselves naturally in a place of grief. However, your gratitude, your generosity, your humour and especially your "to-the-brim, overflowing 'yes' to life" mean the world to us. I have read your letter more than a dozen times already and suspect I will be reading it more in the months and years to come. It was generous and so thoughtful that, in the early stages of recovery, you took the time to write us.

What happened to you on January 25th, and your sharing that with us, fills in a final, vital missing piece to that late January weekend. When it became clear that we could not have the miracle we wished, we stepped back and let other miracles occur. We want to honour the wishes of our son.

You speak of your exceptional health care team of doctors and nurses waiting for your new heart. We had a remarkable team of doctors and nurses doing what they could to breathe life into our boy but nurturing his life, his organs, for whatever lie ahead.

The organ transplant network and healthcare teams deemed you the best match for our son. That obviously is a medical decision. On a completely different level, as you shared your pre-transplant life and post-transplant commitments, I sensed your love, hope and optimism. It does seem like a perfect match. And I suspect my son is grinning in agreement.

Let me introduce you to my son through a few stories. It is in the details where his spirit, his personality, his character, come alive. And I hope that you will see just how right the doctors were, without their actually knowing, the right match that this is for you.

My son was this impulsive, fun-loving, fast lane, people-first individual. We seemed to be always catching up to him. At school, from the earliest grades, he must have misunderstood the teacher that there were extra marks to be the first finished every assignment or exam, regardless of the quality of the work or the right answer.

He always wanted to be first done, first out the door, first for what is next. (If your heart ever races a bit, understand it may take a while to get used to a slower pace of life!)

My son loved sports. Out of the blue, when he was twelve, he decided he was going to be a goalie. Playing for average teams, the only thing better for him than getting thirty shots a game was to have forty fired at him. There seemed to be a lot of close losses, 2–1 or 3–2, with my son the first star or tournament all-star. Neither his mom nor I could stop those shots from the stands, as much as we tried. When I would go to the dressing room after a game and loss, wondering what mood he would be in, there he was in the centre of the dressing room changing his gear, laughing, joking, and [being] the ringleader for a story or another joke for his teammates. He never seemed to know or care what the score was or who won. Fun and friends were everything to him.

He had this infectious zest for life — sports, travel, the outdoors, and especially his friends and family.

When a friend of his heard the news of the heart transplant, she said the recipient better know how big his heart is. As a parent, you try to pass on core values on respecting others, treating people right, doing the right thing. I suspected my kid learned those lessons, but it was in the final vigil with him and his friends and in an exceptional Celebration of Life after that we heard dozens of stories confirming this. They told us how he lit up a room when he walked in, how he was always there for them, fighting their battles for and with them, be it with an employer, a landlord, or a distant parent, whatever. He had a special fondness for those who seemed to be vulnerable, hurting and in need of love.

Our son was incredibly brave. When dangerous seizures surfaced in his later teens, he was deemed a candidate for major and risky brain surgeries. When the choices were presented to him, it was obvious what he would do. There was no doubt that our goalie was going to take this shot at life. He would do it twice over four years, endure enormous pain for another shot at a normal life. He always chose life.

And I became convinced someone whispered to him that he may not have a long life. He was bound and determined to have a full life. And in many, many ways he did. We are grateful for that on so many levels.

I will close because otherwise this will be a book. Be well. Be healthy. Be you. Enjoy (eventually) the golf course, the treadmill, the cold beer. That will make my son the happiest, knowing this. You referred to your now strong and love-filled heart. I hope this news on your donor confirms how strong and full of love it is. His love and strength, [and] yours, are indeed a good match. We will remember you and your family who have endured your illness and this extraordinary turn of events. I remain confident that all will be well, for all of us.

Donor's Dad

And from Suzanne:

His dad has conveyed much of the sentiment that I share, but as a mom there is a little more I would like for you to understand.

Despite being much loved, our son's life was not an easy one. I only tell you this as it is my hope that the courage and strength he had will transcend to you. No matter the difficulties (and there were many) he always picked himself up and managed to be positive about life and its possibilities. A lesson he leaves me as I try to deal with the depth of sorrow and grief that overwhelms me with his passing.

His father has told you about his generous spirit and sensitivity. I still remember our discussing the organ donor card that came with his driver's licence. There was not a moment of hesitation on his part — his answer was that if ever it were to happen of course he would donate whatever he could to help save another life. Know that his gift to you was sincere and intentioned.

I would like for you to know that I send much love and hugs to that heart of yours. Your letter has meant more to me than you will ever know. I hope that you continue to recover well and find some of the strength he has given you.

I would be grateful to hear how your recovery is progressing if you are inclined to share with us.

My most sincere best wishes for happy and healthy years ahead.

Mom

Suzanne's note at the end of our letter signals a desire to at least keep in touch. We want to know how Adam's heart recipient's recovery goes.

Bekkaa
March 20, 2012
I hope everyone is having a good day, and don't forget: Beauty comes in many colors!

It is weird writing a letter in which I cannot fully disclose my son's story — for example, to have to fudge the part of his hockey years when he, as Rebecca, played for a girls' hockey club. I figure that the gender information will be an identity giveaway.

But I still wonder about the rules for anonymity, for not contacting one another. A quick Google search gives me the answer to the rationale for those rules in Ontario. Health information is protected by privacy and confidentiality laws, and the TGLN Act (under which the Trillium Gift of Life Network was established) requires anonymity for donors.[1] Anonymity is meant to protect both recipients and donor families, ensuring that neither is subject to unrealistic expectations nor a relationship they don't feel comfortable with. I follow the

1. Trillium Gift of Life Network Act, ontario.ca/laws/statute/90h20.

rationale, up to a point. The burden can be enormous on both sides. The recipient is recovering. The donor family is grieving. Many people may not be able to find the words to express their gratitude, given the extraordinary circumstances by which life has brought these two sides together. There can be walls of guilt, false as they may be. One family may want to meet when the other side does not. And human nature being what it is, a good connection without judgments on either side may not be made. I am also aware that the heart recipient is at risk for an organ rejection. Can we bear further sorrow?

What I do not know, though, is that Adam's heart transplant recipient is eager to meet us, and is doing something to fix that.

And that he is rather clever and a good detective.

I will soon learn that he began sleuthing the news, looking for possible donor matches from deaths that happened around the time of his heart transplant. He read our letter several times and put together rather vague references, "hints," he called them — the information that the donor was a hockey goalie, that he had epilepsy, that there was a Celebration of Life. The heart recipient knew the day or weekend of the death of the donor. When he put those words and phrases into a Google search, the hit was immediate.

Obituary
Adam Prashaw April 22, 1993–January 24, 2016
Adam Daniel Prashaw ... died Sunday, January 24, 2016 after a seizure-related drowning.... Throughout high school Adam was an excellent goalie within the Kanata Girls' hockey association.... A Celebration of Life will follow at 4:30 p.m....

He is 99.9 percent certain that he now knows the name of his donor and his donor's family.

We still do not know him. That changes three weeks later.

I am on the computer late these nights. Adam's death, my lack of sleep, the writing of thank-you and other follow-up letters have me up most nights. I am tired. The Facebook notification I read doesn't jump out at me. New Facebook friendship requests are coming in from many friends of my son as well as from organizations.

"Heart Recipient" wants to be my friend.

I click a quick acceptance and go to bed.

The next day, I am busy and forget the request.

The following morning, still in bed, I hear a clear voice in my head, "Facebook Heart Recipient." *Thank you, Adam!*

I get out of bed right away and go to my computer. On Facebook, I search "Heart Recipient." Instantly, I know who this is as I look at the page he cleverly created specifically to meet me. I am his only friend on this page. I will joke later with him that he needs more friends!

He doesn't give his name, not yet knowing the details of his donor's death and wanting to be respectful about our circumstances, which are still unknown to him. I learn that he is fifty-three, closer to the age Suzanne thought he was. With no mention of kids in his letter, I had guessed that he might be in his thirties; I also learn later that he had to edit a first draft which had introduced his family. I start writing a message to this man when I spot his personal message to me. He hopes that we can introduce ourselves by name to one another soon, but he gives me one last chance to ignore this message by saying that he will accept it if we do not want to make actual contact.

The man has my son's heart. Of course, I want to meet him and know more!

I call Suzanne with the news. By the time I am done errands a few hours later, I am back on the computer to notice that she, too, is a friend of his on Facebook. Now he has two friends! Within an hour, I learn that John Dickhout of Welland, Ontario, is Adam's heart recipient. He now lives near Dunnville, Ontario, where he went to high school. This jumps off the computer screen — my dad spent most of his childhood in Dunnville. I have relatives there. *It's a small world, Adam!*

We are astounded that John tracked us down, wondering how he has done it. Adam died in late January. We got the news in mid-February that four of Adam's organs were donated, the kidneys and liver to women and the heart to a man. We received the heart recipient's anonymous letter in March, appreciative that he wrote it so early in his recovery.

And it was April when we sent our reply to TGLN, figuring that it would still be a few more weeks before the recipient would receive it.

This is racing to a finish so quickly that I suspect my fast-lane Adam is choreographing introductions. I meet Suzanne and Mike that same night on her back deck. She has dug out our first donor family letter to him, still wondering what clues had led him to us so quickly. We guess at what they are, too — the Celebration of Life, the epilepsy, the hockey goalie, and the dates — and put those facts in the Google search, just as we later discover that John did. We are stunned to see Adam's face staring at us from the computer screen from an online, moving tribute the Kanata Girls Hockey Association posted, which included the newspaper obituary.

There is so much more to say and share with this man. It is apparent that he feels the same way.

First, we learn much through an exchange of Facebook messages. Then I travel to John's Welland home on June 10 while on a trip through southern Ontario for my sixty-fifth birthday to visit family, and then to Detroit to watch the Toronto Blue Jays. John is young looking, now a healthy fifty-three. His wife, Lynn, is an intensive-care nurse. John has two daughters: Jamie, twenty-five, and Kristen, twenty-three. I like his humour. In one of many exchanges, he notes that his youngest daughter was born a little over a month before Adam, "giving me bragging rights that I now have the youngest heart in the family." He is an international contact centre training professional and is involved in amateur and professional theatre.

After a remarkable morning chat on his back deck, I prepare to say goodbye. Lynn is in the kitchen and reminds me that she is a nurse. She has a stethoscope. Would I …?

WOULD I?

As I put the stethoscope to John's chest, I hear this loud, strong, fast-beating heart — his heart, Adam's heart. Is this how a racehorse's heart beats?

There are no words. I anticipate tears then, but they do not come until later, on the drive home on Highway 401. I have to pull over.

I enjoy every health update from John and Lynn, delighting to learn of his astonishing recovery — how he is feeling fitter, stronger, healthier, and freer every day.

Rick listens to John's (and Adam's) heart in Welland.

He was a non-smoker and was physically fit, but he'd had a mild heart attack while living and working with his wife in the Philippines in March 2013. Tests discovered that his heart was seriously diseased and, with the risk of sudden death, for the next three years, he needed a pacemaker and defibrillator. In October 2015, he went on the transplant list. As his health deteriorated, he had difficulty walking up a flight of stairs. He couldn't lift his hands above his head to wash his hair.

Rather than getting a number and waiting one's turn, those needing an organ transplant have to wait for the right match from a donor. Even though John was told not to expect a heart transplant until the summer of 2016, the match came sooner. He got the call Sunday night, in the early hours of January 25, about eleven hours after doctors pronounced Adam dead in Ottawa.

Three months later, he is beating benchmark targets for cardio fitness stress tests set for six months post-recovery. He is on the treadmill and lifting weights, and he expects to be swinging a golf club soon. He has the green light to participate in the 2016 Canadian Transplant Games in Toronto in August.

Suzanne, Mike, Lauren, David, and I, along with many of my family, are at the finish line to cheer him on in his 5-kilometre race, in which he achieves a personal best post-transplant time and an overall fourth-place finish against a tough, strong field. He confides that he wanted a medal. Adam must feel right at home with John's competitive DNA. Of course, nobody running that race is a real opponent. We are cheering everyone, including an amazing group of transplant-recipient kids who run a 1-kilometre race.

My hockey goalie kid is undoubtedly impressed. We are impressed. Adam's heart is beating amongst us. John's heart now. John's irrepressible joy. He is being John, living life to the fullest. What unconditional love on Adam's part. The unconditional gift that keeps on giving to our world.

> Bekkaa
> October 17, 2010
> Wheewwww!~ Oh soooo tired!! just played two games first @ 5 then 2nd @ 7 almost played 3rd game between the two but they didnt allow me since i wasnt on game sheet!! :P lol but won 2-0 for both :D <3 2 shutouts!

I mention that I have decided to contact a few journalists to determine their interest in the story. I want to magnify the good that I am already witnessing here, to shine a light on Adam's courage, his epilepsy, his gender journey, and now his organ donor story. Kelly Egan, an *Ottawa Citizen* columnist, comes to mind. I don't know him personally but I enjoy reading his articles, in particular the columns he has written on interesting people's lives. I feel connections with those people after reading Egan's narratives.

Egan interviews Suzanne, John Dickhout, and me. His story, "The Brave Heart: In Death, Ottawa Man Gives Life to Ailing Stranger," appears online the night before I drive to Toronto to cheer for John at the Transplant Games. The next morning, I go to a corner store to buy several copies of the newspaper. In the store, I grab one newspaper to locate the article. I flip through every page of every section. I can't find it. I wonder if it is only being published online. When I put the newspaper down on the pile, I see the story. Page one, "above the fold," as they say.

Now I grin. My Adam likes the limelight. Page one headline story in his hometown works for him. He will enjoy the pictures that have been published, especially the "Rebecca Prashaw hockey goalie" photo along with his grown-up, "on the Russell rock," guy picture.

Here is how Egan began his story.

The Brave Heart: In Death, Ottawa Man
Gives Life to Ailing Stranger[1]

John Dickhout underwent a heart transplant on Jan. 25 and 22 days later, his cleaved chest still healing, typed out his speechless gratitude to the anonymous donor.

"How can simple words do justice to explain to anyone how their choice has given me the most significant, life-giving, perspective-changing gift of my life? You have given me my life back, and I am forever eternally grateful!"

And yet he didn't know the half of it — how brave the heart had been.

It belonged to Adam Prashaw, who was born a girl, Rebecca, on April 22, 1993, but was transitioning to a man. And that wasn't all. Diagnosed with epilepsy at age five, he underwent two lengthy brain surgeries to get the condition under control, the last in November 2015.

Even Dallas gets a mention!

At his Kanata condo, [Rick's] sock feet were tapping on the floor. Dallas, the beautiful black-lab mix that belonged to Adam, hugged his knee.

Now this has to make Adam happy.

Adam found his voice and his courage to tell everyone who he was. Well, page one, above the fold, in your own city's newspaper is definitely coming out!

1. Kelly Egan, *Ottawa Citizen*, August 6, 2016.

Two days after John's race, CBC's Natasha Fatah interviews John, Suzanne, and me live in Toronto on the national news channel. John is wearing his gold medal from the Transplant Games' golf tournament.

Both the Dickhouts and I will meet again and continue communication. It seems that both sides have feelings to wade through in our contact. We recognize John's immense humility, his awareness that while his family is getting a life back, our family is losing a life. But it's clear that the contact, feelings and all, is worth it. To move from it being an intangible recipient and an unknown donor to real people with names and stories changes everything for all of us. It's such a personal decision for any donor or recipient family to make, but for me, it has been so precious. It helps that John is determined to make the most of his new heart, and his new life.

The media work does move me to that good, hard pain again. And it massages the grief. Unfortunately, it still cannot pull me out permanently from those deep, deep waters.

Bekkaa shared

March 5, 2012

Life's a climb... but the view is great

CHAPTER 18

Keep Us All Safe in the Storm

I CANNOT ESCAPE the worst part of my loss: that this is my child. It doesn't matter that he is twenty-two. He is my kid, forever. So many people speaking or writing their condolences tell me that they cannot imagine what it must be like to lose one's child.

They are right.

I am a father without being a father now. I sense a few parents pulling away from me, unable to "go there." Who wants to talk about that? I suspect a few may find it too hard to even make contact.

*   *   *

May our children bury us.

That's what makes this so wrong, so cruel.

*   *   *

Again, on Facebook, a few months after Adam's death, I read a post from Doug Krystia, who was in my church youth group long ago in a Sudbury parish. Doug and Tammy Krystia had recently lost their son, Josh, a young teen, after a tough, five-month bout of cancer. He and his family know my grief. And I theirs, somewhat. Grief is so unique, so personal, so different for everyone, but there are unspeakable bonds.

One day, he writes a private Facebook message. "How do we get through this? As dads, we are supposed to protect and save our kids. Where do we go from here? How do we survive it without it eating us up? Sorry bad day today. I am pissed off with God and I don't know how I get over it without going insane. Our kids aren't supposed to go before us. It's wrong. It's unacceptable."

As he would say another time, "It sucks, and I don't know how or why it exists."

He didn't need to apologize. Their Josh. My Adam. We loved our boys more than life itself. I have those "pissed off" days, too. If I'm not mad at God, I am mad at myself, for not saving Adam.

* * *

My "what if" days.

What if I had paid to break his lease to get him out of that high-rise apartment building with its hot tub and pool?

What if I had pushed more to get him to come to California in January?

What if I had tried harder to get him to agree to the biofeedback and acupuncture treatments to help with the epilepsy?

What if that elevator in his high-rise building hadn't been so damn slow?

What if Adam had listened more to our warnings about being careful?

What if he had fallen backward, on the tiles, instead of forward, into the tub?

What if another tenant had arrived for a swim and found him in time?

What if the new seizure had happened anytime and anywhere else but that exact moment and place?

What if we had gotten him a seizure dog?

So many "what ifs" that whirl me in a vicious circle. They are useless.

*   *   *

In my parish ministry, I observed how men and women can grieve differently. It would be misleading to state absolutes here, but I often found that women tend to grieve more through memories, the lived experiences with their lost loved ones, while men tend to grieve about the future, the "lost, not going to happen" years ahead without their loved one.

In fact, at times, I find myself in both places, Adam's past and Adam's future, grieving the lived memories and grieving the lost future. I do seem less upset, though, when I go to those memories of my much younger child — the ball park, the soccer field, the hockey arena, the graduation ceremonies, the friends.

Is it because I experienced them that they do not hurt as much? Or is this the "guy thing" on grieving? Thinking of the future, I weep bitterly over what will never be — seeing Adam with his shirt off, growing a beard, walking down the aisle on his wedding day, holding his child, becoming a grandparent. That stings.

I turn to my faith for stability and hope. I do believe that I will be reunited with Adam. Of this, I am certain. Of course, I wonder much about how, where, and when. I am reading an intriguing book, *Matthew, Tell Me About Heaven: A Firsthand Description of the Afterlife*, in which a mother writes about her telepathic communications with her seventeen-year-old son who died in a truck accident.[1] From a place called Nirvana, Matthew answers his mother's questions about the afterlife — relationships, the presence of animals, communication with earth, our composite souls, reincarnation, pre-birth agreements, and more. It confirms some of my life-after-death beliefs and stretches others. There are some details I could take or leave, but the book underlines how enduring and vital our connection is with those who have died.

---

1. Suzanne Ward (with Matthew Ward), *Matthew, Tell Me About Heaven* (Camas, WA: Matthew Books, 2002).

But this God of mine, well, that's a bit more complicated. It's been quite the "crooked, straight" faith journey — from my Roman Catholic upbringing, priesthood, and studies in Rome in preparation for teaching in the seminary in London, Ontario; to the end of those studies, my broader immersion in ecumenical, then interfaith, then Indigenous spirituality; to leaving the priesthood and getting married. My faith is as much a "roaming" as "Roman" now, and finally, the death of a child has distilled everything. I am not in church as much these days. There's no single religion that can contain or fully express my God of many names, this God whom I've discovered is very much "she" as well as "he." Adam will surely bless those divine pronouns. Jesus's teaching remains a core part of my faith — his actual teaching and not the way that it is preached perversely by some. My Catholic prayers come in handy in times of trials and tribulations. They certainly did at the Ottawa Hospital – General Campus in January. I go to my angels often, to my spirit guides, too. I pray every day — that is, I talk with God.

Through it all, God's personal, faithful, and forgiving love has been more or less constant. More or less. Ha! There's the rub. Job's cursed sense of abandonment shows up as well. The two are my constant companions. I had had many conversations about this while counselling and listening to others, now it's my turn to ask how God could let this happen. It's a crisis of faith, a curse of the heavens, a gnawing search for answers. Since Adam drowned, I have felt God's consolation many times, and I have also found myself shaking my fists heavenward in those "pissed off," "How could you, God?" moments. Indeed, if the truth be known, it's a conversation that has been going on for over half a century now. The God that I preached in ministry and the God that I have experienced so far in life is the God who showed up that tragic weekend, joining us in our suffering, ministering to us in the chaos — through people and events — yet who inexplicably had no Batman-like miraculous act to perform for us. As usual, I am left putting foot after foot forward in faith, with plenty of questions and doubts, all laced with lamentations.

Epilepsy Ontario interviews Suzanne for an article on Adam's life. Suzanne is quoted: "Everything that led to the day that Adam died and the day that John received his heart were destined to be, whether I like that or not … It was meant to be."[1]

I agree. A divine plan. I'd be wise to leave this search for answers at her eloquent comment. We do seem caught up in a much bigger plan that is, for me, more destiny than a powerless, predestined fate, a plan where we play an active role but do not ultimately get total or absolute control, a plan that includes parts that we will definitely not like. This plan embraces what happened to Adam in the hot tub on January 22, but there is much, much more: our child's conversation with her mom about being an organ donor, Pati's comments about organ donation in California, the "angels of the airlines," Kevin and Asia, getting me home in time for that sacred thirty-six-hour final vigil with my son, and especially, Adam's 2014–2016 journey home to himself, Adam's exceptional choir of friends, Dr. Cardinal, the nurses, Adam's family, the Trillium Gift of Life Network, organ recipients, and so much more. I recognize fragments of the plan in many people and places in Adam's story.

Adam seemed to muster his own internal strength to change and yet still recognize that life has a plan.

Bekkaa
April 17, 2013
All things happen for a reason, some accidentally, some on purpose, some good, some bad. Their there to help show you this thing called life, and some lessons but there is one that could have all those and still be right for you. And that's love, you'll do anything for it.

I think back to when Rebecca once "played church" as a kid. She might have been seven or eight years old. Rebecca wanted to be the priest, of course. She did her share of bowing and genuflecting, and then she led a procession to an altar that she had made, with an

---

1. Deron Hamel, "In Death, Ottawa Man with Epilepsy Is Providing Life," Epilepsy Ontario, August 25, 2016, epilepsyontario.org/in-death-ottawa-man-with-epilepsy-is-providing-life.

upside-down wastepaper basket covered with a towel as the taber-
nacle. I remember her sermon:

> God is big. Very big. God is bigger than me or Dad or
> Mom or anybody. God is bigger than our house and
> our street. God is bigger than Russell. God is bigger
> than the sky. God is very big. Amen.

Good theology there.

*　*　*

Questions circle questions.

My love for Adam is unbreakable, forever. My belief in where he
is now, in what he experienced the weekend he died, helps my grief.
I do believe that the January weekend was
Adam's ultimate, whole transition. I believe
that he crossed over to his full self.

Everything Adam wanted — freedom
from seizures, surgeries, meds, visits to the
Neuro, and a cure for epilepsy; freedom
from binders, breasts, and monthly periods;
freedom to be shirtless, to be everything he
understood as Adam, and more — he now
has. There is a boy in the mirror. He is free
of hate, hurt, judgment, discrimination,
prejudice, laws, and everything else that
hindered him. He is home.

> Adam
> July 15, 2015
> I can't wait till the day I
> can actually be in pictures,
> go swimming without a
> shirt or binder not having
> to hide anything...that'll
> be the best day of my
> life! 😂 💪 #ftm #trans
> #feelingcomfortable
> #cantwaitfortheday

This is THE transition, is it not? On New Year's Eve 2015, he
embraced the new year, looking ahead to transitioning to a man, to
Adam. He wanted his hope to rise. Well, I believe that the January 22
weekend did that. He is now Adam. This is a good place for my sorrow.
It is real. I believe it. If I can just keep the focus on Adam, on where he
is, on what he is up to now.

One night, surprisingly, the storm's waves subside a bit, like the old man forecast. I distinctly recognize what is changing. I am in bed, calm, chatting with Adam. Previously, those pillow conversations were more chats about Adam to God and the gods, to angels, spirits, to my parents.

But, this night, I start talking to Adam.

First, I want him to know his ancestors better, now that he is among his new family. The Prashaws, with the anglicized French surname that can be traced back through Île Perrot on the St. Lawrence River at Montreal to Brittany, France. On my maternal side, the Beatons of Mabou in Cape Breton, tracing back to Scotland. I ask him which ancestors on my side of the family greeted him that Friday afternoon in the hot tub to help him to cross over.

Of course, Adam would have recognized his grandma, my mom, Gertrude Beaton Prashaw. Rebecca was ten when my mom died. Rebecca enjoyed her visits to North Bay, both to see Suzanne's parents nearby and her grandma at her apartment, and later at her independent-living residence.

This night in bed, I tell Adam stories about my dad, Dick Prashaw, whom he had never met before but now knows. I sense that Dad and Mom are definitely two of the souls who helped Adam cross over that January weekend. I suspect that Adam and Dad are a perfect match for each other. They share a love of humour — Adam's silliness, Dad's perpetual clowning, never taking himself or others too seriously. I want Adam to know about my dad's military service, his years fighting as a D-Day Dodger in the Italian campaign in the Second World War. The term *D-Day Dodger* is Lady Astor's, an ill-chosen moniker for the men in uniform who missed D-Day in France because they were fighting in Italy; something they had been doing, in fact, for months or even years before June 6, 1944. From listening to the radio and being online, Adam seemed connected to world events. On Remembrance Day each year, he gave a shout-out to the brave soldiers who fought in the wars:

Adam
November 11, 2015
Lest we forget 🖤 😢 thank you to all of our amazing soldiers for fighting for their loved ones and our

country. You are amazing people. But wish it didn't
have to happen this way. Lest we forget to all my
family who have fought in the war and who are still
here and in the army ❤️ love you so much. You are
all amazing, strong, and supportive fighters.

His grandpa was one of those amazing soldiers. Now I want Adam
to know how brave his grandpa really was. These past two years, I have
been researching his wartime story, prep for a book in the works that is
actually evolving into the love story of Mom and Dad, wrapped around
the wartime story of their hometown of London, Ontario, and Canada.
My research has so far failed to uncover the specific act of heroism that
earned my father a coveted postwar mention-in-dispatch (awarded for
valiant conduct, devotion to duty, or other distinguished service). Dad,
typical of many veterans, talked little about his years in uniform, its
horrors or its daily grunge and boredom. I heard vague references to a
middle-of-the-night river swim behind enemy lines to bring important
intelligence back to company headquarters. One night, I urge Adam to
get Dad to tell him that story. On Remembrance Day 2016, I am comforted by the image of Adam in the company of Dad, Mom, and Dad's
Perth Regiment pals, hearing their stories of 1941 to 1945.

Courage meeting courage. I tell Dad about how courageous his
grandson is — about his epilepsy and how he endured and bounced
back from all those seizures and two brain surgeries; his extraordinary
transgender journey; how he donated his organs and saved lives. This is
Adam's mention-in-dispatch!

Two heroes of mine.

I let Adam know how thrilled I am that he has met my favourite uncle, Bill Stotesbury, his wife, Dorothy, and their three basset
hounds, Ralph, Brutus, and Leslie; those dogs chased my brothers
and sisters and me around cottages in northern New York State and
North Bay during many summer childhood vacations. Bill took a
pass on believing in God after a young priest informed him once that
there were no dogs in heaven. You know better than that, Adam. I
have no doubt that Ralph, Brutus, and Leslie are up there beside Bill,
at his feet, when they are not chasing you. It must be quite the canine

choir with Murphy, Molly, Josée, those basset hounds, and others. *Adam, can you get Ralph, Leslie, and Brutus to chase that priest around heaven's gate?* Just a small favour.

I keep up with the introductions.

How strange that my Adam meets my brother Danny before me. Danny was my parents' first-born. He lived only one day. In *Matthew, Tell Me About Heaven*, Matthew tells his mother that in Nirvana, where our bodies are more flexible and etheric, young people "continue to grow until they reach maturity in body that would correspond to healthy, robust Earth humans thirty to thirty-five years in age."[1] Interesting! The reverse happens for older folk, who grow down, younger, to reach thirty to thirty-five. Yeah! I am happy about this heavenly Benjamin Button plan to lose a few years, where I can hit a permanent pause button at thirty-five. I am certain that Danny and Adam now enjoy the earthly years they never reached.

Adam
September 28, 2014
Beautiful day today wish
it was like this everyday! :)
#beautifulday #summer/fall
#ftm #transgender

* * *

The rough waves are still absent the next few nights, so I continue this chat with Adam. We revisit a few legendary parent-child episodes, dad-daughter and dad-son conflicts.

There is the shoplifting incident at a nearby Zellers store in the mall when security hauled Rebecca and a friend into the store's office. Rebecca called me to tell me where she was. At the time, it was terrible news. Now I suspect that my kid could rob a bank and I would be fine, if it meant having my son back.

The shoplifting incident comes to mind because this week, sorting through a treasure chest, I found an award-winning *mea culpa* letter that my kid wrote to me in green crayon:

1. Ward, *Matthew*, 54.

Dad:

I was caught stealing with Steph. it was the first time I've stolen and I regret doing it. I stole costume for to-night. I had a long talk with the officer and I learned it was a disgusting/horrible thing to do and I'm sorry.

Dad, the dance is tonight and I know stealing doesn't give me the right to go but would really like to and we paid. I understand the reaction I got and going to get and punishments. I'll do work round the house or anything to pay off the bill. Anything. Sorry dad for disappointing you and barely talking to you at supper. I'll do better. I'm sorry ❤ I've realised that it was totally wrong to do this and that it could affect life, like your job, school, friend etc. And I should have thought of this. I hope I can go to the dance. I love you, Rebecca.

My kid. Nothing like mustering charming chutzpah to repeated-ly get up off the canvas when life jabs. Confess your crimes, throw yourself at the mercy of the court, accept whatever punishment might come, AFTER the dance.

I grin. This is so my kid. Being in politics, I recognize a good speech-writer, too. Steph now works across the street from my condo. I make a copy of the letter from her "partner in crime." I deliver it to Steph. I want to believe that they went to the dance. Steph says they did.

Do you see things any differently now, Adam? I do. I ask for his for-giveness for any anger, my rush to judgment.

I revisit with Adam the reasons why I pushed for the biofeedback and acupuncture treatments, how certain I was that they might cut the stress and otherwise support seizure prevention. Now I see more of Adam's perspective. Adam had had his fill of doctors, hospitals, medical practitioners, and counsellors. Adam was tired of needles. No love of his cousin, Natalie Ramon, nor of his hometown of Sudbury could convince him to say yes to acupuncture. *Adam, I understand your refus-al. Adam, drop by Natalie's clinic now, okay?*

As we chat on the pillow several nights in a row, it dawns on me. I am still Adam's dad.

Of course I am!

Death cannot kill the one fundamental relationship that binds us together. My love as Dad is stronger than any sorrow or bitterness or anger. Adam may have uncoupled from epilepsy and from the body that was not all him. He and I have not split. Stuck where I am, it isn't the relationship that I want, exactly. But it is real. And now I find myself still parenting Adam, tentative at first in this new way of being his dad, introducing him to ancestors and to our family history, still teaching him, seeking and offering forgiveness, explaining those other forms of medical intervention, asking my busy son to find time to be with his ancestors.

> Adam
> July 12, 2014
> I am still here aren't I?

Parenting is not finished.

Adam has things to teach me, too. This kid, my teacher on pronouns and transgender things, is teaching me through life, suffering, death, and more.

This kid who raced through life made it to his finish line. He lived his life. He was true to himself. This kid who always tried to get every test, every piece of homework done quickly, damn the results, beat me to the other side. And there was no stopping him, as much as we threw a few roadblocks his way.

I am amused, just a little. Adam accomplished the one job asked of each of us: he lived, and fully. Just not long enough.

From time to time, my grief shuts out the wisdom that friends share. My sister Jude emails me a reflection on death being nothing at all, simply a move by your loved one to another room, next door.

Death Is Nothing at All[1]

Henry Scott-Holland

Death is nothing at all.

It does not count.

---

1. Henry Scott-Holland, "Death Is Nothing at All," familyfriendpoems.com/poem/death-is-nothing-at-all-by-henry-scott-holland.

I have only slipped away into the next room.
Nothing has happened.

Everything remains exactly as it was.
I am I, and you are you,
and the old life that we lived so fondly together is
    untouched, unchanged.
Whatever we were to each other, that we are still.

Call me by the old familiar name.
Speak of me in the easy way which you always used.
Put no difference into your tone.
Wear no forced air of solemnity or sorrow.

Laugh as we always laughed at the little jokes that we
    enjoyed together.
Play, smile, think of me, pray for me.
Let my name be ever the household word that it always was.
Let it be spoken without an effort, without the ghost of
    a shadow upon it.

Life means all that it ever meant.
It is the same as it ever was.
There is absolute and unbroken continuity.
What is this death but a negligible accident?

Why should I be out of mind because I am out of sight?
I am but waiting for you, for an interval,
somewhere very near,
just round the corner.

All is well.
Nothing is hurt; nothing is lost.
One brief moment and all will be as it was before.
How we shall laugh at the trouble of parting when we
    meet again!

I instantly hate this message. Reading it, I scream silently that death IS SOMETHING, not nothing. I scream that death is a lot MORE than my kid moving next door. But the more I read it, the more that I thrash in this sea of grief, the more I seem to touch the universe that is so much larger than this earthly time we have. There is something real and consoling in thinking of Adam as having just moved next door, that everything is normal, that I should just carry on. My own SNAFU moment. To tame death a bit. "My kid living next door" is both absurd and yet utterly true now. On the one hand, I miss the physicality of his being, but on the other, I find myself chatting with him, joking, admonishing him, introducing him to others, telling stories with my Adam day and night. Is it Adam that I hear laughing when Dallas sneaks onto my bed before dawn to do what she did to Adam every morning — play, lick me, wake me up, throw off my covers, lay her head on my neck — way too early in the morning?

Adam
January 5, 2016
Usually how I wake up every morning.. Lol silly sure loves the cuddles 🐶 😊 #dogsofinstagram #cute #squishesoflove #labboardercolliemix #sillyDallas #everymorning

One Flew Over the Cuckoo's Nest moment, talking to the spirits. Surely the staff in white coats are at the door to take me away. Or is this crazy time why Adam finds it so easy to move in? Am I in an altered spiritual and mental state, more receptive to Adam? Or is it that Adam's presence in my mind draws me to that state? I can't figure it all out, but Adam's presence is real. Waves large and small, scars taking me back to my love for my son.

* * *

My artist sister is breaking through my walls yet again. Jude had been a healing arts practitioner at a Virginia hospital, letting art do its healing with patients facing serious illness, dying, and death. She writes a blog post on this experience; these words are another life jacket:

Keep Us All Safe in the Storm[1]

The reality is that we don't forget, move on, and have closure, but rather we honor, we remember, and incorporate our deceased children and siblings into our lives in a new way. In fact, keeping memories of your loved one alive in your mind and heart is an important part of your healing journey.

— Harriet Schiff, author of *The Bereaved Parent*

The suffering is too deep for words, no matter all the words written.

As another friend put it, "When there are no words, the other organs weep."

The sliding glass doors at the front of Carilion [Roanoke Memorial Hospital] open and suffering enters.

This suffering is not limited to the patients in their rooms or the family and friends who attend them. Today, while walking through the glass doors into the volunteer office, I discovered that sorrow had also entered; recently, two women each lost an adult son and a third lost a twenty-two-year-old nephew.

Hopefully, our visitors and patients discover what greeted these volunteers: compassion. One of the women who lost her son, a long-time volunteer, said, "I needed to come in today to volunteer. My son was so proud of my work with cancer patients."

I know that with suffering and sorrow, hope enters and resides in this hospital.

After leaving the volunteer office to return to my Healing Arts table in the lobby, the first note I read that was left in my small clay boat read: "Her story will continue in heaven."

Our stories of suffering and sorrow, of hope and healing, of giving and receiving compassion continue

1. Jude Prashaw, "Keep Us Safe in the Storm," Carilion Clinic, carilionclinic.net/blogs/keep-us-safe-storm-jude-prashaw.

to walk through these hospital doors each day. Many stories are penciled on notes and placed as a wish or a prayer into my clay boat.

- may this hospital heal everyone that enters it
- stay strong, have hope
- heal my sister
- soar with the angels, Adam
- born a miracle
- I care for you

And the last note of the day, a note that softens the sorrow, that speaks to whatever story we carry in our hearts, that helps us believe we are not alone:

- keep us all safe in the storm

Jude Prashaw
Artist in Residence

*   *   *

I am Rick, a Prashaw, a guy, among other things. I keep busy. I hunker down. I learn a few survival skills, as my organs weep and the small boat I find myself in tosses on those immense waves in the storm. I want my Adam back. I can't have him back the way I want him back. I slowly, grudgingly, learn the ways that I can have him back — through his family, his friends, Facebook, the happiness of the heart recipient, John, and my choice to be generous and true to myself and others.

These are all precious lifelines.

That weekend in the hospital, I felt that I was in a celestial "tug of war" with my God and the gods.

Beside the hospital bed, I imagined the heavens pulling skyward while I pulled back in an earthly direction, with Adam the prize. But I realized at last that Adam was not between the heavens and earth. Adam was now pulling gently against me. Adam had crossed over. Hard as it was to imagine, I sensed that Adam did not want to come back. Once I knew Adam's whereabouts and wishes, the tug of war was done.

This grief thing is so on me, so on those of us left behind.

The anger at the departed is part and parcel of the package. Irrational, right?

Why were you in the hot tub that day?

Bekkaa
January 27, 2010
life just keeps getting better

Why didn't you get out while your friends went to the apartment?

Don't you remember the parent talks about those seizures, their dangers, the danger of water?

Did you think that you were invincible, my Batman?

I can hear his answers so clearly.

I was not alone in the hot tub. My friends were there. They only left momentarily to get something.

I didn't think that I needed to get out of the tub.

I had had no seizures for two months.

The surgery went well.

The check-up a few weeks ago was amazing.

The doctors were confident. I was confident. You were confident.

I am shocked by my death.

And, yes, I am sorry I was in the hot tub then.

Shocked by your death, Adam? I never thought of that before. I have been thinking too much about me. I can't be mad at my Adam. I never could be, for long. Putting my parenting script aside for a moment, for the most part, I liked very much his living as he did, a bit on the margins, with his friends.

I don't have all the answers. I sit in a stew of questions and wonder. I cling to certain truths and mull the mysteries. I find myself in a sacred place that terrifies me. Cheryl Strayed, in *Tiny Beautiful Things*, describes this place in a letter she writes to "Living Dead Dad," a man trying to recover from the death of his own twenty-two-year-old son at the hands of a drunk driver. She says we who grieve are in the "obliterated place," equal parts destruction and creation, pitch black, bright light, water and parched earth, mud and manna. Exactly![1]

---

1. Cheryl Strayed, *Tiny Beautiful Things* (New York: Vintage, 2012), 283.

We have loved Adam. Adam was, and is, loved. I am certain that he knew how loved he was the entire weekend of January 22–24. He knew it in the days after and in that church and museum on Wednesday, January 27. I believe that he crossed over on a wave of extraordinary love from family, friends, and the health care team at the Ottawa Hospital – General Campus.

Yes, I forgive him, easily. Honestly, I don't think that there is much to forgive.

The grief has not killed me yet. That's a surprise. I work on being gentle with myself when those crazy "what if" thoughts bite.

I need to protect my heart and energy now. This is never-ending work. I know that I need to slowly integrate Adam's Celebration of Life and the experience of his wake into my life.

The depths of life call.

Bekkaa
January 18, 2013
Here I come 🖤 🖤

CHAPTER 19

Fragments

You may encounter many defeats, but you must not
be defeated. Please remember that your difficulties do
not define you. They simply strengthen your ability
to overcome.

— Maya Angelou

January 2017 to March 2018

IT IS A YEAR since Adam drowned.

Jude's painting of the selfie my son took minutes before he died
hangs at the top of my stairs. It is the first thing that I see every
morning and the last at night, before heading to my bedroom. I kiss
Adam good morning and good night. He can't bail on those kisses
anymore, as he partly succeeded in doing with my hugs those last
few years of his life. I teased him about this "guy thing" with his half
hugs. Hugs or not, his love is a given. Many days, looking at the
painting, I see a serene, relaxed smile on Adam's face. There are a few
days when I look twice, catching a smirk or scowl or puzzlement.
There's mischief, too, every now and then. I need the morning and
night kiss to manage my day.

These days, threads of Adam's story nurse the ache and memories.

I watch his Montreal Canadiens hockey team more than I ever did, cheering my son's hero, Carey Price, though still only as long as he is not playing my own favourite team, the Ottawa Senators. In the kids' vernacular, Price is having "a sick season," with shutouts and repeated First Star selections, he's a "human wall" in the nets. I sense that my kid's spirit may have season tickets at the Bell Centre.

Suzanne tells me that she spotted a beautiful, strong cardinal outside her home soon after Adam's celebration. Later, for the first time, a new flock of cardinals moved into her backyard and garden. We remember Dr. Cardinal.

I am still on Facebook a lot, Adam's and mine; among other things, it helps me to keep track of his close friends. Their posts, their inevitable raw emotions — the loves, hates, instant and repeated "life-and-death" emergencies, comments like "life sucks" and "I want this to end" — bring me strange comfort, drawing me back to Adam's daily reality. Every now and then, I throw his friends a surrogate Adam "love" or "like." They call him by special nicknames, "Broski" or "Badam"; they hurt, too, and like me, spot Adam's Batman reminders everywhere.

Their words of love remind me of what a special friend Adam is. They post on his page that they miss his "funny face," "heart-breaking smile," "3 a.m. conversations," "the long, random talks," and "his willingness to be so open, so accepting."

I ask Brittney Palmer for the names of the five kids who put those "forever friendship" bracelets on their wrists after slipping one on Adam in the casket. Brittney tells me, "lol," that the five are now fifteen and she doesn't know all the names!

I still find it hard driving on that part of Elgin Street downtown where Adam lived and died at his high-rise. I had avoided looking at that building for months, until John Dickhout paid a visit to Ottawa with his wife, Lynn. One day, we parked at the Museum of Nature on our way to see Adam's boss when John innocently asked where Adam had lived. I looked up to point out the building, a block away. I told John and Lynn how rare it was that I looked there. John touched my shoulder.

That visit by John and Lynn in the summer of 2017 was remarkable on so many levels. They wanted to meet Adam's sister Lindsay, and other family members. Their time in Ottawa also moved me through other grief walls. As the recipient of Adam's heart, John wanted to express personal thanks to Dr. Cardinal and also to the hospital nurses and to Joel, Adam's boss. I am grateful for what all these people did; they had been on my "must see" list, too, except that I hadn't gotten around to doing so for months. I guess I am stuck in some ways.

With John and Lynn, we had an extraordinary, positive series of encounters, all around. At the end of each conversation, John went out of his way to tell everyone that Adam, a "beautiful, wonderful, and thoughtful son," had given him "the greatest gift one can receive, my life!" He and Lynn wanted the health care specialists to see the positive results of their work — that John had his life back; Lynn, her husband.

Both Dr. Cardinal and Kristen Dupuis, the ICU hospital clinical manager, commented on how rare it is for this follow-up contact with families who have experienced, as we did, both a tragedy and a transplant. Like the worlds of church and politics that I've worked in, health care systems do not do follow-up well or at all. Life hurtles health care personnel to new emergencies, new lives to save. Dr. Cardinal told us that John is the first recipient of a heart from one of his patients that he has met in thirty-five years as a doctor. Working in ICU and Emergency, he is usually on the other side of the transplant equation, dealing with the grieving families and their decisions on organ donation.

We had a heartwarming chat with Joel and two of Adam's staff colleagues. We shared some work stories and laughs. Joel praised Adam's work, noting the ease he felt in assigning my son to different, high-demand café positions. He did not notice the memory challenges that we had heard about at other jobs. Joel told me how much the memorial Celebration that his staff helped to prepare and that they experienced had touched everyone deeply. He told us that his café had since won a national award and that, at the ceremony, he dedicated it to Adam.

That same night, again at John's urging, we invited three of Adam's friends for supper at the Elgin Street Diner. After all the stories and dessert, John made them the same offer that I had heard in Welland. "Do you want to listen to your friend's heart, my heart?" He had a stethoscope. Ciarra, Kendra, and Ashley took turns listening. I will never forget the look on their faces. Tender mercies.

Rick with the paramedics who rescued Adam: Dan, Laurie, Kevin, and Christian. Missing: Bob and Eric.

John and Lynn Dickhout meet Adam's friends. From left to right: Rick, Ashley Mary-Lynn, Kendra, John, Ciarra, Lynn.

I am grateful for John and Lynn's visit, which nudged me forward and cleared up some of my "to-do" missions.

*   *   *

I feel Adam's hands shoving us all forward.

While reading more literature on organ donation, it dawns on me that there is another group that I want to meet and thank. Their names are Christian, Kevin, Laurie, Dan, Bob, and Eric. They are the six Ottawa paramedics who responded to the 911 call to the apartment building and who resuscitated Adam on the third and final try. I've been wanting to thank them. I want them to know the rest of Adam's story, what their actions meant to his family and friends and his four organ recipients. Their resuscitation meant that he went to the hospital alive and we got those precious, final thirty-six hours to deal with what happened and say our goodbyes.

I flew a red-eye from California to have the most important two days of my life with my son. His brother flew in from Edmonton to be with him. A sister returned from Quebec. Some family came from London and Toronto.

I cannot imagine us not having had that precious time with Adam or him not experiencing all our love, all that we told him. Surely that is enough to be grateful for, but there's more. As John and Lynn Dickhout came into our lives, I realized that these paramedics not only rescued that final weekend for us, they rescued Adam's wishes to be an organ donor. Only because he was in the hospital and on those machines was he even eligible to be an organ donor. The rules for organ donation are that the potential donor must die in hospital and while on life support — organs are not suitable for transplant without oxygen and blood flow. (Tissue donation can happen under a wider variety of circumstances.) As during the early meetings with Dr. Cardinal and the nurses, there was a precious feeling in that room with the paramedics. With all his seizures and frequent trips to Emergency, Adam knew first-hand the good service that they provide.

It seems that Adam is still in good hands, for it seems that Adam isn't really gone. In fact, Adam is showing up elsewhere. There are appearances, messages, and other "coincidences" sprouting up for family and friends. I visit Atherton Drenth, a certified medical intuitive and holistic energetic practitioner, in Guelph. Before Adam's death, I had made an appointment because a few other family members who Atherton had treated reported positive experiences of healing, as well as release from past hurts or illnesses. After Adam's death, I decide to keep the appointment. Atherton is known for her healing gifts and clairvoyance. Her businesslike demeanour and appearance suit my healthy, semi-skeptical side. After an intake review, I am not on her treatment bed five minutes before Atherton reports that Adam has appeared. I did not mention to Atherton either Adam's name or his transition from girl to boy. It is here on her treatment table that I learn how shocked Adam was by his death in the hot tub, how ancestors accompanied him across to the other side, how fine he is now, and his abiding, steadfast love for us. He remains keenly interested in what's going on here. I hear from Atherton that he's busy now in a trans youth group, whatever that means. The news of his shock about his death and the trans group meetings have a special "ring of truth" for me. Atherton later tells me that she has a son named Adam, too.

There is more news, still.

I learn from others that Adam has visited Natalie Ramon's acupuncture clinic in Sudbury, as I suggested to him one night in bed. Meanwhile, Victoria Sharpe, a friend of Adam's who was trying to sell a ring online, is shocked when she gets a text from a prospective buyer with Adam's phone number and Adam's name appearing. She is confused and a bit creeped out until the conversation with the buyer confirms that the man just got a new telephone number, and yes, it's Adam's number. Adam seems to be busy!

* * *

Another of Adam's organ recipients contacts us. The recipient of his right kidney writes anonymously to express her heartfelt gratitude for the generosity and compassion in our act. Until that letter arrived via the Trillium Gift of Life Network, I have to admit that I never thought about my "right" versus my "left" kidney. She tells us that, before her kidney deteriorated and dialysis began, she was an active person, exercising regularly, running marathons, skiing, biking, skating. It seems that my hockey goalie has a thing for getting formerly healthy, active people back on track. Like with John's letter, the kidney recipient's news makes Adam's gift real. It does not erase our heartbreak, but it does connect me in real ways to my son. My prayers for the four recipients become yet more concrete.

Bekkaa shared
April 28, 2012, Ottawa
Each of us represents a star in Heaven. Sometimes we shine with the rest, sometimes we twinkle alone and sometimes, when we least expect it, we make someone else's dreams come true.

* * *

Adam
February 13, 2015
Big cheers and thoughts to my sister Lauren Mann (Quebec team) in the Scotties Tournament of Heart!! 👏 👍 I'll be cheering for you this week, wish I could of came! 🖤 kick some 💥💥!!! 💪💪

In February 2017, Lauren, now curling for Eve Bélisle's rink, sweeps the Quebec provincial curling qualifiers with a perfect 7–0 record. At the 2017 Scotties, a few journalists will tell the remarkable story of Lauren's curling, her brother Adam, and heart recipient John Dickhout, who, with his wife, Lynn, joins us in St. Catharines for the Scotties Tournament of Hearts. Lauren tells CBC reporter Devin Heroux that the pain is still very real: "The positive I was able to take out of it was really focusing on the curling. Because I know I didn't want to live the rest of my life saying I never came back to the Scotties because of that."[1]

---

1. Devin Heroux, "Closer to the Heart: Curler Feels Late Brother's Heart at the Scotties," February 22, 2017, cbc.ca/sports/olympics/winter/curling/scotties-quebec-lauren-mann-1.3994445.

Curling connects Lauren and Adam "in both a good and bad way," given the tragedy that interrupted her 2016 path to the Scotties. TSN highlights the "hearts" story — Adam's, John's, the Tournament of Hearts — in an exceptional two-minute video that airs nationally. TSN shows John cheering in the stands for Quebec, "the two families close, brought together by a man [Adam] he never met, who will always be a part of him." The video ends with Lauren throwing a stone that slides across the heart symbol on the ice. TSN's Vic Rauter reports that our family is willing to share the story to encourage organ donation, "to help some other John."[1] Lauren and Eve's team have a terrific week, going 7–4 in the round robin, just missing the playoffs in a very competitive field.

I suspect my Adam loves the national audience!

*　*　*

Despite all of the positives, I still feel a huge sense of loss. This grieving is on me, not Adam. I have had too many precious experiences and communications with my son since his death. I have zero doubts about his own happiness, joy, and new life now. The grieving is all mine — no son, no contact, no texting, no meeting up downtown, no sports together, and so much more. No future, as I saw or wanted it.

There are other kinds of contact, though. The quiet in bed at night seems to help me hear Adam speak. It was there I heard his clear words, "heart recipient," reminding me to get up to discover John Dickhout's message to us on the computer. On the same pillow, almost a year later, I hear the words "park bench" when I am at a loss as to how to advise Gender Mosaic on what to do with its memorial fund for Adam. A Google search identifies the City of Ottawa memorial park bench initiative. Gender Mosaic will help me pay for a park bench with a special plaque featuring Adam's name and his invitation to sit down, relax, and rest a while. The bench will be across the street from his favourite Elgin Street Diner.

1. Kevin Pratt, producer, "Lauren Mann's Unique Connection to a Fan," February 24, 2017. The video is no longer available from TSN, but is viewable on YouTube at https://youtu.be/Lm4tOyLln4w.

In March 2018, we are at another finish line to cheer John Dickhout as he runs his own "Amazing Race" — this time the Running Room's Hypothermic Half-Marathon right in Kanata. It's so incredible — a winter run, in his donor's hometown, shadowed by a film documentary crew, all unleashing a media frenzy. He completes the ten kilometres in sixty-three minutes, just over his one-hour goal. Filming the race is a terrific group of film students from Niagara College who will produce *Racing Heart* as part of their course, with plans to enter the documentary into film festivals.[1] Ironically, the director, Andrew Dickhout, is a cousin of John, but they had never met. At an initial meeting, John shared his pre-transplant bucket list of seven goals. The last goal was to run a marathon. The students knew right away what their film project would be. John confided he did not like running in the cold, but course deadlines dictated a winter race and the kids spotted the "perfect" location of Kanata, where Adam had lived. An Ottawa CJOH CTV news story triggered other stories: Global News, CBC's *As It Happens* (who interviewed John), a Disney news site, and the New York–based *Epoch Times*. A friend of John's living in Australia watched a news story there. I sensed Adam running beside John and enjoyed every step of the race.

> Adam
> September 26, 2015
> Well here it is! For those who couldn't make it tonight, unfortunately. Here's me @Hunter Downe and my friend @Chad Charming doing our duet! We were second up first set 😉 haha weren't as good as some of the performances we saw tonight. 😎 Buuuuut...I didn't care, I had a blast either way!! 😄 🎤 and perhaps do it again soon. Thanks for a great night Canada's Capital Kings!!

Times like this, I surprise myself, landing in new, beautiful places, in the universe of Adam's friends, being with the Dickhouts, speaking about organ donation, or finding new friends, my friends, who are transgender.

I circle to the final fragments in Adam's story.

* * *

---

1. Directed by Andrew Dickhout and produced by Sean Elliot and Ella Guclu.

Facebook Dad

I am forever grateful that Adam accepted me as his friend on Facebook. That was no big deal for Adam. This was the kid who invited his parents to stay in the doctor's office or come for appointments with social workers or trans health counsellors.

In his last few years, while we lived in the polar-opposite Kanata and downtown universes, I did crave actual visits from him, phone calls, and heart-to-heart conversations — he squeezed many of those in while mostly enjoying being twenty-two, young, and on his own downtown. On Facebook, though, Adam did visit and love so many friends and family, myself included.

> Adam shared
> TeenTimes's post
> Sept. 19, 2015
> @Ashley Mary-Lynn 😂
> 👇 all the time
> That amazing moment when you and your bestie look at each other, know what you are thinking and both laugh

There, I observe his joy in connection with people and his genuine capacity for finding friends, often online first and then in real time. He finesses the humour or craziness in many things.

Facebook is a ringside seat to my kid's fight for his life, his loves and emotions, his cursing, his humour, wicked and otherwise, his news and sports reports, and so much more. It is my window to his friends, his girlfriends, his community. It is not an Ottawa that I otherwise visit often!

On Facebook, I witness his hard life. I notice his soldiering on. I marvel at his positive side. I am impressed at his writing: smart-like, even with the cognitive deficits from all those seizures. But now, especially after his death, I visit Facebook to remind myself how he lived, loved, and laughed, and the tonic he was to so many friends.

With Facebook, there is no parental temptation to go peek at a diary. This *is* his diary, published online, for the whole world to see. I laughed when Facebook asked me from time to time if I knew Adam D. Prashaw — a question that Facebook puts to users to suggest other people to "friend" and expand their networks. Do I know Adam D. Prashaw? Oh boy, do I, and don't I. Indeed, Facebook helps me get to know much better the same Adam who lived in the next room for all those years. My kid.

Being on Adam's Facebook page tested every parental bone in my body. I am eternally grateful for this social media site. Eternally, literally! Facebook encapsulates a seven-year diary of my kid's highlights, lowlights, events, feelings, and more.

Though it's a memorial page now, Adam's page offers friends the chance to come together to tell more stories, post more pictures, lament how much they miss him. Adam lives on that page. It's where I heard Victoria's ring story. Facebook introduced me to John and Lynn Dickhout. Facebook leads me to "Everglow," sweet salvation for my soul. It's where I grieve and flee from grief, a place in which I learn of an old man and a shipwreck metaphor that will guide me home. It reminds me of other years, the good times that his long, hard suffering obscured.

Indeed, I touch Adam's life and love on Facebook. Adam still communicates there.

* * *

Epilepsy

Disease and illness afflict the loved ones of too many families. It is hardest when it strikes our children.

Epilepsy is a disorder. Its causes are numerous: sometimes it is the result of disease and illness, sometimes the product of brain damage, sometimes a genetic predisposition, and often its origins are unknown. But whatever its roots are in a particular person, its effects can be devastating. It dominated my child's life between age five and ten, and then, especially, from seventeen to twenty-two. When doctors diagnosed epilepsy after that morning "Ferris-wheel" seizure at the breakfast table in Russell, Ontario, it seemed scary, but we still thought that it was manageable.

It wasn't cancer, thank God. It wouldn't kill our kid, or so I thought. But the onset of the second, more serious seizures at seventeen did introduce life-threatening risks, a dangerous, untimely cocktail exactly when our adolescent was bent on speeding to adulthood and his independence. Kids feel invincible in those young years. As parents, we reluctantly played the "killjoy" role, periodically reminding our kid about the dangers and how to manage the maze of threats. He hated the reminders. I hated reminding him some days.

We tried not to make too big a deal of the epilepsy. Adam was bound and determined to live a full and normal life, epilepsy and all. He took his meds unless he forgot or got confused. He'd tease online about "skipping the meds to stir up some fun," but a check-in would confirm that he was kidding. The "home invasion monster" metaphor best captures what epilepsy felt like all those years. It did lurk in the shadows, especially from 2011 onward.

There are no precise numbers for people with epilepsy in Canada or the Province of Ontario. Most often, the estimates tend to be between 0.5 and 1.0 percent of the population. A 2015 study reported that there are approximately 90,000 people living with epilepsy in Ontario, including 15,000 children 17 years old or younger. Project that percentage across the country, and an estimated 287,000 Canadians are living with epilepsy.[1]

Our kid was among the epilepsy patients who were predicted to benefit from surgical intervention. Adam went for the surgery twice, a testament to his courage. We backed him. I am so grateful to the Montreal Neuro's health care team, to Dr. Olivier. I believe the surgeries helped Adam, although we never got the total cure or the longer second remission that we hoped for.

It is hard to know how many people die from causes directly or indirectly related to epilepsy. It is a small number. Sometimes, the cause of death listed on a death certificate may not mention epilepsy or seizures even when they may have been contributing factors. The general finding is that epilepsy is associated with a two- to three-fold increase in mortality in developed countries, but "the risk of drowning in people with epilepsy is raised fifteen- to nineteen-fold compared with people in the general population."[2] People with epilepsy whose seizures are not controlled have an almost forty times higher risk of mortality than those in remission.

1. R. Ng, C.J. Maxwell, E.A. Yates, K. Nylen, J. Antflick, N. Jetté, S.E. Bronskill, *Brain Disorders in Ontario: Prevalence, Incidence and Costs from Health Administrative Data* (Toronto: Institute for Clinical Evaluative Sciences, 2015), 78–79, ices.on.ca/flip-publication/BrainDisordersInOntario2015/index.html.
2. G.S. Bell, A. Gaitatzis, C.L. Bell, A.L. Johnson, J.W. Sander, "Drowning in People with Epilepsy: How Great Is the Risk?" *Neurology* 71, no. 8 (2008): 578–82, ncbi.nlm.nih.gov/pubmed/1871111.

In the end, epilepsy pulled Adam under. Adam chose not to take a pass on life; he chose to be active. Adam did not want to be babysat or tethered, ever. He was in the water as a baby, taking swimming lessons as a young child. I have fond memories of watching him make dozens of dives from his grandparents' houseboat on Lake Nosbonsing near North Bay. Certainly, we taught him the dangers of seizures in the water. We educated his friends as they came into his life. But life, the plan his mom talked about in that Epilepsy Ontario interview, has its way of overruling other, best-laid plans. I appreciate Adam's confidence about beating epilepsy after the second surgery and his optimism after his post-surgery appointment in Montreal in early January, three weeks before his death. He had reason to believe that those seizure days were behind him. He was with his friends that day. They left only briefly. I fault none of them. Who could conjure up the absurd and cruel timing of that seizure in such a narrow window of minutes? Looking at that final picture he took, reviewing his Facebook posts those final days, I sense his peace that moment before his death, the light shining down from the heavens.

Bekkaa
March 26, 2014
Happy Purple Day! ♥ Happy to see there is a day to support those like me with epilepsy... if you know anyone or wanna support those with epilepsy wear purple today! :) ♥ I'll go to work today with purple tie maybe lol

In the end, I choose to bow deeply to epilepsy, but not as deeply as I do to the doctors, nurses, and the epilepsy organizations that work tirelessly to cure and halt the progress of the disease.

I think of all the families and especially the people who live with epilepsy, and I feel the solidarity of sorrow and pain with all those families whose kids are sick with other threatening conditions and diseases or who mourn loved ones who have died. There are many Adams out there.

I will do my part to support education and work for the cure. I will wear purple on Purple Day for Epilepsy, which is held on March 26 each year. Purple Day is a Canadian grassroots initiative that has spread around the world. March is Epilepsy Awareness Month in most parts of Canada. In the United States and Australia, Epilepsy Awareness Month is in November. The United Kingdom holds an Epilepsy Awareness

Week in May. There is also International Epilepsy Day on the second Monday of February.

The symbol of epilepsy, the purple ribbon, was one of Adam's many tattoos. It will be part of the second tattoo I get to celebrate my son's life. I have to come up with a tattoo that captures hockey, epilepsy, transman, and organ donor. Adam will guide me on that, as he will on other work to support epilepsy organizations, including the Canadian Epilepsy Alliance, "a partnership between grassroots epilepsy organizations Canada-wide dedicated to the promotion of independence, quality of life, and full community participation of persons with and affected by epilepsy, through innovative support services, advocacy, education and public awareness."

*   *   *

Transgender Journey

I told my Rebecca, as a small child, that I loved her "to the moon and back, three times." I don't recall adding "as long as you are a girl, and love just boys." It is love, period, no conditions, not love predicated on a specific gender identity or specific sexual orientation. That's easy to say, and then it demands a life to live it out. It's unconditional love, punctuated by a million typical, parental screams, missteps, and judgments.

> Adam
> January 22, 2016 3:52 p.m.
> Hot tub time 😎 😊
> #hottubtime #confidence #goodtimes #ftm #presurgery #timewillcome #transgender

It was a few months after Adam's drowning when I had this jarring realization reading his very final communication (yes, the selfie picture in the hot tub): the very last word Adam ever communicates is *transgender*. It's his last hashtag on that final selfie. How appropriate.

While transgender never fully defined or captured who Adam is, it's impossible to tell his story without highlighting his transition from girl to boy that intensified in those final four years of his life.

I am no expert on transgender people or their issues. I am Dad to a trans kid. Adam is my first teacher, he and some of his friends. Along with my own reading and learning, they grew my thinking, grew my loving, and grew my acceptance.

To appreciate the daily realities and the demands for justice for transgender people, look to pioneers and activists like Toronto's amazing Susan Gapka, visit resource centres, and read the literature.

Adam, though, did teach me so much.

I lived in smaller places in northern Ontario like North Bay and, later, Sudbury. I know that in some towns, there are now some services for transgender kids and also LGBTQ groups. There are even parades that, for at least one day in the year, recognize this group of people living in our midst, part of our communities. But I can't recall knowing or hearing about a transgender person when I was growing up there. My sister Margie, a teacher, progressive in every way, told me that she could count on one hand the number of trans kids that she knowingly taught in four decades of teaching. These kids would usually go deep into the closet, withdraw into themselves, given the gender-polarized world they lived in; some would need to leave for bigger cities to find more acceptance. Some would inevitably suffer from mental health issues, addictions, and self-harm.

A new generation of teachers tell me that, in some places, bigger cities for sure, there is more public recognition of these kids. I hear conflicting reports, though, on how much better it is, whether many more kids feel able to come out, and how many more services there are in some communities. I am told that now more trans kids find love, support, friendship, and positive role models. Still, they can remain vastly under-supported and enough will still leave for the bigger cities, where they can discover more kids just like them. Wherever they are, I know their reality can be harsh. Transgender tenants might be denied public housing. They face abuse at school. Many face increased violence if incarcerated.

During a Christmas visit in 2015, a month after Adam's surgery and a month before his drowning, my brother-in-law Jeff Connor was visiting Ottawa. One night, after we drove Adam home to his apartment, Jeff had some questions for me as a dad. His own son was preparing to come to Ottawa for university. Jeff was trying to imagine the unimaginable: a child coming out, announcing that he is not the gender that he was determined to be at birth. He wanted to know what that was like for me. I struggled to find the right words for Jeff that night.

I rambled about parenting Adam. I didn't want to make it out to be more than what it was. I never saw any radical change in my kid. Adam was never "girly-girly."

I told Jeff that I remember how absolutely happy I was at the birth of my child. I believed that my kid was a girl and discovered soon enough this "tomboy" Rebecca was not what many people imagined a girl to be. I didn't give it that much thought. I loved her. Like most parents, I found raising a child a hell of a ride, surfing their (and your) successes and failures, victories and defeats: the schools, report cards, trophies, bragging rights, illnesses, and setbacks. Rebecca filled up my life. When she awkwardly came to announce that she liked girls, still thinking that she was a girl, that was okay by me, too. I have a beautiful nephew whom I love who is gay. I have many friends and working colleagues who are gay or lesbian. My parents modelled a way to accept people. As in every family that I know, my brothers and sisters and I occasionally announced news about our lives that must have been disappointing to our parents, given their own values and perspectives. However, nothing that we told them derailed their love for us. I will always remember telling my mom of my decision that I, a Catholic priest, was going to marry and how she, as difficult as that had to be, asked if I had a picture of Suzanne and her children to show her. My mom and dad were role models for acceptance. I am fortunate to have opportunities to practise this way likewise in life.

When Rebecca said she was a lesbian, my biggest worry was how to protect her. I feared that she would face discrimination, that people, acting out of ignorance, fear, or hate, might hurt her. I told Jeff that when Adam surfaced a few years later, again it was not like a stranger suddenly appeared. I looked at my child and he was the same kid, with a new name. For Adam, of course, adopting his "new identity" meant much more than simply changing his name. It was huge for him. In truth, I guess it was huge for us, too. Still, I don't remember having to make a new decision to love him. I loved my kid and accepted him for who he was, as he was discovering who that was. For Adam, there must have come a point when he decided that the pain he would feel if he didn't change would be worse than the pain of the change itself. Pain does that to us. I have known that life-changing pain myself.

Adam's story sensitizes me to read the news differently. I'm better at spotting the stories on transgender people.

There is Kenny Cooley, a trans kid and football player whose story, covered in the media, allegedly led to his firing from a McDonald's restaurant in the Halifax area.[1] There is also Chrystopher Maillet in Ottawa, who fought a Charter of Rights case, demanding that OHIP cover the costs of gender reassignment surgery that had taken place prior to the lengthy approval process.[2] Then, there is Jesse Thompson, an Oshawa teen who won a human rights case to dress in the arena dressing room of the gender with which he identifies.[3] He has overturned the long-held dressing-room policies of Ontario's minor hockey league — rules Thompson says ultimately outed him to his teammates and exposed him to harassment. Thompson's complaint culminated in the posting of transgender-inclusive policies for the Ontario branches of Hockey Canada, including a rule stating that players who identify as trans can use the dressing room corresponding to their gender identities. What courage, Jesse! Adam and Jesse are hockey teammates forever.

I become aware of the alarming statistics involving the transgender

> Bekkaa shared
> September 8, 2011
> If you're gay, it's a sin. If you're bisexual, you're confused. If you're skinny, you're on drugs. If you're fat, you're a slob. If you're dressed up, you're conceited. If you speak your mind, you're a bitch. If you don't say anything, you must be miserable. If you cry, you're a drama queen. If you have male friends, you're a whore. If you defend yourself, you're a troublemaker. You can't do anything without being criticized. If you're proud of who you are repost this, love me or hate me, but you will never change me.

---

1. Haley Ryan, "Halifax LGBTQ Group Demands Apology from McDonalds," *Halifax Metro News*, September 22, 2016, metronews.ca/news/halifax/2016/09/22/halifax-lgbtq-group-demands-apology-from-mcdonalds.html.
2. Jake Kivanc, "The Barriers to Sex Reassignment Healthcare Faced by People in Ontario," Vice News, June 4, 2015, vice.com/en_us/article/the-problems-with-access-to-sex-reassignment-in-ontario-980.
3. Wendy Gillis, "Rights Fight Prompts New Inclusive Rules for Ontario Hockey," *Toronto Star*, September 7, 2016, thestar.com/sports/hockey/2016/09/07/ontario-minor-hockey-moves-on-transgender-inclusiveness.html.

population — considerably higher than average numbers are victims of murder, sexual assault, self-harm, homelessness, and suicide.

They can face a lifetime of rejection from their own families or potential employers. I read about the one hundred anti-LGBTQ bills being introduced in the United States. I followed the "bathroom bill" debate in North Carolina. I confirm how under-supported the trans population is in all resources and services.

What does this do to me? First, it takes me back to the fears that I had for my Adam and all of his friends. His coming out in that powerful and passionate post in 2014 stoked my parental pride and unspoken fears at the same time.

It is scary.

On June 13, 2016, Murray Sinclair, chair of the Truth and Reconciliation Commission in Canada, spoke about this parental fear in one of his first speeches in the Senate of Canada after Prime Minister Justin Trudeau named him a senator. On the night of the horrific Orlando shooting at the Pulse nightclub, Sinclair said that he was celebrating the thirty-third birthday of his openly gay daughter. Sinclair told a hushed chamber that he and his wife, already dreading the dangers she faced because she is a woman and Indigenous, felt even more afraid than ever. He said she was already "living a life of enhanced danger just by being female," something that was increased by the fact that "she was in a higher at-risk group because she was an Indigenous woman.... We told her about the fact that among Indigenous people, being a two spirit was traditionally a position of respect and honour. Ceremonies, we have been taught, are enhanced if done by or with two-spirit people present, for it is believed that they embody the strengths and spirits of both man and woman and bring a special healing power and medicine to every special event."[1]

Sinclair wanted to speak personally about how it felt as a parent to hear that an American filled with hate for lesbian, gay, bisexual, transgender, queer, and two-spirit people had carried his legally purchased

1. Tonda MacCharles, "Senator Murray Delivers Emotional Tribute to Orlando Victims," *Toronto Star*, June 14, 2016, thestar.com/news/canada/2016/06/14/senator-murray-sinclair-delivers-emotional-tribute-to-orlando-victims.

machine gun and pistol into a bar and started killing everyone he could. Sinclair said:

> We want to protect our kids from physical and mental abuse, the hurt, the discrimination. We have learned to shield them and to heal them. [But] society's dislike and disrespect for those who are gay and transgender has been a part of Western thinking for many generations. The enhancement and recognition of their right to be who they are and their right to public protection of those rights does not sit well with far too many people, the shooter in this case being representative of that.[1]

I knew Sinclair from my Church Council on Justice and Corrections days, working on healing justice. Now his words penetrate bone, marrow, and soul. Flashing in my mind is the worry I had about protecting Adam from this hate and discrimination.

I was sickened when I saw the first television news report of the Pulse nightclub massacre — a security guard killing forty-nine people and injuring dozens of others in Florida. These "kids," these Adams, were the people in that club. Horrific. It is inconceivable to think of what they experienced that night. Adam taught me how sacred those clubs are, places where they can be themselves, feel free, sometimes for the first time in their lives. Hate can find them anywhere.

It is why there is work left to do: for them, for ourselves, for our world.

I am back at the library one night this fall when I notice a *Walrus* magazine cover on trans youth. The author, Mary Rogan, weaves her personal story into her coverage of the long, hard-fought progress for rights and the struggle to raise awareness of gender as an issue of identity, not sex.

"Gender isn't something most people think about critically," Rogan writes. "We don't have to explain to each other what it feels like to be settled in this 'male' or 'female' experience of ourselves.... We're thrown off balance when something as elemental as gender is questioned."[2]

1. MacCharles, "Senator Murray Delivers Emotional Tribute."
2. Mary Rogan, "Growing Up Trans: When Do Children Know Their True Gender?" *Walrus*, September 12, 2016, thewalrus.ca/growing-up-trans.

Adam induced me to think critically about something I hadn't thought much about at all: my own gender and the gender identities of others. Slowly, I began to uncouple sex and gender, to think about the binary understanding of sex and gender and the notion of a "default" gender state. Adam changed me as a parent and as a person. Adam taught me that transgender issues are about so much more than bathrooms, locker rooms, or dressing rooms, as important arenas as each might be to someone at any given moment. Commenting on Facebook about the new federal legislation C-16 (which added gender identity and gender expression to the list of prohibited grounds of discrimination under the Canadian Human Rights Act), Susan Gapka says that

> strategically speaking, pronouns are this year's washrooms — a planted distraction from the immediate task — our Trans Human rights. The legislation is about equality before the law for trans and non-binary people, access to employment, housing, health care, mobility rights and social inclusion. The legislation is also about freedom from harassment and discrimination in these areas of our lives. Focusing on pronouns and washrooms reduce the debate to the opposition's claims and attacks our most vulnerable which human rights legislation is designed to protect.

Adam
October 31, 2014
First ever job where I need
I.D. pass! Don't I feel fancy! ;)
#fancy #sexy #silly

Like everyone else, transgender people should have their inherent human rights recognized. Recognizing transgender rights gives transgender people the things that others who are not transgender may have taken for granted: a life for everyone, no matter who, to love whom you love, be who you are. I grew to appreciate that all of us didn't necessarily get the right body parts to go with our gender identity. Nature can screw up.

And, I suspect Adam would add, death stare and all, get the pronouns right. They matter.

I am so grateful for people like Nichelle Bradley, Dr. Jennifer Douek, and Dr. Wallace Archibald, who helped my son's transition. I am immeasurably consoled that my son wore Adam on his ID tag at work at the Museum of Nature Café. That was so respectful to him.

I will always remember that note on the whiteboard at the Ottawa General Hospital in Room I-28 that identified my kid as Adam, no matter what the health card said.

Human dignity. Human rights, in oh-so-small, simple, yet powerful ways.

The weird thing about Adam being so driven about becoming "all boy" is that he wanted the change so he could finish being "a trans man." He wanted to cross over to what he understood as the "new normal." The Rebecca chapters would always be a precious part of his story, but they wouldn't be like some scarlet letter hanging around his neck forever, the one-and-only way people would see him.

We do label people. We can reduce them to a condition or an issue. Adam reminded me that this is about people, not vaginas and penises. On Adam's Facebook page, a few months after he died, I read this remarkable post from a young trans man who was heading back north to live in a smaller community. All he wants is the chance to be himself, to decide for himself who and what he tells others, to avoid the stigmatization. He gives his friends a heads-up. He does not wish to be known or introduced as a trans guy:

I move soon and felt I'd share a few things before I do so. For those who know me in [name of place] I'd appreciate when meeting new people or being introduced that it's just [person's name] not [old name] who used to be a girl. My story is for me to share with whom I feel comfortable sharing it with.

I've had the opportunity here in a big city to meet people without them knowing my past and just knowing me as [name] so I'd appreciate the same courtesy. I just want to be me please! So I'd appreciate if in new crowds not to be discussing my story. If you're in a group of people, please don't feel the need to use me as a discussion piece and gossip about the "tranny" who's moved to town. Please respect that I'd like to just live my life as me ... the man I always was ... and no surgery questions please ... what I've done for surgery is none of anyone's business.

I'm looking forward to reconnecting with everyone but please respect who I am and the rough ride I've had getting here.

Just want to be me! Adam seconds that.

I recall my somewhat awkward, hesitant telling of Adam's news to my own friends and work colleagues. Family, especially those who were Adam's Facebook friends, knew the news and followed every twist and turn of his journey. But who else should I tell, and when? It is, after all, Adam's story, so his timing must be respected. *You want to just be, just live, not let your story define you.*

But, not surprisingly, Adam gave me carte blanche to tell the world. Still, this didn't enlighten me on any timing norms for disclosure. Some work colleagues and friends did not see Rebecca for years or weren't as much in our lives as family. It wasn't a story to tell quickly.

I did whisper Adam's news to a few. I started referring to Adam on my Facebook page. I remember one friend messaging me, asking "Who is Adam?" Others figured it out. I did want Adam to disclose his news himself as more of my friends came into his life. Like him, I didn't want the trans news to dominate or define him.

Now, I know that there are others who need support for their journey.

I have come to love Adam's friends. It is not hard to know why Adam loved them, too. How could I walk away from them? They loved Adam in life and in his dying and death. They love him still. They made such a difference in Margie's preparation and celebration of the service for their friend. That afternoon, in the atrium of the Museum of Nature, I caught a glimpse of how it should be every day. These "kids" stretched many of us in those final days with Adam. There's a lot more stretching to do. I will push the Ontario government forward on its late, slow promises to change policies for approvals and funding regarding gender reassignment surgery. There is so much education needed. There are letters to write, burdens to share as more families have these hard conversations.

Transgender people could use some allies to stand up to the hating trolls on social media and the online news site commentaries.

University of Toronto law professor Brenda Cossman says it well: "At the end of the day, this is about people. It's about trans and gender and non-binary people. These are our children, our siblings, our nieces, our nephews, our friends, our neighbours. How bloody hard is it to simply treat these people with respect and dignity?"[1]

*   *   *

I love my boy, my "boy in the mirror." The kid who didn't know all the right terms but discovered the courage, first at a pub breakfast with a girlfriend, to tell her mom who she thought she was, and then, a few years later, to tell us all who he was, what a few intuitively knew long ago.

He discovered a courage and will to get it right, to take us along for the journey.

I savour Margie's final words at Adam's Celebration.

> Adam
> July 15, 2015
> Beautiful day today wish it was like this everyday! :) #beautifulday #summer/fall #ftm #transgender

The beating of our own hearts calls us to be
our true selves.
Calls us to be our best selves;
Calls us to be what we might become;
The breath of our neighbour calls us outside ourselves;
Calls us to be companions;

1. Rosie DiManno, "New Words Trigger an Abstract Clash on Campus," *Toronto Star*, November 19, 2016, thestar.com/news/gta/2016/11/19/new-words-trigger-an-abstract-clash-on-campus-dimanno.html.

Calls us to be allies;
Calls us to be partners;
Listen, we must heed the call of our own hearts;
Where love and truth, caring and justice are born.
Listen, we must heed the call of others to gather together
for some great purpose
where passion and fidelity, compassion and equity are
nourished.

Adam had come to love who he was in his short, plentiful life. I wanted so much more but, really, what more could I want for my kid.

* * *

Adam and Adam's Dad

People tell me that Adam's story is exceptional — his epilepsy, his brain surgeries and seizures, his transition to a boy, and his donation of the organs that saved four lives. On the one hand, I get that, but still I want to resist, even though I know that his story touches countless other families who also suffer through illness, heartache, and tragedy. On the other hand, as proud as I am about those highlights in Adam's story, my son is so much more. He didn't let any of those headlines define or contain him. I tend in the end to go to the heart of my son's story. Pure and simple, he is Adam, previously known as Rebecca, our son, our brother, a grandson, a nephew; a work colleague at Farm Boy, sub shops, and the Nature Café; a neighbour, a Facebook friend; girlfriend to Ciarra, Jesse, and others, and boyfriend to Chelsey; Carey Price fan, athlete. He is quite ordinary, normal, like all of us, in his own unique and, yes, devilish way. I see other Adams on the street and in our communities.

He got to his finish line.

As I complete his story, I learn of the death of our beloved Leonard Cohen, singer, poet, lover. His words have seen me through a dark night or two. I read his words from a 2008 interview: "The emergency never ends. Everybody's heart gets broken. Everybody gets creamed."[1]

We got creamed. Sadly, Adam got creamed.

I will go to the light, to some joy and peace. It is what Adam wants. It is what I want.

We move forward and understand what is in the rear-view mirror, step by step. Moving forward matters.

> Adam shared
> September 12, 2015
> Courage is being
> scared to death ... and
> saddling up anyway.

I am Adam's dad. That is the only name that matters now. There are my other names — "Rick," or "Richard" if my mom was on the warpath looking for me, "Father Rick" for eleven sweet years — but the twenty-two years and counting as "Adam's dad" identify me now.

I've commented on our lot as parents, wiser now from my own experience, as we often are. What is that parent job description again? Part crapshoot, balancing act, hanging under the high-wire acts as our kids perform? My many revisions to the parenting manual. Ha, what parenting manual?

I joked that it was a good thing I put off parenting till I was forty-one years old. I shifted from parenting with Suzanne in Russell to parenting solo in Kanata, from the bliss of "hands-on" parenting to figuring out the gig of distant, empty-nest parenting and those surprising new meeting places, like when I became a Facebook Dad and when I began all the texting and messaging to chase my kid. I learned that parenting is about tidying their room and sending money and being guard on the watchtower.

And the best surprise of all, given the deadly circumstances, is that it is not over. I am still Adam's dad.

Adam did have a hard life, although it was woven through with all the fun that he manufactured. Every parent wants their kid to be happy, to have an easy life, to be who he or she is, their truest, authentic self. Like some parents, I didn't mind if there was a bit of adversity to toughen the character for life's challenges. Adam had way more adversity than we could ever wish.

---

1. Elizabeth Renzetti, "The Solace of Art: Leonard Cohen in a Time of Darkness," *Globe and Mail*, November 11, 2016, theglobeandmail.com/opinion/the-solace-of-art-leonard-cohen-in-a-time-of-darkness/article32818006/.

Would I do it again knowing what I know? Where do I sign up?

* * *

In a final tribute, Lindsay captured Adam's outstanding attribute: "Courage is a word we have long associated with Adam. Over and over again, friends and family have spoken of his courage. Adam's transition wasn't one of solitude, but one which invited so many to witness both his struggles and his victories. He openly shared his intimate thoughts and feelings with the world."

Adam got back on the horse after every tumble. Suzanne wrote this tribute in a thank-you letter to family, friends, and colleagues after the wake and Celebration of Life: "His life was not easy, but he always pushed on. I loved his open spirit and was in awe of his courage. In the days that followed his death, I witnessed the incredible number of lives he touched and was given a glimpse of the love and friendship he shared with so many people from so many different walks of life. I had no idea."

We heard about his tolerance, his strength, his capacity to forgive. I knew Adam was courageous and so alive. I didn't know nearly enough, though, the extent of his courage or how bravely he chose life. It was because of that courage that Adam, most importantly, found his voice. Adam unwaveringly charted his course home to himself. I take comfort from those last posts that he was being ministered to.

As for me, I learned to listen better. Adam pushed me past boundaries I hardly imagined. He made me better — I sense a better parent, I hope a better human being. There has been no greater blessing than giving life to him, once, starting from that day in Sudbury in 1993, and now twice, through these words that we co-author.

The world is changing for the better. Adam is helping that happen. Soar, Adam, soar.

Adam
January 13, 2015
Love you

Postlude

I slipped into the Kanata Farm Boy for gluten-free bread and fresh salmon for supper. The express counter line was fairly short this time.

"Hi, Dad," chimed Adam at the cash register.

"Adam?"

"That's my name," he said, looking down on the name tag on his Farm Boy shirt.

"Last time you were here, it said Rebecca."

"That's another life ago."

"How ARE you?"

"I'm good, all good, fine."

"You look great. Still fast helping people through this line?"

"Yep."

"Remembering all those codes?"

"Simple."

"Did you lose your razor?"

"Ha! Good beard, eh? Grew it in two weeks."

"Looks good."

"Thanks."

"Can you come for supper?"

"Dad, I am really busy."

"Ha! Some things never change!"

"Pedro has a pickup basketball game and then we are skateboarding. I have acupuncture with Natalie. The trans youth group has a meeting tonight."

"Trans youth group?"

"Yep. New friends. We meet a lot."

"But you are all guy now?"

"Yeah, but there's a lot to understand. It takes a while to become Adam, remember?"

"I do remember. Not bored?"

"Never. So much to do."

"Stressed?"

"Blessed. Relaxed!"

"Annoyed?"

"Ha, no time for that!"

"All good?"

"The best. I am going back to school, too, trying to decide if I want to work with kids or animals."

"Amazing. Supper soon?"

"Absolutely."

"Dallas wants to see you."

"I am in the woods with you every day."

"Nice. Don't forget your family, eh."

"I KNOW, DAD."

Acknowledgements

As certain as the hugs from family and friends carried me that week in January 2016, so many have hugged *Soar, Adam, Soar* through to publication.

I treasure the generous, positive first readers: my brother, Marty; my sister, Jude; and a wise Jen Ball, who shares the wonders of parenting and whose nightly love notes in the margins I woke every day to. I forgive Jude for that nudge (or was it a shove?) to share my grieving with the universe. Kevin O'Connor, a nephew, gave wise counsel on Adam's path.

The hugs keep going to Sudbury, as friend and editor Colleen Humbert remembered a long-ago pastoral kindness and offered a remarkable polishing of the manuscript. She handed me over to a Toronto friend, Jody Colero — Groucho Marx's twin, I swear. Jody's good cheer and networks nursed the manuscript along. Jody also lead me to Ron Hay, a musician turned lawyer whose counsel and story of his late father, Rev. Eldon Hay, and his Dr. Seuss Pride hat, blessed the book's journey.

Finally, a university friend, Peter Lockyer, introduced me to Beth Bruder at Dundurn Press. Her first two questions, with acquisitions editor Scott Fraser, confirmed my story was home at last:

"How did Adam come out to you?"

"Did you really name her Rebecca Adam?"

What a treat to have your story loved to life by these consummate professionals: Scott Fraser, Dominic Farrell, Laura Boyle, Jenny McWha, Michelle Melski, Elham Ali, and the entire Dundurn team, as well as Catherine Dorton and Tara Quigley.

I am indebted especially to the experts and activists who advised me — those in the healthcare, social work, epilepsy, trans, and organ transplant universes. I cherish the counsel from Susan Gapka and Kate Hewitt. Any mistakes still here are Dad's, not the experts'.

I thank Adam's mom, Suzanne Corbeil, and aunt, Sandra Corbeil, for sharing photos and facts. I am in awe of Adams friends who checked facts, offered advice, encouraged this project every day and revealed so many more treasures about my son. I will love them forever.

Last, and truly first, is a thank you to Adam, my co-author. He took me by the hand through his Facebook page, choosing text, revealing that it would be best to print the whole posts rather than paraphrase them, assured me his selfie was and would be the cover (quality of picture notwithstanding), and woke me up on my pillow a few nights to introduce his heart recipient and the City of Ottawa memorial park bench program. Adam kept me going every second of every day, all the way to print.

How appropriate, given this son of mine, for all the news of *Soar, Adam, Soar* to thrive on my Facebook, as his and my friends offered leads, advice, and encouragement.

I am so grateful and, yes, gratitude IS everything.

Image Credits

Aaron Helleman: 152

Adam Prashaw: 96, 178

Added Touch Photography: 25

Ashley-Lynn Deschamps: 49

Chelsey Faucher: 45

Jean-Pierre Trottier: 222 (top)

Jude Prashaw; Photographed by Jennifer Scrivens: 151

Lynn Dickhout: 198

Rick Prashaw: 35, 155, 222 (bottom)

Sandra Corbeil: 82 (left), 115 (bottom), 141

Scott Saunders, Peaceful Ram Photography: 115 (top)

Suzanne Corbeil: 13, 18, 19, 47 (top and bottom), 82 (right), 144

Of Related Interest

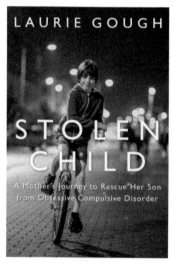

Stolen Child
A Mother's Journey to Rescue Her
Son from Obsessive Compulsive
Disorder

Laurie Gough

Although Laurie Gough was an intrepid traveller who had explored wild, far-off reaches of the globe, the journey she and her family took in their own home in their small Quebec village proved to be far more frightening, strange, and foreign than any land she had ever visited.

It began when Gough's son, shattered by his grandfather's death, transformed from a bright, soccer-ball-kicking ten-year-old into a near-stranger, falling into trances where his parents couldn't reach him and performing ever-changing rituals of magical thinking designed to bring his grandpa back to life.

Stolen Child examines a horrifying year in one family's life, the lengths the parents went to to help their son, and how they won the battle against his all-consuming disorder.

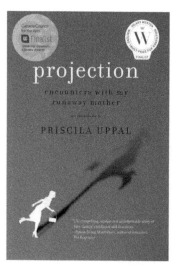

Projection
Encounters with
My Runaway Mother

Priscila Uppal

In 1977, Priscila Uppal's father drank contaminated water in Antigua and within forty-eight hours was a quadriplegic. Priscila was two years old. Five years later, her mother, Theresa, drained the family's bank accounts and disappeared to Brazil. After two attempts to abduct her children, Theresa had no further contact with the family.

In 2002, Priscila happened on her mother's website, which featured a childhood photograph of Priscila and her brother. A few weeks later, Priscila summoned the nerve to contact the woman who'd abandoned her.

The emotional reunion was alternately shocking, hopeful, humorous, and devastating, as Priscila came to realize that not only did she not love her mother, she didn't even like her.

Projection is a visceral, precisely written, brutally honest memoir that takes a probing look at a very unusual mother-daughter relationship, yet offers genuine comfort to all facing their own turbulent and unresolved familial relationships.

**You Can Have a Dog
When I'm Dead**
Essays on Life at an Angle

Paul Benedetti

Paul Benedetti has a good job, a great family, and successful neighbours — but that doesn't stop him from using it all as grist for a series of funny, real, and touching essays about a world he can't quite navigate.

Benedetti misses his son, who is travelling in Europe, misplaces his groceries, and forgets to pick up his daughter at school. He endures a colonoscopy and vainly attempts to lower his Body Mass Index — all with mixed results. He loves his long-suffering wife, worries about his aging parents and his three children, who seem to spend a lot of time battling online trolls, having crushes on vampires, and littering their rooms with enough junk to start a landfill.

BOOK CREDITS

Developmental Editor: Dominic Farrell
Project Editor: Jenny McWha
Copy Editor: Catharine Dorton
Proofreader: Tara Quigley

Designer: Laura Boyle

Publicist: Elham Ali

DUNDURN

Publisher: J. Kirk Howard
Vice-President: Carl A. Brand
Editorial Director: Kathryn Lane
Artistic Director: Laura Boyle
Production Manager: Rudi Garcia
Publicity Manager: Michelle Melski
Manager, Accounting and Technical Services: Livio Copetti

Editorial: Allison Hirst, Dominic Farrell, Jenny McWha,
Rachel Spence, Elena Radic, Melissa Kawaguchi

Marketing and Publicity: Kendra Martin, Elham Ali,
Tabassum Siddiqui, Heather McLeod

Design and Production: Sophie Paas-Lang

dundurn.com   dundurnpress
@dundurnpress   dundurnpress
dundurnpress   info@dundurn.com

FIND US ON NETGALLEY & GOODREADS TOO!

DUNDURN